TEACH YOURSELF
DRESSMAKING

By

ISABEL HORNER

INTRODUCTION

" SOME women dress—others merely wear a few
clothes ! " a witty old lady once remarked. . . .
The art of dressing is well worth studying. Many
so-called beauties owe their reputation entirely to
the fact that they are rich—or clever—enough never
to wear anything unbecoming. Luckily the styles
of to-day are so varied that there is no need to do
this in order to be fashionable. " Dress up to your
individuality " is a good motto. In adopting this a
woman must study herself diligently, to find out
the colours, fabrics, and styles which set off her good
points—every woman has a *few*, at any rate—and to
conceal her bad ones—few escape *some* ! Aids to
attractive dressing are provided by magazines, newspapers, cinemas, theatres, and dress parades.
Thanks to these, the provincial woman is now as well
dressed as the Londoner.

Smart ready-mades can be bought very inex-
pensively, it's true. But there is, or can be, a
cachet about the specially made frock which is
absent from that bought " off the peg ". Materials
are so cheap, too, that a girl with a knowledge of
dressmaking can quickly, and at little cost, copy or
adapt a style to meet her own needs. There are
some lucky women who seem to have been born
with a needle and scissors in their fingers ! These

v

can make, apparently as easily as a spider spins a web, a frock which simply cries out " Paris " to all observers. But less-favoured ones need not despair, for dressmaking is an art which can be learnt by anyone who will apply herself to it wholeheartedly. While dressmaking can be attempted with confidence by the amateur, it should at the same time be taken seriously. Of no other art can it be said more truly that it is the little things which count. For instance, we all know the girl who talks so glibly about " running up a frock in a few hours ". And doesn't the result proclaim the method ! This is the culprit who brings home-dressmaking into such bad repute. No, the old virtue of taking pains cannot be discarded with impunity.

This book has been written to explain the " Hows " and " Whys " to the woman of no experience. Dressmaking has its rules, of course, and there are standards of workmanship which must be attained if the finished results are to pass muster. But what seems so puzzling to the uninitiated is as clear as the daylight when the process is explained. It is strange that while the appellation " Home-made " is so highly esteemed when applied to cakes, jams, and other eatables, it is often a term of disparagement in connection with clothes. This, however, is not inevitable, and I guarantee that any girl of average intelligence can, by diligent practice according to the directions given in this book, turn out creditable work which will transform the despised label of " Home-made " into an enviable one.

ISABEL HORNER.

CONTENTS

CHAPTER I
YOUR EQUIPMENT

THE right tools are all-important. That doesn't mean that they are necessarily elaborate or expensive, for many of the items or their substitutes are to be found in any ordinary household. For instance, no sensible carpenter would attempt to make a chair with a penknife, a twopenny hammer, and a handful of tacks; but I have seen a woman try to cut out an evening frock in expensive material on the top of an eiderdown quilt with a pair of nail scissors, and afterwards begin to " run it up " with sewing-cotton of contrasting colour and a coarse crewel needle! I won't venture to describe the disastrous results to both frock and quilt.

The special tools are few, but they are well worth buying. I will give first a list of essentials, and then one of desirables; and if you start with the first, you can add the items of the second as it is convenient.

ESSENTIALS

1. Sewing-machine—hand, or treadle, or electric. I put this amongst the " essentials ", because, except for very thin fabrics made with much fullness, you cannot make a frock smartly and firmly by hand, while for tailored work it is indispensable (see Chapter II).

2. Large, smooth and firm surface for cutting out, at least 40 inches wide and 54 inches long, and larger if possible. Use a table if you can; a folding one is convenient, as it can be hidden when not required, but, failing that, a large piece of plywood may be placed on a small table. In the last resort there is always the floor, which can be covered with brown paper or newspaper. Remember that the bed is always taboo!

3. Scissors—three pairs: cutting-out (8 or 10 inches long); a small pair (4 or 5 inches long); buttonhole scissors (small, with a gap in the blades which makes unnecessary the piercing of a hole in starting). Keep all these in good order, never use them for cutting paper or string, or for any other purpose than dressmaking, and have them sharpened when required. (Make long cuts on glass paper with them occasionally, to keep them in good condition.)

4. Needles—of best quality. Long ones, Nos. 6 to 8, for tacking or fly-running; sharps, Nos. 8 and 9, for general sewing; betweens, Nos. 9 to 12, for very fine work.

5. Pins—steel for preference, as these don't make large holes or soil delicate fabrics. They must, however, be kept free from rust, and an emery cushion is useful for this purpose.

6. Pincushions—a large one for general use, and a small one on a strap for wearing on the left wrist when fitting.

7. Stiletto—for piercing holes for eyelets, and for marking fitting-lines on cotton fabrics.

8. Tacking-cotton—in two or three colours, for tacking-up, and for marking fitting-lines.

9. Tailor's chalk—in two or three colours, for marking fitting-lines, etc. Sold in flat cakes at a haberdashery counter.

10. Thimble—a smooth one which will not fray thread or fabric.

11. Tape-measure—marked with inches (subdivided into eighths) on both sides.

12. Long ruler or yard-stick—for ruling long fitting-lines. A blind stick will serve.

13. Padded skirt-board—for pressing. Also long padded rollers for pressing skirt-seams; short padded rollers for short seams such as those of sleeves (a rolling-pin wrapped in flannel will serve in an emergency); clean cotton cloths for pressing.

14. Iron—either electric or flat, from 5 to 7 lb. in weight. If a flat iron is used, a gas ring will be necessary. Keep bathbrick and cleaning-cloths handy, as the iron must be scrupulously clean.

15. Kitchen soap—for pressing.

DESIRABLES

1. Tailor's goose—10 to 12 lb. in weight, for coats and heavy cloth garments.

2. Very light iron—for fragile fabrics. A pair of old-fashioned curling-tongs is useful for pressing narrow turnings in thin materials.

3. Sleeve-board—for pressing sleeves. Can be bought uncovered cheaply. Must be padded with blanket or flannelette. A child's cricket bat, similarly padded, makes a good substitute.

4. Tailor's cushion—for pressing sleeve-heads of coats, curved seams, darts, etc. (How to make one is described below.)

5. Dress-form—made to your personal measurements if possible. (How to adapt one of standard size is explained on pp. 13–17.)

6. Sleeve-form—for fitting sleeves. (Directions for making are given on pp. 17–18.)

7. Pinking-shears—for neatening seam and other turnings.

7. Tracing-wheel—for marking fitting-lines on cotton materials.

9. Sheets of cardboard—for protecting tables when using a tracing wheel.

10. Tweezers—for picking out tacking-threads.

11. Full-length mirror.

12. Under-bed chest—for storing garments during their making.

13. Waste-paper basket—for holding waste material and snippings.

14. Dust-sheet—for protecting the floor.

TO MAKE A TAILOR'S CUSHION (Fig. I, p. 13)

Cut four pieces of strong, washed, unbleached calico, to the shape shown in Fig. 2. Stitch two of them together, leaving a few inches open at the narrow end. Turn right side out and stuff with rags, very tightly, then sew up the opening. Now stitch up the remaining pieces, leaving the wider end open sufficiently to allow it to slip over the cushion. Sew up the opening, and remove the cover for washing when required.

TO ADAPT A DRESS-FORM TO PERSONAL MEASUREMENTS

If you can afford it, you will find a dress-form made to your own measurements a profitable investment. It will enable you to make your frocks, etc., in little more than half the time which would be necessary without it. You will have an exact

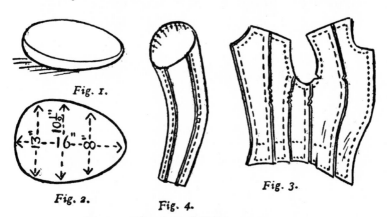

Fig. 1.

Fig. 2.

Fig. 3.

Fig. 4.

Fig. 1.—Tailor's Cushion.
Fig. 2.—Diagram of Tailor's Cushion.
Fig. 3.—Foundation Lining Bodice.
Fig. 4.—Foundation Two-piece Sleeve.

reproduction of your own figure, so that you can judge what will suit it much better than by looking in a mirror. The made-to-measure form costs a few pounds, but if you do not wish to spend so much, buy one of standard size, which you can easily transform into a duplicate of your own figure.

Before making this purchase, cut out in strong unbleached calico a tight-fitting bodice with two-piece sleeves, of the type shown in Figs. 3 and 4, extending the part below the waist to about 8 or 9 inches. (Directions for cutting out are given in Chapter VI.) Tack it up as described on pp. 80–2, and get someone to fit it on you according to the instructions on pp. 88–9. The bodice should be fitted *very tightly* directly over the corset, or, if this is not worn, over the vest. The sleeve must be fitted skin-tightly. Stitch up all the seams, excepting those at under-arms, but including the centre-front edges. Cut down the turnings to ⅜ inch, snipping them at intervals of 1 inch, and press them open over a roller, as described on pp. 179–80.

The Dress-form

There are two types of dress-form. The cheaper one is for the bodice only, stopping short at the hip-line. You can stand this on a table, or, better still, if you have an old plant pedestal, you can glue or screw the form to this, and then cut off the legs to make the completed form correspond to your own height. The other type is mounted on a pole-stand which can be adjusted to any height by a screw, and thus is very useful for testing the skirt length (see Fig. 5). This form may or may not have a wire framework to hold out a skirt. You should buy a form which is 2 inches smaller in the bust than yourself. If you choose it personally, the salesman will allow you to try your calico bodice on the various forms until you find one which satisfies you. It is essential that its back length from nape of neck to waist should be as near your own as possible—a difference of $\frac{1}{2}$ inch either way may be adjusted, but more than that creates a difficulty.

Padding the Bodice

Run a fine tacking-line in coloured cotton round the waist-line of the bodice, and similar ones round

Fig. 5.   *Fig. 6.*

Fig. 5—Dress-form for Fitting.
Fig. 6.—Padding a Dress-form (back).

neck and armholes; also mark the sleeve pitches (or points of inset) on the armholes with large crosses in coloured cotton. Take wadding of natural colour and place a layer of it all over the form, then with a long needleful of cotton catch the wadding to the form at intervals with the diagonal tacking shown in Fig. 22 on p. 54. The slanting stitches should be long, and need not be uniform in size, and they should not be drawn tightly enough to flatten the wadding. Place the lining bodice on the form and draw the back into place. First see that it fits down well into the waist and pin it there. Now take small pieces of wadding and pad out the back where needed. Pad firmly and evenly, and avoid lumps. When the back is finished fix the under-arm edges to the form temporarily with pins placed horizontally about 1 inch apart; also pin round the back neck, back armholes, and along the shoulder seams (see Fig. 6, p. 15).

Now pad the front similarly, and be sure to keep the centre-front seam straight from neck to waist-line, pinning it to the form at both these places. As the padding progresses, pin round the neck and armholes, then turn back the under-arm edges and pin them over those of the back, taking out the former row of pins as you do so. Take strong sewing-cotton and sew down these turned-in edges firmly, using a short needle. Turn in the neck edge all round and sew it to the form, unless the neck of it is too small for the bodice. In that case do not turn in the neck of the bodice, but pad the form with wadding. Then take a strip of calico cut on the bias (see p. 68), turn in the upper and lower edges, and stretch the strip round the neck with its ends at the front. Fold one end over the other and fell it into place. Cut two circles of calico to fit over the armholes, turn in their edges all round, and fell them over the armhole turnings.

THE SLEEVE-FORM

Before turning the calico sleeves right side out, cut two pieces of wadding to the shape of the upper and under parts, leaving no turnings. Tack each piece to its corresponding piece of calico, then turn right side out. Cut an oval piece of calico to fit the open space at the wrist of each sleeve, then turn in the edges of the ovals and fell them over the wrist edges. Now stuff very tightly with rags.

Fig. 7.

Sleeve Form for Fitting.

Something is needed by which to pin the sleeve-forms to the shoulders of the dress-form when in use, so cut out four pieces of calico to the measurements given on the diagram in Fig. 8. Stitch each pair together round the curved edges on the wrong side, turn them right side out, then place over the top of the upper sleeve with edges matching, and run together on the sleeve fitting-line.

Fig. 8.

Diagram for Shoulder-piece.

Now cut out two circles of calico, large enough to fit over the arm-holes, and, if necessary, flatten the sides a little. Turn in the edges, pin them over the sleeve turnings (you may now find it needful to add a little more stuffing), and sew all round. The sleeve-forms can then be pinned to their respective shoulders by means of the shoulder-pieces. (It is useful to have two sleeve-forms, though some people manage with one only.)

A FOUNDATION SKIRT

If the dress-form has no skirt framework, a tight-fitting skirt of unbleached calico will be an advantage. In this case cut the bodice off 2 inches below the waist-line, then cut out a plain skirt in at least four gores. This should measure not more than 45 inches round the lower edge, and it should be 6 inches shorter than your own skirt measurements from waist to ground (see p. 31). Have the skirt fitted skin-tightly round waist and hips, and leave open one seam for about 8 inches from the top, to enable it to slip over the dress-form. Pad the form round the hips, if necessary, then sew up the open seam, turn in the waist edge, and fell it to the form (see Fig. 5, p. 15).

YOUR WORKROOM

You are lucky if you can have a special room for your sewing, where you can work undisturbed, and in which all your apparatus can be stored. But this is not always feasible. However, it is sometimes possible to make your own bedroom or a guest-room do duty as a workroom also, in the following way. If there is a large cupboard, all your equipment can be housed in it, except perhaps the sewing-machine. Failing a cupboard, a recess will serve. Two or three shelves may be installed to hold materials and small implements, and curtains will conceal these, as well as dress-forms, ironing-boards, folding table, etc.

The latest cabinet sewing-machine is an ornament to any room, but there is an older type of ostrich-like character—that is, though it hides its head, it fails to conceal its ugly legs! It is an impossible piece of furniture, anyhow, but with a little trouble it can be disguised and made to serve a double purpose. Have a board made to fit the top, and should the lid be raised an inch or so in the middle, leaving a few inches at each end at a lower level, a strip of wood should be nailed or glued under the board at each end to fit close up to the raised part. Cover the top plainly with cretonne or chintz, and make a petticoat of the same in four parts, the open ends coming at the corners. Arrange a triple mirror on the top, and you have an attractive dressing-table. When you wish to use the machine it is only the work of a moment to lift up the board and deposit it, with outspread petticoats, on a small table, or the bed, without disarrangement.

It is an advantage to spread a dust-sheet on the floor when sewing, as it protects the carpet from tiresome snippets, and can be picked up and removed in a few moments, leaving no signs of sewing.

THE PIECE-DRAWER

The home dressmaker should certainly set aside a drawer or large dress-box in which to store scraps of spare materials which she may collect. Nothing really comes amiss, as even the most unlikely things " come in " for trimmings and neatenings. Ribbons, odd bits of silk or satin, linen, buttons, hooks and eyes, and other fastenings—none of these should be rejected. Pieces of linen provide good interlinings for collars and cuffs when a little firmness is required. Old starched collars and cuffs cut to the shape of the diagram on p. 69 will serve for sleeve extenders. Men's silk ties, unpicked, washed or otherwise cleaned, can often be used for pipings, little bows, button coverings, etc. Little bits of cord make loops for buttons or hangers for coats, frocks, and skirts, and old wrist-watch ribbons are excellent for the latter purpose.

When discarding any old garment, cut off from it, and keep, all worth-while buttons, hooks and eyes, press studs, etc. I long ago made it a rule never to buy anything in the way of dressmaking sundries until I had looked in my piece-drawer. It is astonishing what a lot of money can be saved in this way in the course of a year. There is a tale told of a Victorian needlewoman who boasted that she had never used more than one length of tacking-thread in all her years of dressmaking. She carefully withdrew her treasured length of cotton after each time of using and put it away for future work. However, I don't advise economy carried to such lengths, especially as later on I shall have much to say on the necessity of adequate tacking.

CHAPTER II

THE SEWING-MACHINE

THE newest models in sewing-machines show no outward sign of their essential function, and they are expensive; but it is possible to get, at very moderate prices, re-conditioned machines which are perfectly satisfactory. *Do get one of good quality,* even though its looks are not very attractive. Remember that it is going to be your indispensable helper in all your dressmaking efforts, and its conduct will make or mar the results, so it is worth a little sacrifice, if needs be, to obtain one upon which you can rely for satisfactory work. Whether you buy one run electrically, a treadle model, or a hand machine depends upon your taste and your purse. Good work can be done on a hand machine, but it is slower than a treadle, which leaves both hands free to manipulate the fabric. The electric model is, of course, ideal.

Take the greatest care of your machine. Keep it in a dry place—avoid damp like the plague. Never leave it uncovered when not in use. Oil it regularly with the special oil sold for the purpose. Clean the works methodically with a small, stiff paste-brush dipped in paraffin. If the machine has been out of action for some time and you find that it runs stiffly, probably the old oil has clogged the works; so remove both upper and under threads, fill an oil-can with paraffin and apply it to every nut and screw, then work with a piece of old material under the presser foot to absorb all the oil which will drain out. Do not stop until the needle works cleanly; then clean all the parts and oil sparingly in the usual way.

From time to time the foot-plate should be removed, and all fluff and ends of thread which may have collected can be removed with an old toothbrush or a pipe-cleaner.

Be sure that you thoroughly understand your special machine. (Some machines have their little " ways ", and need humouring if they are to give perfect satisfaction.) The shop where you bought it will send you an instructress and also supply you with a book of detailed information concerning your own particular model. Master it before you attempt any work, then practise stitching plain seams and hems, after which you should become familiar with the hemmer, tucker, ruffler, etc., and other attachments. Learn to work rhythmically and at a fair speed. Jerky movements are bad for the mechanism and produce bad stitching.

NEEDLES AND THREAD

Your instruction book will tell you what numbers of needles to use with different fabrics, and failure to employ the correct ones will cause puckering, breaking of thread, and other faults. Be very careful, in removing work, not to bend the needle, and it is best to draw out the material to the back instead of to the front. Never work with a blunt needle—replace it at once.

Your instruction book will also specify the correct numbers of cotton and silk to use for various fabrics and with needles of different sizes. Use silk for all fabrics except linen and cotton, as silk is more elastic and stands the strain of wear better. Do not, for economy's sake, use silk for the upper and cotton for the under threads, when doing ornamental stitching, as the strain will thus be unequal and one or both threads may break. Mercerised cotton is suitable for cotton and linen goods. When stitching coloured material choose silk or cotton a shade darker, as it will appear lighter when used.

HINTS ON STITCHING

Always test your stitch on a spare piece of fabric, and practise until you get a perfect result. Regulate the size of the stitch to suit the material. As a rule, thin fabrics need a smaller one than thick materials, as these take up more thread, and thus shorten the stitch. Always tack all parts to be stitched—never machine over pins, or you may break the needle, besides puckering the fabric. When stitching near a fold it should always be pressed on the wrong side first, as in this way it is easier to get the stitching even. Always keep the turnings to the right when stitching seams, with the main part of the material to the left. Be sure to stitch all seams in a garment in the same direction, either all up or all down, and if the fabric has a " nap " you must stitch with it, not against it.

Do not pull the material as it is pushed forward under the presser foot, but simply guide it in the required direction. In seams stitch just outside the tacked fitting-lines, as the machining will be much tighter than the tacking. A good deal of time and thread are wasted by stitching short seams one by one and breaking the thread after each. The quickest, safest, and most economical way is to have all pieces of work tacked ready, and immediately one has been stitched, to go straight on to another. When all have been stitched, the needle should be worked on to a spare piece of material, which can be left until the machine is again required. The threads between the different pieces are then cut. This plan, however, will not serve when the stitching is of an ornamental nature and the ends of thread must be fastened neatly. Here when the end is reached and the needle is in its highest position, lift the presser foot and draw out the material to the back with a few inches of both threads. Cut the threads, leaving 2 inches on the material. Take hold of the upper thread coming from the needle and carefully pull it out until there are about 3 inches, otherwise when work is resumed the needle will unthread. On the material just stitched the upper thread should be drawn through to the wrong side and both ends tied there. Sometimes it is necessary to insert the upper thread in a sewing-needle and to work a few back stitches to fill in a gap in the machining.

When joining two pieces, as in a seam, if one edge is more on the bias than the other, keep this uppermost, and tack closely, so that it is not pushed along by the presser foot. (As there is an exception to every rule, it may be necessary, in order to have the bias edge uppermost, to reverse the rule given on p. 23, and to stitch the seam with turnings to the left and the main part of the garment to the right.) Thin fabrics, such as georgette, lace, net, etc., should be tacked to tissue paper and the fabric kept upwards while being stitched. The paper can easily be torn away afterwards.

GATHERING

There is a special attachment for gathering, but it can be done quite easily by machine without it. Make the stitch as large as possible, then stitch the single material in the ordinary way. After this draw up the upper thread to the required fullness, then regulate this and draw up the under thread to keep it firm.

CHAPTER III
PAPER PATTERNS

A GOOD paper pattern is just as important to the successful fashioning of a frock or other garment as the plan drawn by a competent architect is to the building of a beautiful house. The lines and seams of a garment are not placed just where they are simply to make it fit—that can be done with seams running in any and every direction—but they are planned with deliberate intention to flatter the figure and to give pleasure to the eye of the beholder. Have you ever thought why any particular building delights your eye? It may be bare of any ornamentation and devoid of colour, and yet the sight of it is satisfying, and even delightful. This is the result of correct proportions and skilful placing of lines, curves, and masses. So it is with a well-cut frock.

THE COVETED CUT

That highly prized and mysterious quality called " cut " is the product of many years of study and practice on the part of the modeller, and, with true artistry, every line will tell and be indispensable. Ask two cutters, one of the first grade and the other of the second, to model the same design, and note the result. The model of the first will have well-proportioned pieces and graceful lines, whilst that of the other will somehow be all wrong—it will irritate even the uninitiated with its faulty lines and ill-proportioned pieces. If you have never thought of this before, begin to notice other people's frocks; compare one with another; decide why this pleases you and that does not; find out what makes your friend, whose figure is really not so good as it might be, look dumpy and broad in one frock and positively graceful in another. You will find yourself studying these things unconsciously as you go along the street or meet other women in a room, and it is surprising how interesting they can be. In this way you will learn, without knowing it, the foundation principles of intelligent and successful dressmaking.

Do not, therefore, begrudge money spent on a good paper pattern. Accompanying it you will find a leaflet giving amounts of material required and instructions for making, as well as a " layout " showing you how to plan out the pattern to the best advantage.

YOUR MEASUREMENTS

Besides studying the figures of other women, you should make yourself familiar with your own, and know its measurements and peculiarities. Don't be alarmed! I am not suggesting any pronounced abnormality, or even anything just slightly noticeable; but there are many figures, to the casual observer perfectly symmetrical, which yet deviate a little from the normal, thus necessitating some adjustment of the pattern. So enlist the aid of a friend to take your measurements, and enter them on the list given on pp. 28–31. You should retain your usual posture, even if this is a bad one! Some women who habitually stoop, for instance, will suddenly become very erect at the sight of a tape-measure, or at the approach of the fitter; but they will relapse into their customary posture when wearing the garment, so that it is ruined from the point of view of fit.

A well-fitting and rather plain frock, or plain blouse and skirt, should be worn over the usual corset or belt, and lingerie, and the shoes should be of the customary type. The measurer should tie a piece of string round the waist, pulling it down well and keeping the knot exactly in the centre-front. The string serves to indicate the waist-line. Length measures need only be taken on the right side of the figure, unless it is one-sided, when the corresponding measure should be taken on the left side also, and the two marked respectively " right " and " left " on the list. The tape-measure should be in good condition, as if it is much worn it may have stretched, and therefore the results of its use will be inaccurate.

LIST OF MEASUREMENTS (Figs. 9 and 10)

Bodice

1. Length of back. Hold beginning of tape on nape bone under left thumb, carry tape down to waist-line with right hand.

2. Length of front. Keep left thumb as before, but let tape swing round over right shoulder and down to knot on waist-line at centre-front.

3. Height of under-arm. Hold beginning of tape in armpit with left thumb and carry it down to the waist-line with the right fingers.

4. Width of bust. Place tape round fullest part

of figure, rather loosely, but on no account allow it to droop at the back.

5. Width of waist. Take this just sufficiently

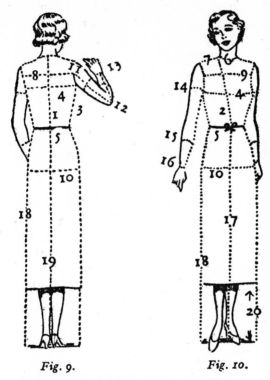

Fig. 9.   *Fig. 10.*

Fig. 9.—Taking Measurements (back).
Fig. 10.—Taking Measurements (front).

easy to allow the tape to slip round. Pull it down well.

6. Width of neck. Take tightly round base of throat.

*7. Width of right shoulder. Take from the base

of throat, about 2¼ inches from nape bone, to top of arm, and mark last point with a pin.

*8. Width of back. Measure across from armhole to armhole, about a quarter of the way down between nape and waist. Mark at right armhole with a pin.

*9. Width of chest. Take across front at same level as width of back. Mark as before.

10. Width of hips. Take easy round fullest part of hips, from 7 to 8 inches below waist-line, according to the figure.

Measures marked * depend upon fashion, and vary from time to time.

Sleeve

11. Width of armhole (right arm). Take tightly with tape meeting on top of shoulder, and just touching the three pins.

12. Armhole to elbow. Right arm must be held straight out from the side, then bent as in Fig. 9. Hold beginning of tape under left thumb at back of armhole, and then with right hand carry it to the elbow.

13. Elbow to wrist. Keep tape at elbow as before, but let left thumb drop from armhole and place it on the elbow. Carry tape to wrist-bone and subtract figure at elbow from that at wrist to give correct measure.

14. Width of upper arm. Take easy just below armhole, and allow an inch extra.

15. Width of lower arm. Take easy half-way between elbow and wrist and add one inch.

16. Width of wrist. Take easy at the joint.

Skirt

Width of waist. As for bodice.

Width of hips. As for bodice.

17. Front length. From knot on waist-line to ground.

18. Side (right) length. From string to ground, over fullest part of hip. (Measure left side, if necessary.)

19. Back length. From string to ground.

20. Desired height from ground.

Note any idiosyncrasies of figure, such as round-shouldered, hollow-backed, etc.

BUYING YOUR PATTERN

Buy your frock, blouse, or coat pattern by the bust measure. Remember that the measurements given on the pattern are those of the figure, and not of the pattern itself, so that in choosing a full or loose style you must still buy by the plain bust measure, as the fullness has been allowed for by the cutter. Even for a coat, where the actual bust measure of the garment must be larger than that of the frock, you must still observe this rule. The patterns are usually graded with a difference of 2 inches between the sizes—*e.g.*, 32, 34, 36, etc. If your bust measurement happens to be an intermediate one—33, 35, 37, etc.—get the next larger pattern and adapt it in the way which will be described later on. There is an exception to this rule, however. Should your bust be large in proportion to any other part of your figure, it will be wiser to buy the next smaller pattern and enlarge the pattern in the way described later.

Buy skirt patterns by the hip measure, and if you can't get the exact one, buy the next size larger and adapt it as will be described. When buying a frock pattern, and your hips are large in proportion to your bust measure, buy one by the latter and adapt on the hips according to the rules to be given.

ADAPTATION OF PATTERN

The less fitting you do in the tacked-up garment the better, so that your pattern should be as perfect as possible before cutting out the material. If you are an exact stock size, you are lucky! There are several ways of adapting a stock-size pattern to individual measurements. The aim in each one of them is to preserve the original fitting-lines of the pieces—that is, the outside edges—so that all alterations, as far as possible, should be made inside these lines.

Examine the Pattern

Open out the pattern, sort out the pieces, and compare them with the layout which accompanies them. Read the instructions and examine all marks and type on the pieces. Patterns vary, but there are always notches on the outside edges to enable you to put the parts together easily, joining one notch to one, and two to two, and so on. Sometimes there are perforations where one part has to be laid over another, and then one hole goes over one, and two over two, etc. Then there will be printed directions on various parts, such as " Place to lengthwise fold ", " Place on the bias ", etc. All these are most important, and must on no account be ignored.

Turnings or No Turnings

One thing must be borne in mind carefully, or confusion may result. Some brands of patterns are cut out on the exact fitting-lines, therefore extra material, known as turnings, must be allowed outside them to sew by. Other brands have the turnings allowed on the pieces, and the fitting- or sewing-lines are indicated by perforations or tracings. Both kinds have their advantages, and which you shall use is simply a matter for your own preference. It is, however, a good plan to keep to the same kind, or mistakes may arise.

First Method of Adaptation

Remove your frock and get someone to pin up the pattern on the right side of your figure and make any necessary alterations; or, if you have a dress-form adapted to your own measurements, you can test the pattern on this.

Second Method

Lay all parts of the pattern on the table, matching the notches, and with edges touching if no turnings are allowed, or with turnings overlapping if turnings are left on the pattern. The shoulders must, of course, be left open. Now with the tape-measure apply your own personal measurements in the position in which they were taken on the figure. Apply the bust and waist measures (using half) and, unless for a perfectly tight-fitting bodice, allow a little ease, according to the style and fashion— no hard-and-fast rule can be given. (This also

B (Dress)

applies to the width of chest.) If the bodice has a V-neck or crossover front, place the centre-front to a ruler or the table edge and measure to this.

Third Method

This entails more trouble, but saves time in the end. Cut out, tack up, and have fitted on you (right side of figure only) a tight-fitting bodice and sleeve in unbleached calico, such as is described for the adaptation of a dress-form on p. 13. Discard the unfitted half, then cut off the turnings of the fitted pieces on the corrected fitting-lines. Mark the notches with pencilled crosses, also the sleeve insets, and pencil in the waist-line on all pieces. Now lay all these pieces on the bought pattern and make any necessary alterations, allowing ease as described for the second method, and paying particular attention to armhole and neck curves, shoulder and under-arm edges.

HOW TO CORRECT THE PATTERN

Bodice or Blouse

1. Back or front too long. Is the excess between neck and bust, or between bust and waist, or at both places? Wherever it is, correct by pinning a tuck across, thus keeping the under-arm height in accordance with your own (see Fig. 11, A and B).

2. Back or front too short. Correct in same places as No. 1, by cutting pattern straight across and inserting strips of paper as required (see Fig. 12, A and B).

Note.—For a round-shouldered figure the back of

the stock-size pattern may be too short and the front too long, while for the over-erect, hollow-backed figure the opposite will be the case.

3. Back too wide. Is the excess width across the shoulders, where the back width measurement was taken, or is it just below the neck? For the first

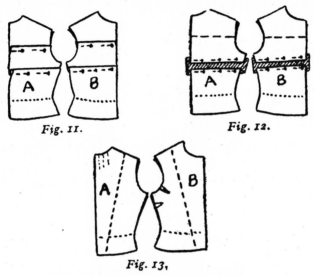

Fig. II.   Fig. I2.

Fig. I3,

Fig. II.—Shortening Bodice Pattern.
Fig. I2.—Lengthening Bodice Pattern.
Fig. I3.—Altering Width of Bodice.

make a downward tuck slanting from middle of shoulder to waist-line, finishing there about 2 inches from centre-back (see Fig. 13A, above). This tuck may be graduated as required. (Should the pattern have a seam running down from the shoulder, the alteration will be made here.) If the fullness is just below the neck only, make tiny pin-tucks about 2½ inches long; these must be made in the material also. If, however, the material is very thin the back must not fit too tightly, and instead of making the pattern narrower, pin tucks may run down from back neck and shoulders to give the required easy fit.

4. Back too narrow. If there is a seam running from the shoulder to the waist, separate the pieces and insert paper as required. If there is no seam, make a cut running down from shoulder in a slanting direction to the centre-back of waist-line (see Fig. 13A), separate the pieces, and insert a strip of paper to the necessary width.

5. Front too wide. The excess width may be either across the chest and bust, or just below the armhole, or at both places. If at the former place make a slanting tuck from shoulder to the waist-line in position shown in Fig. 13B (or, if there is a seam in this position, take in here); if at the under-arm, make a downward tuck there. If fullness forms at front armhole, make a small dart running from it diagonally to the bust-line, or else make a small horizontal dart on the under-arm edge about 2 inches down, and paste on a small piece of paper above to restore the armhole curve.

6. Front too narrow. If front is in two pieces, separate them as required and insert strips to give the required width, afterwards cutting exactly through the middle of the strip. A little extra may be added to the under-arm edge if too narrow here. If the front is in one piece, cut downward from middle of shoulder to waist (as shown in Fig. 13B) and insert a strip to the required width.

Note.—In an over-erect or " sway-back " figure the front will be long in proportion to the back, and probably also wide, so that in the pattern the front may have to be both lengthened and widened and a small dart made in the under-arm edge as described in No. 5. The exact opposite happens with a round-shouldered figure. For this the pattern front will be found both too long and too wide, whilst the back may be both too short and too narrow. When the shoulders are unusually round, a dart running downward may be made in each back shoulder.

Sleeve

1. Too long. Corrrect excessive length by making tucks across the pattern, either above or below the elbow, or in both positions, as needed. Do not shorten at the top of the sleeve, as this will make the sleeve narrower, and do not shorten at the wrist edge by more than 1 inch (see Fig. 14).

Fig. 14.

Shortening Sleeve.

2. Too short. Make cuts across in one or both of the positions shown in Fig. 15, p. 38, and insert strips of paper to give desired length.

3. Too wide. If a two-piece sleeve, make a small tuck down the middle of each in the position shown in Fig. 16. If a one-piece pattern, make a tuck straight down the middle from the highest part.

4. Too narrow. If a two-piece sleeve, cut each

part down the middle (in position shown in Fig. 16) and insert strips of paper. These need not be the same width all the way down, but may be regulated in accordance with the required width. If the sleeve is in one piece, cut down the middle from the highest point and insert a strip of paper.

 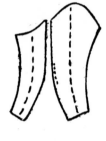

Fig. 15.   *Fig. 16.*

Fig. 15.—Lengthening Sleeve.
Fig. 16.—Altering Width of Sleeve.

Coat

Work on same principles as for bodice, but adaptation cannot be as exact here. Pay particular attention to neck and armhole curves, but it must be remembered that stretching and shrinking of the cloth can do much in the way of removing slight fullness or giving ease.

Skirt

Decide how high from the ground you wish your skirt to be, and deduct this figure from each of your own personal length measurements. Test the pattern by these figures.

1. Too long or too short. If the difference is not

more than 1 inch, this may be taken off or added at the lower edge; but if it is more than that, work thus: to shorten, if not more than 1½ inch, make a tuck across each piece just below the hip-line, and these tucks must follow the shape of the lower edge. If the excess is more than 1½ inch, take away half of this in a tuck as just described, and take away the remainder in another half-way between the first one and the lower edge of the skirt. Correct the sides of the pieces with a long ruler or yard-stick.

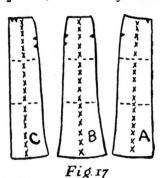

Fig. 17

To lengthen, cut the pieces across where directed for the tucks and insert strips of paper as required. Correct sides as before.

Fig. 17.—Gored Skirt. A—half-front; B—side; C—half-back. Broken lines indicate where pattern should be altered to lengthen or shorten it; crossed lines show where alterations may be made to make the skirt wider or narrower.

2. Too wide or too narrow. For a two-piece skirt, if the difference on the half-skirt is not more than 1 inch, this may be taken off or added at the straight side of each piece; but if more than 1 inch, or if there are more than three pieces in the pattern, it is better to make a tuck down the middle of each piece to make the skirt narrower, or to cut each piece exactly down the middle and insert strips of paper to make wider. In these ways the original proportions of the pieces are retained (see Fig. 17).

A Circular or Umbrella Skirt

To adjust the length, first draw a curve about 10 inches below the waist and another half-way between that and the lower edge (see Fig. 18). To shorten, take up a tuck on each of these lines, and to lengthen, cut along each curve and insert a strip.

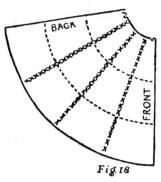

Fig 18

Fig. 18.—Lengthen or shorten the pattern of a circular skirt in the positions shown by broken lines; make it wider or narrower where indicated by crossed lines.

To adjust the width, divide the waist and lower edges into four equal parts and connect by downward lines (see Fig. 18). To make narrower, make tucks on these lines; to make wider, cut down the lines and insert strips of paper. When a skirt is desired wider round the hips, it is unwise to make it wider round the lower edge also, unless it is to be lengthened in addition; so in this case the pieces should be separated sufficiently at the hips to give the required increase, and then the lower edges may meet. It may then be necessary to make one or two small darts at the waist on each half of the skirt.

Frock

The adjustment of this will be a combination of bodice and skirt methods. If the frock has a waist seam, the fitting is much reduced; if without one, the following hints are useful. When the front part of the skirt pokes forward at the hem, make a small horizontal dart on the side edge of the front piece, about 2½ or 3 inches long, and about 3 inches below the waist. This shortens the front piece, so the lower edge must be lengthened. If the back falls in at the lower edge, lift up at the shoulder, and, if this is not sufficient, make a horizontal dart on the waist-line, about ½ inch deep in the middle and tapering off to nothing at each side seam. Conceal this dart by a belt.

Of course, it is not claimed that after any of these adjustments of the pattern your frock or other garment will need no fitting at all, but the process will certainly be simplified considerably, there will be no waste of material, and less danger of spoiling the original cut of the garment.

CHAPTER IV

MATERIALS AND LININGS

SOME people seem to find difficulty in appreciating the important part which the grain of the material plays in a garment. It needs, however, only a little consideration of the method of weaving to make it all quite clear. Woven fabrics have a foundation of lengthwise threads, called the warp. A shuttle, filled with thread of a rather weaker calibre, is then passed from side to side under and over the lengthwise threads. This is called the weft. The turning at each side is called the selvedge (or " self edge "), and it will usually be found that this is rather tighter than the main part of the fabric, and therefore it is generally snipped at intervals when it comes on the seams of a garment, to counteract this tightness (see Fig. 19).

PLANNING OUT

In planning the cutting out of a garment, it is essential to arrange that the warp threads should run straight down the figure on all the principal parts, thus ensuring the correct " hang ". If the centre-front or centre-back, or the upper part of a sleeve, for instance, should be the least bit off the straight grain, these parts will twist noticeably. Of course, every rule has its exceptions, and some of these are : the belt of a frock, and the yoke, collar, and cuffs of a striped shirt blouse. Here the warp threads are arranged to run round the figure in positions where there is strain, and at the same time the arrangement of the stripes has a decorative effect. From time to time, also, fashion

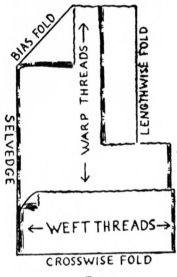

Fig. 19

Fig. 19.—This diagram should be studied before beginning to cut out material.

decrees that stripes should run in various directions on the different parts of a frock, so the home dress-maker must always be on the alert to observe current vogues. Luckily all paper patterns are accompanied by layouts giving the correct placing of parts, so these changes of fashion need cause no difficulty.

Frequently the method of cutting garments with

the warp threads running downward is called " cutting with the grain ", and that of cutting them with the weft threads running downward " cutting against the grain ". If you have a piece of material without a selvedge and you find it difficult to tell which are the warp threads, try folding it in both directions. It will fold much more easily downwards—that is, with the warp threads—than across, or with the weft threads. Another plan is to unravel the material in both directions and to pull the threads with the fingers. The weft threads will break much more easily than the warp.

CUTTING ON THE BIAS

But besides " cutting with the grain " and " cutting across the grain ", there is a third method, known as " cutting on the bias ". The bias is the exact diagonal between the warp and weft threads, and it can be found by folding over the straight weft thread to lie level with the selvedge or warp thread— the fold thus formed is exactly on the bias. If you test this, you will find how very pliable this fold is, and that a bias strip of even width, if stretched along one edge only, will become curved. This is the reason why most trimmings, facings, and neatenings are cut on the bias. Sometimes, too, it is the fashion to cut entire garments in this way, either to produce a clinging effect or to give variety in the case of stripes and plaids.

Most fabrics have a right and a wrong side—the right one being that which is uppermost in the weaving. Generally the two sides are so different that it is impossible to mistake them, but sometimes they are very similar, and then the following points will guide you in distinguishing them. Woollens, when sold folded, have the right side inside; when without a fold, but rolled, the wrong side will generally be outside. But this is not an invariable rule, for many silks when sold rolled have the right side outside, and linens and cottons, whether sold folded or single, usually have the right side outside.

There are also fabrics made with one side bright and the other dull—both equally attractive—so that one may be used for the main part and the other for the trimming. This has decided merits for the economically minded dressmaker, for if a frock of this kind becomes faded or soiled, it can be unpicked and re-made on the reverse side.

CLOTH WITH A NAP

Some woollens look and feel the same when viewed and felt lengthwise from either end, and with these, so long as the warp threads run correctly, some of the parts may be placed upside down if they fit in better that way, thus often effecting a great economy in material. (It is important to find out this when buying.) But others feel smooth when the hand is passed along the warp threads in one direction, and rough when passed the opposite way. These fabrics, such as face cloth, camel hair, etc., have what is called a "nap". Besides feeling smooth and rough in opposite directions, they also look light and dark. With these fabrics all parts of the pattern should be arranged so that the material will feel smooth when the hand is passed down the garment when worn. Failure to observe this rule may produce annoying results, as in the case of an economical wife who made a dressing-gown of camel-hair cloth for her husband's birthday. When she showed it to me she confessed she was not quite satisfied with it, and asked why it looked so peculiar—which it certainly did. The long hairs ran correctly downward on back, under sleeves and pockets only, and on all other parts they ran upward! The cause was obvious.

PILE AND NON-REVERSIBLE FABRICS

In pile fabrics, such as velvet, and velveteen, the pile should run up the figure, so that when the hand is passed downwards when wearing a garment the material will feel rough; also looked at downwards it will seem dark, while viewed upwards it will appear light. Panne velvet is the exception to this rule—it should be smooth downwards when worn. Occasionally velvet can be obtained which looks the same from either end, but all the pieces of the pattern should be cut the same way.

Many plaids, stripes, and floral patterns, while they have no nap, yet have some difference when viewed up or down the warp threads, which makes it essential to decide which shall be the top and which the bottom, and then to lay out all the parts with their top ends in the same direction. One has seen ludicrous effects if this has been neglected, when a reckless cutter has condemned herself to wear a frock on which giant roses stood on their heads on various parts.

WIDTHS OF STANDARD MATERIALS

Formerly any material up to 36 inches in width would be sold unfolded and known as " single width ", whilst wider ones would be folded down the middle and termed " double width "; very wide folded ones would be classed as " extra double width ". The majority of materials are now sold folded, whatever their width, but when less than 36 inches wide they are still called " single width " by the trade, which might lead the puzzled amateur to propound a conundrum : " When is double material not ' double width ' ? " . . . " When it's ' single width ' " (that is, less than 36 inches wide). On the other hand, there are some materials of 36 inches or more which are sold single and rolled, as the fold would spoil their appearance—for instance, velvet, brocade, and tinsel fabrics. Here are the standard fabrics and their respective widths. Varieties of these are also put on the market under different names, but they are all included in one of the classes in the following list.

WOOLLENS

Harris tweed : 28 inches.
Light woollen dress cloths : 52 to 54 inches.
Serge and gabardine : 54 inches.
Suiting : 54 to 56 inches.
Faced cloth, velour cloth, and similar coating cloths : 54 inches.
Scotch, Irish, and Yorkshire tweed : 54 inches.

COTTONS AND LINENS

Plain and printed dress cottons : 36 inches.
Voile and mercerised lawns : 36 inches.
Spotted muslin : 30 inches.
Plain organdi : 44 inches.
Embroidered organdi : 36 inches.
Linens : 36 inches.
Linings : 36 inches.

SILKS AND RAYONS

Plain and printed marocains, satin, taffeta, crêpe-de-chine and other crêpes, spun silk, broché silk, and most other silks : 35 to 38 inches.
Shantung, both natural and dyed : 33 to 36 inches.

VELVET, ETC.

Velvet : 35 to 36 inches.
Velveteen : 27 to 36 inches.
Tinsel brocade, lamé, etc. : 36 inches.

GEORGETTE, CHIFFON, NINON, ETC.

35 to 36 inches.

LININGS

Linings have a threefold purpose—they give substance and support; they add warmth; they enhance the appearance of the garment when the inside is exposed (as in the case of coats and cloaks) or when they show through a transparent outer material. The quality of the lining should always be appropriate to that of the material of the garment. For instance, the appearance of an expensive lace frock would be quite spoiled if a cheap cotton-backed satin foundation showed through it, while on the other hand the effect of quite a cheap muslin can be much enhanced by being made up over a good silk. It is often possible to use up discarded silk and crêpe-de-chine frocks for the linings and foundations of others. Taffeta is ideal when a standing-out effect is desired, and satin or crêpe-de-chine when a clinging one is essential. When a cheaper one is necessary, artificial sik or rayon may be substituted for taffeta, and mercerised lawn or shantung for the softer fabrics. For frocks of thin, but not transparent, material, a lining of jap silk or net is often used for the bodice.

Tight-fitting Bodices

When tight-fitting bodices are in fashion—for instance, in the case of an evening bodice without sleeves or shoulder-straps, or other visible means of support—a tight-fitting boned bodice lining is a necessity (the pattern would probably be of the type shown in Fig. 3, p. 13, but cut to the desired shape round the upper part). For good-class work taffeta should be used, and the lining would either be cut to the same shape as the material and the two stitched up together, or the lining would be made separately (except for under-arm and shoulder seams, where the two fabrics would be stitched together) and the material draped over it. (How to bone seams is described on pp. 210–11).

Coats

All cloth coats look better for the addition of a lining, even though one is not required to give warmth. It improves the " hang " of a coat, and it also lengthens its wear, as it saves the cloth from a certain amount of friction. Satin, crêpe-de-chine, and broché silk are all good, while shantung is hard-wearing and when patterned is very effective. Coat linings are cut looser round the figure than the coat, as the cloth will stretch, whilst the lining will not, and would tear unless the extra width were provided. Cloaks and evening coats are lined similarly, but the latter call for very handsome lining materials. Sometimes quilted satin or broché will be used, and this can be bought by the yard, and although it can be made by machine, it involves a great deal of labour and causes no saving of expense. Coat linings are made separately and felled in as explained in the chapter on coat making.

INTERLININGS

Interlinings are often inserted in garments for the sake of extra warmth. For instance, domette or flannelette may be placed between the cloth and lining of a coat, thus increasing the warmth considerably, and in fact a summer coat, if not too summer-like in aspect, may often be wearable in winter in this way. For evening wraps of velvet and brocade—tinsel or otherwise—an interlining of domette or wadding is essential, both to give substance and to supply the necessary warmth. The little house- or coffee-coats of fragile material also need a similar interlining for the same reason, otherwise they would give to the figure and would have no shape of their own.

There are two ways of setting in an interlining, and you must choose that which is most suitable for your own need. (1) Cut it to the shape of the outer material and seam it up with it, afterwards setting in the lining in the usual way. (2) Cut it to the shape of the outer material without turnings, and after the seams have been made in the material, place the interlining on each piece and tack it to the turnings. A wadding interlining must, of course, always be applied in the second method, and as a rule it is laid over a foundation of firm, but not stiff, muslin, and tacked to it, and then the wadding is thinned off all round close to the edges.

STIFFENINGS

Book muslin, tailor's linen, and tailor's canvas are all used to stiffen collars and cuffs, bows, trimmings, etc. They are usually cut on the bias, for the sake of pliability. Machining in straight or zigzag rows gives extra firmness. Horsehair—sold by the yard in ribbon width—is employed to stiffen paniers and to give bouffant effects to draperies. Pleated frills of lace-edged muslin, or gathered ones of " pinked " taffeta, are sewn inside the lower edge of ground-length skirts when a wide, sweeping effect is desired. Crescent-shaped pieces of canvas, or small pleated frills of stiff muslin, are sewn inside the upper part of the armhole to extend the fullness of large sleeves, and to give a broad appearance to the shoulders.

TIPS

1. When handling velvet avoid pressure by the fingers, and when necessary, to avoid marking, place a scrap of velvet with pile downward against the pile of the large piece and hold the two layers between the thumb and finger.

2. See that the style you have chosen for the garment is suitable for the material—that is, a firm material for a tight-fitting garment, to take the strain; and a full, easy style for a thin, stretchy material.

CHAPTER V
FOUNDATION STITCHES

SOME of the stitches described in this chapter are used in ordinary household sewing, others in embroidery, but many are peculiar to dressmaking. I advise the reader to study them with needle and thread in hand and to try each stitch in turn in accordance with the directions, thus making certain that she is familiar with all. It is essential for good hand-stitchery that it should be done both quickly and lightly. Heavy, laboured sewing produces garments which can only be described as " stodgy ", for the less handling they have the better. " Lightness with firmness " should be the dressmaker's motto.

TACKING

This is a temporary stitch used to keep two or more pieces of material in position for permanent sewing, or to indicate fitting or trimming lines. There are several varieties of this stitch. Begin with a knot on the right side when great firmness is not required, but when tacking up skirt or bodice seams for fitting begin with two back stitches, otherwise the tacking will not hold. Special tacking-thread is sold which is quite suitable for light work, but it is not strong enough for fitting seams, or for any seams in firm material.

53

Even Tacking (Fig. 20)

The simplest form, used for seams, hems, facings, outlining shapes, etc. Stitches should be of the same size on both sides, but may vary in length on different pieces of work to suit the special purpose. For instance, for long, straight seams in firm material

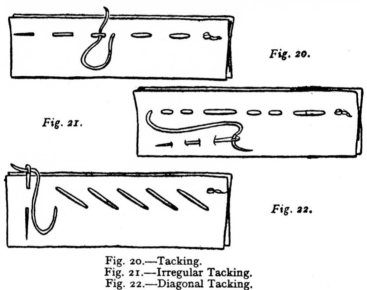

Fig. 20.

Fig. 21.

Fig. 22.

Fig. 20.—Tacking.
Fig. 21.—Irregular Tacking.
Fig. 22.—Diagonal Tacking.

stitches may be much longer than when tacking a curved seam in thin fabric.

Irregular Tacking (Fig. 21)

For springy fabrics. Make first a long stitch and then two short ones.

Diagonal Tacking (Fig. 22)

To keep together two large surfaces, such as a coat and its lining. It can be worked from right to left (as shown), or upward, by turning the fabric half-way round; it can also be worked from left to right, or downward, if again you turn the work half-way round. This stitch is used for seams in velvet or other pile fabrics, but is worked much more closely. In this case the stitches are taken from right to left, the needle being inserted in the turnings and brought out on the fitting-line straight below, to avoid marking the pile.

Tailor Tacking or Thread Marking (Fig. 23)

For marking the fitting-lines on two pieces at the same time. Take a long length of double cotton, threaded in a long needle. Begin without knot or back stitches. Make running stitches covering about ⅜ inch on both sides, but

Fig. 23.—Tailor Tacking.

leave every alternative stitch on the right side as a loop. about ¼ inch in length. Draw the two layers of material apart gently and cut the threads between them.

Withdrawing Tacking-threads

After stitching, a long tacking-thread may often be taken out by pulling from the knot end, but in the case of delicate fabrics, velvet, or anything which crushes easily, it is best to snip the stitches on one side and draw them out from the other. When removing tacking from the *right* side of any pile fabric cut the stitches on the *wrong* side and withdraw them from the right.

RUNNING (Fig. 24)

This is a quick method of sewing seams where great strength is not required, also for tucks. It is worked from right to left, and is really like the first type of tacking (Fig. 20) on a small scale, as the

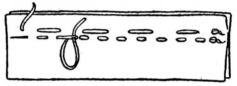

Fig. 24.—Running.

stitches should be $\frac{1}{16}$ inch in length, or smaller, in proportion to the material. With practice several stitches may be taken on the needle at once. For very thin materials there is a variation of this stitch known as " fly running ", in which the fabric is held upright by the fingers of both hands, while the needle is also held between the right thumb and first finger near the point and is shaken in and out, forming small stitches, very quickly. The needle is never drawn out completely, but the material is worked off the eye as the point works its way along.

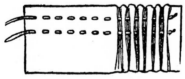

Fig. 25.—Gathering.

GATHERING (Fig. 25)

This is worked just like running, but the thread is drawn up afterwards to the desired fullness.

Two or more rows of evenly spaced gathers are known as shirring or gauging. When gathering a long length it is advisable to divide both it and the piece to which it is to be sewn into an equal number of spaces, thus ensuring regularity of the fullness.

BACK STITCH (Fig. 26)

This can be used for a seam when great strength is required and a machine is not available. The stitches must all be of equal length, with no space

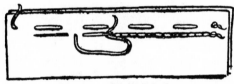

Fig. 26.—Back Stitch.

between them. They progress from right to left, but each one is actually worked from left to right, by putting the needle into the end of the previous one.

STAB STITCH

Often used through two or more layers of thick material where running or back stitching would be impossible. The needle is simply passed upward and downward through the material. This stitch can be used to simulate machine stitch, back stitch, running, etc., and is useful for filling in small gaps in stitching.

FELLING, OR DRESSMAKER'S HEMMING (Fig. 27)

Used to secure a folded edge or a selvedge to material below. It is worked on the wrong side from right to left. The folded edge must always be tacked into place, as pinning is not sufficient. Insert needle in material just below fold and bring out at front just above it. The space between the stitches depends upon the amount of firmness required. If the lower material is single, only the surface threads should be taken up.

SLIP HEMMING (Fig. 28)

Used to sew a hem invisibly. Tack the hem; first make a horizontal stitch along the fold, then

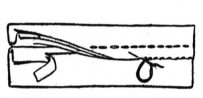

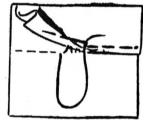

Fig. 27.—Felling.   Fig. 28.—Slip Hemming.

take up only one or two of the surface threads of the material below. The stitches come slightly slanting. The closer they are, the stronger is the result; but when only a light effect is required, the stitches along the fold may be ¼ inch or more in length. In no case should they be drawn tightly. Work from right to left.

SLIP STITCHING (Fig. 29)

Used to join two folded edges invisibly, such as those of a cuff and a coat sleeve, or the edges of a lapel and collar. Edges must be tacked very care-

fully, either together as shown in the diagram
(though here they are purposely separated to show
the stitches) or
meeting on the flat.

Take a tiny hori-
zontal stitch first
in one edge and
then in the other,
the thread going

Fig. 29.—Slip Stitch.

almost straight across. Work from right to left.
Pull up the thread very tightly so that it is invisible.
Although matching thread should be used, yet, if
correctly worked, even if of contrasting colour, it
should be invisible.

WHIPPING (Fig. 30)

Used chiefly for lawn and lace frills. For lawn
the edge must be cut to a straight thread, either warp
or weft, though warp rolls best. Join on the thread
at the right-hand end, then roll the edge of the
material towards you on the wrong side with the

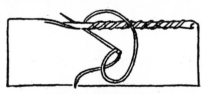

left thumb and fore-
finger. At the same
time work the nee-
dle over and over,
first through the
single material just
under the roll from

Fig. 30.—Whipping.

front to back, then over the roll to the front and
through to the back again. Never pull the needle
completely out but push the material off the eye,
then draw up as required.

LACING STITCH (Fig. 31)

This is used to draw together two edges, usually raw, very lightly. It is chiefly employed for folds to form trimmings, or for strappings. Worked from right to left, taking a stitch first under one edge and then under the other, with the thread slanting across.

OVERSEWING (Fig. 32)

This is sometimes known as top-sewing or seaming. It is only used in dressmaking to join two

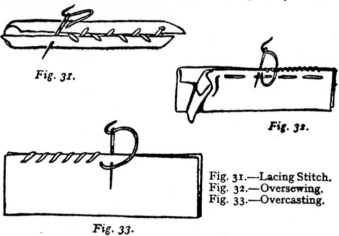

Fig. 31.

Fig. 32.

Fig. 33.

Fig. 31.—Lacing Stitch.
Fig. 32.—Oversewing.
Fig. 33.—Overcasting.

folded edges where they will not be seen. It is a very strong stitch, and is worked from right to left. Tack the two turned-in edges level, then, holding them between the thumb and forefinger of the left hand, pass the threaded needle through the edges of both folds with point coming straight towards you. The distance between the stitches regulates their strength.

OVERCASTING (Fig. 33)

For neatening the raw edges of turnings, either single or double. It is worked similarly to oversewing, but from left to right. In no case should it be worked tightly, or it will contract the edges.

LOOP STITCH (Fig. 34)

Another method of neatening the turnings of a fabric which frays easily. It is worked loosely from

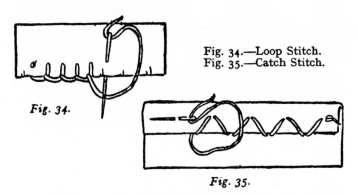

Fig. 34.—Loop Stitch.
Fig. 35.—Catch Stitch.

Fig. 34.

Fig. 35.

left to right. This same stitch, worked very closely over strands of silk, is used for making loops and bars for fastening (see pp. 129–30).

CATCH STITCH (Fig. 35)

For holding down a raw edge which is afterwards to be covered by a lining or facing. It is worked from right to left, taking up only the surface threads of the single material, but going right through the turned-down part.

HERRINGBONE STITCH (Fig. 36)

This serves the same purpose as catch stitch, but is much stronger. It is worked from left to right

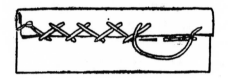

Fig. 36.—Herringbone Stitch.

and, as in catch stitch, only the surface threads of the single material should be taken up.

CHAPTER VI
CUTTING OUT

THERE are some people who would willingly spend days—yes, *days*—trying to solve a jigsaw puzzle who will say : " Cutting out is quite beyond me. . . so many confusing parts in the pattern. . . . I get dreadfully muddled."

That's all nonsense. Planning out can be such *fun*, and just as interesting as a jigsaw, though far more profitable ! I always feel that I deserve a prize when I cut out a garment from ½ yard less material than is prescribed on the pattern. Yes, cutting out can be a really fascinating game—and this is how you play it.

RULES OF THE GAME

1. Essential : a large, smooth surface to cut on, such as is described on p. 10.

2. Assemble your tools so that no time is lost in looking for them one by one as required. They comprise : large cutting-out shears, small scissors, tailor's chalk (in two colours at least), good pins (preferably steel), long tacking-needles, tacking-cotton (in two colours), tape-measure, long ruler or yard-stick, thimble, pincushion, and (perhaps) paper-weights, tracing-wheel, and sheets of cardboard.

3. Examine your paper pattern and test it and

adapt it to your personal measurements as described on pp. 31–40.

4. Be sure, if you are using cloth, that it is guaranteed shrunk, otherwise it must be shrunk as described on pp. 184–85.

5. Find out if the fabric has a nap or a pile (see pp. 45–46). If it has, find out the direction in which it runs and chalk with points arrows downwards.

6. If a patterned fabric, or plaid, which looks different viewed from each end, has been chosen, find the upright position and chalk arrows running downward as before.

7. Always cut out in double material unless otherwise directed. There is always the risk of cutting two sleeves for the same arm, etc., if the material is cut single. With fabrics of large pattern, stripes, plaids, velvet, etc., and when cutting on the bias, it is, however, often necessary to cut in single material.

8. Plan out all parts of the pattern according to the layout accompanying it; failing that, observe the rules to be explained later.

TO PLAN OUT THE PATTERN

If your garment is to be cut out in double material, lay it on the (bare) table with the double selvedges towards you, and if it has a nap or upright pattern, with the top part to the left hand. All creases must have been previously pressed out. If it has been bought folded, leave it in its original fold; if without a fold, lay material right side upwards and lift over the farther selvedge to meet the one nearer you.

Pin them together at intervals of 3 to 4 inches. Should the table not be a very long one, let the bulk of the material rest on a smaller table or a chair at the left hand, with another at the right hand to take the fabric as it moves along. If your pattern has a layout with it, of course you follow that; but, if not, here is the method to follow.

Large Pieces First

Take the largest pieces first, and after planning them to the best advantage pin them temporarily. You will often have to move the parts quite a good deal to get them arranged satisfactorily. Of course, if the material is marked with arrows, you must see that they run downward on all the parts; if not, you can turn them upside down when they fit in better that way. Centre-front and centre-back of skirt will in most cases be placed to folds, also centre-front or centre-back of bodice (or perhaps both). These parts of the pattern will have such directions marked on them. Warp threads must run down the upper and under sleeve from the top to the elbow, and in the case of a one-piece sleeve put the sides together and fold it down the middle; then place this fold on the straight warp thread. Sometimes, in the case of a skirt with narrow front and back gores, and of back and front of bodice, which must all be placed to folds, it is necessary to open out the material to its fullest width and then to fold over both selvedges to meet, thus producing two folds. Again, in the case of wide skirt pieces, it may be necessary to join on small wedge-shaped pieces to

C (Dress)

the bottom of the slanting sides. The joins for these must come on the straight warp threads.

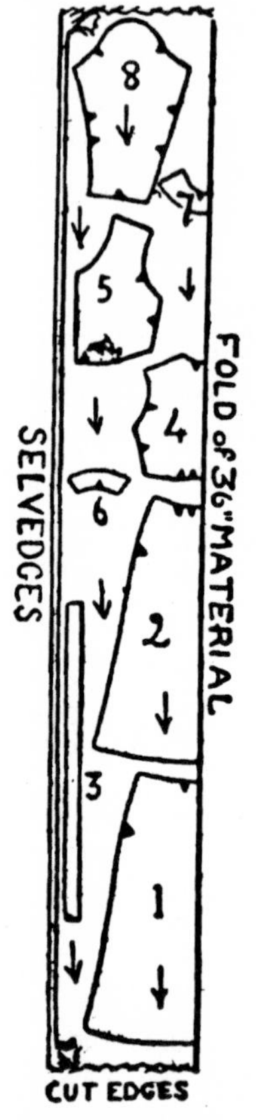

SELVEDGES

FOLD of 36" MATERIAL

CUT EDGES

Fig. 37.—Layout of Frock on Non-reversible Material.

In Fig. 37 is shown the layout of a simple frock in eight pieces—viz., 1. skirt front; 2. skirt back; 3. belt; 4. bodice back; 5. bodice front; 6. cuff; 7. collar; 8. sleeve.

SKIRTS

As before stated, when front and back of skirts are seamless the straight or centre edge must be placed to a fold. When a skirt has several gores they will usually be much narrower at the top than at the bottom, and the front edge of each should be placed on the straight thread, thus throwing the back edge somewhat on the bias; so when the skirt is pinned up a straight edge will go to a slanting edge all round, except at the back, where the slanting sides of the back gore will meet those of the next gores. Occasionally, however, the *middle* of each gore is directed to be placed on the straight warp thread, thus giving a different " hang " to the skirt, as the seams will flare out all round.

COLLARS AND CUFFS

Centre-back of collar and middle of cuffs must have the straight warp thread running down them, and if there is a nap it should be arranged to run down when the garment is worn. Belts should be placed with the warp threads running along the length of the strip. Gathered or pleated flounces are usually placed with the warp threads running down them, but narrow frills may be cut the opposite way if the pattern or weave allows it. Sometimes frills are cut on the bias, and so are most trimmings—folds, pipings, strappings, etc.

CUTTING IN SINGLE MATERIAL

With fabrics of large pattern, stripes, plaids, velvet, etc., it is often necessary to cut out in single material. In such a case it is advisable to cut duplicates in paper of the pattern parts and mark them conspicuously "right" and "left". After they have been planned satisfactorily, cut out all "rights" in material; take one cut-out piece, *turn it over*, and place it on its corresponding "left", with the pattern and grain of thread matching, then cut out to the same shape. Only in this way can you be sure of both sides being exactly alike.

CUTTING ON THE BIAS

When a frock or skirt is to be cut on the bias, the exact diagonal must be found separately for each piece. (How to do this is explained on p. 44.) Then, as a rule, every part which is usually placed on the warp thread must be laid on the bias. You will find, however, all these directions on the pattern. It may be necessary also to cut out right and left sides separately, in order to match a pattern. Fig. 38 shows a gored skirt laid on the bias on single material ready for cutting.   The parts in solid lines show the original pattern—for example, 1. L.—1. left; 2. L.—2. left, etc., whilst the parts in broken lines show the duplicates which have been cut— 1. R.—1. right; 2. R—2. right, etc.

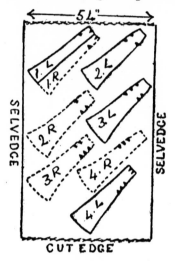

Fig. 38.—Layout of Skirt on the Bias.

BIAS STRIPS

When cutting bias strips from a large piece of material, first find the exact diagonal, then chalk a line, and from this measure the width of strip you require.   Chalk lines in this way until you have the required number.   Be careful with a diagonal material, or with one with a twill, that the stripes or twill run *across* the strip, not along it.   All strips must be joined on the warp threads.   Place two strips with right sides together in the position shown in Fig. 39A. Note that the strips join on the sewing-line, not on the edges of the turnings.   Press all turnings open as in Fig. 39B.   When you require a large number of strips and you have a large piece of fabric to cut them from, chalk the strips on the material, and then cut out on the *outside* lines, leaving a broad strip. Then join the sides of this as shown in Fig. 39C, so that one strip projects at top and bottom.   After stitching, press the turnings open over a roller, then start cutting along the chalked line at the top, and in the end you will find yourself with a long length of the joined strips.

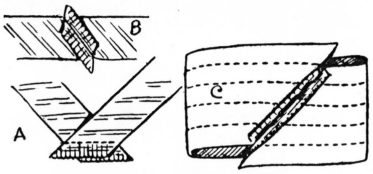

Fig. 39A, B, C.—Cutting on the Bias.

FOR A PATTERN WITHOUT TURNINGS

When planning out the parts, you must, if your pattern is cut without turnings, make allowance for them between the pieces. Here are the approximate amounts when you are using a tested pattern; but if you are not sure of the pattern it is better to allow $\frac{1}{2}$ inch *extra* on what are known as the " fitting-seams "—viz., the under-arms and shoulders. Also, if the material is loosely woven and frays easily, $\frac{1}{4}$ inch should be allowed *extra* on *all* edges.

Bodice

Centre-back and front: if closed, place up to the fold without turning; the same if open, $1\frac{1}{4}$ inch; under-arm and shoulder edges, $\frac{3}{4}$ inch; all other edges, $\frac{1}{2}$ inch.

Blouse

Similar to bodice, with perhaps rather more on centre front, according to pattern.

Sleeve.

Wrist, ¾ inch; all other edges, ½ inch; sleeve set into cuff, ½ inch all round.

Skirt

Centre-front and back : if seamless, place up to the fold; sides of all pieces, ¾ inch; waist edge, ½ inch; lower edge, from ½ to ¾ inch on fragile materials, to 3 or 4 inches on a medium or heavy weight one.

Belts, Pockets, Trimmings

Usually from ¼ to ½ inch, according to fabric.

MARKING THE TURNINGS

When all the parts have been arranged satisfactorily and with the greatest economy, keeping all the spare material in as large and few pieces as possible, pin the pattern pieces to the double material. Place a pin near each corner, and others near the edges of the paper at intervals of 2 or 3 inches. Be liberal with the pins, so that there is no danger of the paper slipping when cutting out the material. Use needles for velvet and fragile fabrics, and for very springy or delicate ones substitute paper-weights for pins or needles.

On all firm materials take a ruler and mark the turnings all round with chalk, crossing the lines at the corners, and not rounding them off. But this will not answer for fragile fabrics, where the turnings must be indicated lightly with needles or pins.

WHEN THE PATTERN IS CUT WITH TURNINGS

Here you can plan out the pattern with the pieces touching at various parts. The rules for pinning are just the same as for the pattern without turnings.

CUTTING OUT (I)

When the Pattern has No Turnings

Take the shears in your right hand, place the left hand flat on the pattern to keep it firm, then cut out on the chalked lines. Make long, clean cuts, keeping the shears close to the table. Cut right to the edges of the turnings, so that the corners are kept sharp. On no account take out the pins.

The fitting-lines must now be marked in some way, so that you will know exactly where to sew. There are three methods : chalking, tailor tacking, and tracing. The first answers well for woollens and cloth of any kind, but for velvet, silk, crêpe, and all fragile materials tailor tacking must be used. Tracing only answers for cottons, and must not be employed even then if the lines are not to be stitched over or covered with trimming, as they cannot be removed.

Chalking

Place the cut-out pieces, with patterns still pinned to them, on the table. Take one piece and lay the left hand flat on the pattern. With tailor's chalk mark all round the pattern edges as close to the paper as possible. Do not use it like a pencil, but push it forward with a driving motion, crossing the lines well at the corners of the turnings. Chalk through any perforations with a different colour, also make a short horizontal line of the same right across the turnings at each notch. When all the pieces have been treated in this way, unpin one pattern piece and separate the two layers of material, placing them with the wrong sides upward.

Take the chalked piece, turn it over, and place it on the unchalked one, matching the edges exactly. (Chalked side will be inside.) Clench the hand, and with it strike the double edges all round, just over the chalked lines, thus driving them on to the piece below. Strike also over perforations and any other marks, then separate the pieces again. Lines will now be blurred, so re-chalk them singly, then place the pieces together again with chalked lines inside.

Tailor Tacking

Take double, soft tacking-cotton, threaded in a coarse, long needle, and work tailor tacking, as shown in Fig. 23 on p. 55, all round each side of the pattern through the two layers of the material. Work right to the ends of the turnings, so that the lines cross. Make one loop through single perforations, and a line of loops where there is a series. At each notch make a little horizontal line of loops in a contrasting colour. Remove the pattern, draw the two pieces of material apart, and cut the threads.

Tracing

Be sure to place cardboard between material and table. Trace all round the edges of the pattern to the end of the turnings, pushing the wheel away from you. Make a short horizontal line on the turning *only* opposite each notch. Do not trace perforations unless they are to be covered—if not, mark with tacking.

CUTTING OUT (II)

When Turnings are Allowed on the Pattern

With the left hand on the paper pattern, and holding the shears as before described, cut all round the paper as close to it as possible. Make long, clean cuts, keeping the shears close to the table, and not lifting the material. On no account cut any notches, and do not remove the pins. Do not cut any darts.

Here is a good way of marking the fitting-lines. Consult the instructions which accompany your pattern, and note the amount of the turnings on the different edges. Now take a ruler and measure these amounts in from the outside edge all round, at the same time outlining the fitting-lines with pins. Each line of pins must go through both layers of material. Now turn to the other side, where you will see the back of the pinned lines, and make a short chalk line over each pin. Mark each perforation and each notch with a pin, and on the fabric side mark with chalk of a different colour. When the material is too fragile for this method the pattern must be removed, the turnings measured inwards as before on the material, and then the fitting-lines must be tailor tacked as described on p. 55.

Transferring the Chalked Fitting-lines

When the material is firm, the chalked lines may be transferred to the unchalked piece in this way. Remove the paper pattern, then separate the two pieces of material and lay them on the table with the wrong side uppermost. Take the chalk and outline the incompete fitting-lines, pushing the chalk forwards. Mark perforations and notches also. Then proceed as described under the heading " Chalking " on pp. 71–2.

Tailor Tacking

With a thin or springy fabric tailor tacking is preferable. After chalking on the under-side over the back of the pins, remove the pins and tailor tack along the pinned lines as described under the heading " Tailor Tacking " on p. 72.

Tracing

Proceed as described under the heading " Tracing " on p. 72, but first measuring in the turnings from the outside edge and drawing them in with a pencil, after which trace through the pencilled lines.

A Word of Caution

Don't *start cutting out in a hurry.* *Give yourself plenty of time, and remember that a wrong cut cannot be retrieved.*

CHAPTER VII
TACKING-UP GARMENTS

THE amateur is inclined to be sparing with tacking and to rely only upon pinning when preparing hems and seams for machining. This is a short-sighted policy, for the unseen work in dressmaking is equally as important as the seen, and well repays all the labour involved. The tailor has a motto to the effect that a well-tacked garment is half-made, and if you have ever examined a tailor-made in its preliminary stages you will see how much time has been devoted to tacking, or " basting " as it is called in sartorial workrooms. So surely the tyro may follow where the expert leads !

Never tack with the material in your hand, but always flat on the table—that is, unless you wish one layer of fabric to be fuller than the other, or to roll slightly, as in the case of cuffs, collars, and lapels, when tacking over the fingers of the left hand is to be recommended. But all tacking of bodice and skirt seams, skirt hems, etc., must be done on a table or skirt-board, and in each case they must be pinned first. Any folds, such as those down centre-front and back of skirts and bodices, must previously be pressed out, and creases must be treated similarly. The folds just mentioned, however, must be replaced by single lines of tacking, as a guide when fitting.

75

BALANCE MARKS

When assembling the different parts of a garment look out for the balance marks, usually notches on the pattern and replaced by chalked or tacked lines on the material. It is very important that these should match exactly, particularly when there is fullness on one edge only. The general rule for bodices and coats is to work from centre-back, adding any pieces at each side until the side seams are reached, then to work similarly from the centre-front, after which these sides and the shoulder edges are joined.

SKIRTS

For a two-piece skirt—back and front, with a seam at each side—work in this way : Open out the front piece and place it right side upward on the table with the waist edge to your right hand. Place back piece on it with right side downward. First tackle the seam farthest away from you. Take a pin, insert it on the waist-line (both layers) where it crosses the side-line, and push it forward on to the turnings; then pin all down the side-line in this way at intervals of 2 inches or so. Lift up the double turnings with the left hand as you pin, to be sure that you are on the fitting-line on both pieces. This done, take a long needleful of strong cotton and, beginning at the edge of the waist-turnings with a double back stitch, tack all down the fitting-line to the bottom with the stitch shown in Fig. 20, p. 54, making a back stitch occasionally for the sake of firmness. The stitches should be about

½ inch long. Now turn the pieces over and tack the other seam similarly. If there are darts, first fold and pin from the top to the point; then tack in the same way, but at the point the stitches should be carried down a little farther, taking up a mere thread of material.

Note.—Any pleats in the middle of the pieces should be tacked before the seams.

A Many-gored Skirt

Pin and tack up the seams on the same principle as before, joining the pieces according to the notches. Begin with the front gore and add pieces at each side alternately until all have been joined. As a rule you will find that a straight edge will be placed to a slanting edge all the way round, with two slanting ones meeting in the centre back, or else a whole piece coming there with the middle to a fold. All the straight edges of the gores will be facing the front and the slanting ones facing toward the centre-back. This is arranged so as to throw the flare towards the back. (Note that if one or both sides of the gores are curved out near the bottom they must be stretched slightly under the iron at this part—the two edges should be placed over one another so that they are stretched equally.) When one is more slanting than the other, this should be placed uppermost in tacking. Care should be taken as a rule not to stretch such an edge, but if the material is very stretchy, and this edge is very much more off the straight thread than that to which it is to be joined, the pinned seam should be allowed to hang for a day. After this the slanting side will have dropped a little and the seam should be re-pinned, smoothing down the excess material to the lower edge of the skirt. Then the seam must be tacked and the excess material on the skirt edge trimmed off to shape.

Note.—All seams must be tacked from the waist downward to ensure evenness.

FROCKS
Simple Model with Under-arm and Shoulder Seams only

Tackle any darts first, which will be as in Fig. 40, either in back or front-half above, and half below waist-line. Press out folds or creases, make a line of tacking down centre-back, then place on the table with right side upward and neck to the right hand. Open out the front and place right side downward on the back piece. First pin and tack the seam farthest from you as described in the paragraph under the heading " Skirts ". Begin at the armhole and work downward as a rule, unless the waist-line is marked on the pattern, in which case pinning should start there and be done upward to the armhole and downward to the lower edge, though the tacking may be done from

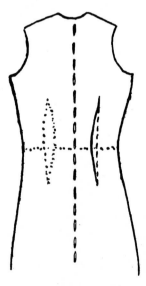

Fig. 40.—Darts in Back of Frock.

the armhole. Then turn the work over and pin and tack the other seam, after which the shoulder seams must be pinned and tacked, starting at the neck-line. If the front shoulder works out a little longer than the back, do not cut if off until the frock has been fitted.

Frock with a Waist Seam

Bodice and skirt must be pinned and tacked up separately, and finally the two parts pinned and tacked by their waist edges.

TIGHT-FITTING BODICE (Fig. 3)

A foundation lining bodice of regulation cut is shown in Fig. 3, p. 13. Though from time to time, for varying periods, it drops out of use for its original purpose, yet it is the ideal pattern for testing stock patterns as described on p. 34, and for adapting a stock-size dress-form to personal measurements. The long seams running from shoulder to waist at both back and front allow it to be easily adjusted to variations of figures. Pin each seam before tacking. First pin the two backs together, starting at the waist-line, and pinning upward and downward from there, then tack from the neck downward, starting with a double back stitch. Now add the other pieces, working from side to side, until the under-arm edges are reached. Work on the same principle as before, carefully matching the notches, but place both pieces flat on the table with the turnings upward when pinning, and keeping the one nearest the back towards you. When you have reached the under-arm edges pin and tack the fronts to the side-fronts, then join under-arm and shoulder edges to those of the back. Pin the shoulders from the neck end. When finished, the waist-line on all the pieces should be continuous all round.

BODICE WITH UNDER-ARM AND SHOULDER SEAMS ONLY

.Many frock bodices are like this, and they may be fairly loose-fitting with a placket under the arm, or they may fasten down centre-front or back. If there are darts in front or back, pin and tack these first. They may run up from the waist, or the bust shaping may be contrived either by a dart in each front shoulder or by one or two small horizontal darts just below the armhole on the side edges of the front. After this pin and tack under-arm and shoulder seams as before described.

BLOUSE

This is tacked up similarly to the previous bodice. If there is a yoke, this is tacked first. Usually the under-arm seams are stitched before the sleeves are tacked into the armholes, but in some models with large armholes and plain, but loose, sleeves these are set in after the shoulder seams have been stitched and before the under-arm and sleeve seams have been tacked up.

SLEEVE (Fig. 4, p. 13)

A tight-fitting, two-piece sleeve (often called a coat-shape sleeve) is tacked up in the following way. Lay the under sleeve on the upper (right sides together) and pin down the middle three times (see Fig. 41A, below). Have the inner curve edges farthest from you, and pin these first. Place a pin in the middle of the elbow curve, then from there pin upward and downward. Begin the outer seam from the top and bottom and pin to where the elbow fullness starts (this is generally indicated on the

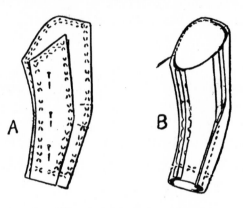

Fig. 41.
A.—Two-piece Sleeve Pinned for Tacking-up.
B.—Two-piece Sleeve Stitched up.

pattern either by notches or traced lines). Keep the sleeve flat on the table while doing all this, and lift over the turning of the upper sleeve to meet that of the under. Gather the fullness on the upper sleeve at the elbow and draw up to meet the under, then tack the seam from top to bottom. Even for a sleeve apparently without fullness round the top its measurement there must be 2 inches more than the width round the armhole. Run a gathering thread round the top edge of the upper sleeve. The position is usually indicated on the pattern, and it starts about 1½ inch above one seam and ends the same distance above the other, though this amount varies in different types of sleeves (Fig. 41B shows this sleeve tacked up).

For a one-piece, tight-fitting sleeve with dart or darts at the elbow, or one running up from wrist to elbow, pin and tack the darts, then fold the sleeve down the middle, bring edges together, and tack from top to wrist.

COAT

Tack up similarly to a tight-fitting bodice or a simple frock, according to its shape, and tack up the sleeve as described for the two-piece sleeve. It is well to cut out collar and cuffs in canvas only before fitting.

VELVET, VELVETEEN, ETC.

Use needles only for pinning, then tack up with the diagonal tacking as shown in Fig. 22, p. 54, inserting the needle in the turnings and bringing it out on the fitting-line to avoid crushing the pile.

CHAPTER VIII

FITTING

THE home dressmaker, in her ardour, is inclined to fit too much and too often, and thus the original lines, which were planned with so much care, are lost. If the pattern has been adapted to personal measurements, as it should have been before the material was cut, then any fitting required should be very slight, and it is very unlikely that many of the defects afterwards described will be present. When you become well acquainted with your own figure you will probably find that one fitting only, at any rate for a simple garment, will be sufficient. But I do beg of you to resist the temptation to slip on the frock, etc., at every stage of its development—it gets so dreadfully crumpled and pulled out of shape in that way, and much time is wasted. Plan your fittings definitely and stick to them.

If you decide on one fitting only, all lengthwise seams should be stitched and fastenings made; sleeves should be finished, but only tacked in; collar, cuffs, and trimmings should be made and ready for pinning on. Skirts should be tacked to the band, and the lower edge may be tacked up. If you prefer two fittings, here is your method of work.

83

First Fitting

Garment must have all seams (except armhole ones) tacked, but not stitched; trimmings made or partly so; collar and cuffs cut out in muslin or canvas. Fit according to rules which follow, mark new fitting-lines with chalk or pins, also position of trimmings. Adjust skirt-band to fit, pin skirt to it. Fit on wrong side of material.

Second Fitting

All seams will now be stitched, pressed, and neatened, fastenings made, and if quite sure of the fit, everything may be finished except the sewing-in of the sleeves. But if not sure, skirt hem may be tacked up only, trimmings, collar, and cuffs simply tacked on, and skirt may be tacked to the waist-band, not stitched.

TIGHT-FITTING LINING BODICE

This will have been tacked up as described on p. 79. Put on the bodice with turnings outside, and pin fronts together at the waist-line. See that the waist-line on the bodice fits well into place on the figure, then pin the front edges together from the waist-line upward and downward. Fit right side of figure only if fitting on the dress-form or another person, but the left side if fitting yourself with the aid of mirrors. Smooth the bodice upward from the waist.

Short-waisted

Unpick shoulder seam, let front and back drop, then re-pin seam. In every case shoulder seam should run straight from neck to armhole, not exactly on the top of the shoulder, but slightly towards the back.

Too Long-waisted

Folds will form round the figure. Unpick shoulder seam, smooth material upward at back and front and re-pin seam. This will raise the bodice at the under-armhole, and this may need hollowing out a little, so make a few short snips here; but do this carefully, and do not make the snips so deep as seem required. Mark the alteration with pins, and trim off turnings after the bodice is removed from the figure. At the moment mark the new armhole curve with chalk or pins.

Too Wide Across Back

Take in not more than ¼ inch at the back seam. If this is not sufficient, take in also at the seam running downward from the shoulder, and perhaps at the other downward seam. Mark new armhole curve, if necessary, as shoulder seam may have to be shortened.

Too Narrow Across Back

Let out centre-back seam, and, if not sufficient, the other two downward seams.

Too Wide In Front

Taking in at the under-arm seam may be sufficient, but, if not, take in at front seam first, then at the other downward seams as required.

In all cases of alteration in width it should be

remembered that the proportion of the pieces must be preserved, and it is better to make a little alteration at many seams than all of it at one. Very often, when it is a case of general largeness or tightness all over, it is best not to make alterations now, but if required smaller to stitch all seams just inside the tackings, and if required larger a little outside them. Remember that the bodice will be tighter when machined than when merely tacked.

Too Tight in the Front

Note the above remarks about general tightness. Let out if required, first at the front seam, then at under-arm, then at the long seam from the shoulder.

Fullness at Front of Armhole

Unpick shoulder seam, stretch front shoulder slightly, or take in seam running from shoulder, then re-pin shoulder seam. If this is not successful make a small dart on the lower curve. This should run diagonally towards the bust. Another plan, if this will not make the under-arm curve too low, is to unpick the under-arm seam at the top for 2 inches and make a horizontal dart on the side edge about 1½ inch below the armhole.

Shoulder Seam Too Long

Length of shoulder seam varies with fashion. Mark any required alteration at armhole with chalk or pins. If the sleeve is a tight-fitting one, this alteration may make it necessary to raise the sleeve head.

Faulty Neck-line

Chalk or pin any alterations. Keep the back neck high, as it always drops a little in wear.

BODICE WITH UNDER-ARM AND SHOULDER SEAMS ONLY

This will probably be in unlined material, so should not be fitted too tightly. Any darts must be tacked, also under-arm seams. There may or may not be a back or front opening; if not, a placket may be made at the left under-arm seam. Slip bodice on the figure with turnings outside.

Too Short or Too Long

As for a tight-fitting bodice.

Too Wide at Bust or Waist

Take in at under-arm seam, and perhaps also at shoulder seam, and re-pin armhole curve.

Too Wide Across Shoulders or Back

If in thin fabric, make pin-tucks about 3 inches long, running from back neck or shoulders, or both. If in thicker material and the fullness is in the middle of the neck only, make three or five darts there, tapering off to nothing about $3\frac{1}{2}$ inches below the neck.

Too Wide on Front Shoulder

Make pin-tucks 3 or 4 inches long; if fabric is too thick for this, make a dart running downwards in the middle of the shoulder.

Too Narrow Across Chest

Let out at front edge (if open).

Too Narrow Across Back

Unless there is a back seam or opening, nothing can be done, except by means of trimming.

Fullness at Front Armhole

As for tight-fitting bodice.

Mark any alterations to neck or armhole curves with chalk or pins, and mark positions for collar or trimmings; also, after fitting sleeve, position of insets of sleeve on back and front armhole.

TIGHT-FITTING, TWO-PIECE SLEEVE

Gather top of upper sleeve finely between points marked on pattern (if not marked, from $1\frac{1}{2}$ inches above one seam to the same distance above the other). Draw up slightly and wind end of cotton round a pin. Pin inset points of sleeve to those of armhole and note the hang. Inner seam should be well towards inside of arm, and at the wrist it should be inclined to run towards the under side, on no account towards top of wrist. Warp threads should run straight down from shoulder to elbow. Fullness on the sleeve head should be graduated so that most of it is just in front of the shoulder seam.

Diagonal Wrinkles on Top of Arm

Probably the sleeve is incorrectly pitched, being too far forward or too far back. Move round as required, and mark new inset points on the armhole.

Too Long

Pin up excess between shoulder and elbow, and when sleeve is removed trim off the top by the amount of the excess. This reduces the width at the top, so both seams may have to be let out a little there. If too long below elbow, take off the excess at the wrist, but do not forget that the sleeve should look quite $\frac{1}{2}$ inch longer than required, as it will shorten after being stitched in.

Too Short

No remedy (except an added cuff)! But it is a fault which is very unlikely to occur.

Too Wide

Take in at the inner seam for not more than $\frac{1}{4}$ inch; if more is required, take in equally at both seams. Remember that the seams are lengthened by taking them in.

Too Narrow

Let out at the inner or both seams. (This shortens the seams.)

TIGHT, ONE-PIECE SLEEVE

Little alteration can be made in this. There may, or may not, be one or two darts at the inner curve at the elbow on the under side. If there is one running up from the wrist to the elbow, some adjustment may be made there.

FULL, UNLINED SLEEVE, SET INTO CUFF

Keep fullness on the top of the shoulder, most of it just in front of the shoulder seam, and do not let it drop to front or back, as it should fall straight down the arm, with the warp threads in the same direction. The cuff opening should be well under the wrist, where the outer seam would come in a two-piece sleeve.

SKIRT

All seams must be tacked, but the top of one should be left open 7 inches or so for the placket—usually the first seam to the left of the centre-front, where there should be a line of tacking from waist to lower edge. Prepare a petersham belt, as described on pp. 189–90. Slip the skirt over the figure with the tacked turnings outside. Pin up the placket, pin the petersham round the figure (wrong side out), and pin the centre-front of the skirt to it, then centre-back and pin at intervals all round. First notice the hang of the skirt. Seams should run straight downward from waist to lower edge, and the skirt should not hang away from the figure anywhere. Correct lower edge if necessary.

If there is to be only one fitting, special care must be taken to mark positions of any trimmings, etc., with chalk, and to be quite sure that everything is accurate. Remember that the skirt will be tighter when the seams are stitched. If there are to be two fittings, at the second all seams should be stitched, pressed, and neatened; hem should be completed except for the final felling or machining; placket should be completed; the waist edge should be sewn to the belt and ready for its final stitching, with the fastenings sewn on temporarily.

Front Poking Out at the Hem

Lift the back at the waist and make a few small downward snips on the edge, then form a new waist-line gradually to the front. But if the abdomen is prominent, this may not be sufficient. In that case unpick˙the seam nearest the front from the bottom upward as far as the hips. Here make a horizontal dart in the edge of the front gore, sufficiently large to make the front hang straight, then re-pin the seam. The front will now be shortened a little by this, so let us hope a good turning is left at the bottom; if not, a false hem might be added on the front piece.

Back Falling In at the Hem

Try the same lifting at the back as described in the previous paragraph.

Too Wide

If wide all the way down, try the effect of stitching the seams just inside the fitting-lines instead of on them. (In any case the skirt will always be a little tighter after stitching up than before—and the more seams there are the greater will be the difference.) If too wide at waist or hips only, take in the affected seams, or make darts. But remember that the waist edge should always be at least 2 inches larger than the waist band; also that it is better to take in a little at all seams than a good deal at one or two, as the proportion of the pieces is thus preserved. A plain skirt should fit snugly round the hips, but it is well to try the effect of sitting down, as a too-tight skirt will wrinkle and strain round the fullest part of the hips.

Of course, though, you may not wish to *sit* in the skirt ! A customer once took back to the shop a made-to-measure skirt and complained that she could not sit in it. She received the haughty reply : " This is a *walking* skirt, not a *sitting* skirt, madam."

Test the Length

Here is a good plan if you are fitting yourself. Chalk the edge of a deal table heavily, then press yourself against it and turn round slowly. After removing the skirt, measure the height of the table edge from the floor, and subtract from this the height from the floor desired for the skirt. This gives you the depth below the chalked line where the skirt should turn up. (For example : height of table from floor 28 inches; desired height of skirt from floor 15 inches; measure 13 inches below chalked line all round to give the line for turning up.) So, after removing the skirt, place it on a skirt-board (waist edge to left hand) and measure this amount all round from the chalked line, chalking a new one as you do so for the turning-up line.

Fitting Another Person (Fig. 42)

If you are fitting the skirt on a dress-form or another person, work like this. Decide how high above the ground the skirt is to be, then kneel on the floor, and as the person or figure revolves slowly, measure this height up from the floor with a ruler and mark at frequent intervals with chalk or pins. (The skirt should be right side out.) After removing the skirt, place it on a skirt-board and connect all the marks to make a continuous line.

Measuring a Skirt off the Figure

If you prefer to measure the length of skirt off the figure, fold it down the middle of the front and back with turnings outside, and pin together round the waist-line. Place it on the table or skirt-board with waist at left hand, and measure from the waist-line all round your own front, side, and back lengths, after deducting the required height from the ground of each measurement. (For instance, front length to ground 41 inches; side length 41¼ inches; back length 40¾ inches; height from ground 14 inches. Then the actual length of the skirt should be : front 37 inches; side 37¼ inches; back 36¾ inches.) Of course, half-way between front and side lengths, and side and back lengths, you must take an intermediate measurement, then afterwards connect all the marks you have made into a continuous, even line.

Fig. 42.—Measuring Skirt Length.

The marks will be on one half of the skirt only, so put pins through the chalked line all round, and then on the other side draw a line over the pins.

CIRCULAR SKIRT

The same principles as before apply here, but there is less scope for alteration. If too wide round the hips, the back seam may be taken in; if too tight there, the skirt may be lifted up all round, the waist edge snipped and afterwards trimmed off. If it fits round the hips but is too wide round the waist, darts may be made as required. Hang up a circular skirt two or three days, to allow for dropping where it falls on the bias, before measuring for the lower edge. It is preferable to do the latter on the figure, as the skirt is then hanging naturally.

FROCK

A frock should hang correctly from the shoulders, and should not rely upon a belt to rectify any faults. Fit the upper part in accordance with the directions given for fitting a bodice with under-arm and shoulder seams only, and the lower part with those given for the skirt.

Front Hanging Away at Hem

Unpick the shoulder seams, let the front drop a little. Lift the back of the frock, re-pin shoulders. If this is not sufficient, make a dart on the front edge of each side seam as suggested on p. 91.

Back Falling In at Hem

Unpick shoulder seams, lift back, and re-pin

shoulders. If this is not sufficient, lift the back at the waist and make a dart running along the waist-line from seam to seam. It should be from $\frac{1}{4}$ to $\frac{1}{2}$ inch deep in the middle, sloping off to nothing at the seams. This dart should be hidden by a belt or trimming. Of course if there is a waist seam the fitting is much simplified.

FIT ONE SIDE ONLY

As mentioned before, it is usual to fit the garment on one side of the figure only—the right if you are fitting another person or on a dress-form; the left if you are fitting yourself. Before removing the garment see that all corrections are marked with pins or chalk, also any alterations to neck or arm-hole curves—inset points of sleeves, trimming lines, etc. Remove the garment care-fully, and if there is an open-ing down front or back with-draw the pins from one side only and retain them on the other side. The corrections must now be transferred to the unfitted side. There are two methods.

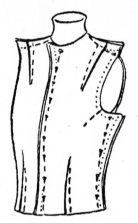

Fig. 43.—Showing Altera-tions when fitting Bodice.

Transferring Corrections—First Method

Chalk in a fresh colour the corrections on both sides of each seam and any other alterations. Be careful also to make new balance marks on seams (corresponding to notches on a pattern). **Remove** the pins and tackings on both sides of the garment. Place unaltered side on the table with right side upward, place corrected side on it (right side downward) with edges level.* Pin together on the new chalk lines so that all the new lines are shown clearly on the other side by the backs of the pins. Now chalk on the other side between the pins to indicate plainly the new fitting lines. Remove pins and draw in these lines correctly with chalk.

Fig. 44—Transferring the Alterations.

Transferring Corrections—Second Method

Work as directed in the previous paragraph as far as *, then proceed as follows. Pin the pieces together just inside the corrected fitting-lines, using just sufficient pins to keep the two layers of material in place. Now make tailor tacking along all new lines with a distinctive colour of cotton. Draw the pieces apart and snip the stitches.

COAT

The fitting of this is described in Chapter XIX.

Fashions in Fitting

The style of fitting varies. Sometimes clothes, to be smart, should fit tightly, at others loosely : so keep abreast of the times.

CHAPTER IX

SEAMS AND HEMS

A SEAM is a method of joining two edges together, either by hand or machine. It should always be pinned and tacked before being sewn, and the material should be flat on the table while this is being done, as described on p. 75. Never machine a pinned seam—it is a frequent source of broken machine needles.

A PLAIN SEAM

This is the very simplest kind of seam. Place the two layers of material one over the other (right sides together, as a rule) with the edges even, and if one is more off the straight than the other, place this uppermost. Pin together at intervals of 1 inch or more, according to the nature of the material. See that all heads come on the fitting-lines and all points on the turnings. Then tack on the fitting-lines and afterwards machine, run, or back stitch on these same lines. Cut down turnings, press them double, then open them and press the single turnings (as described on pp. 179–80), and if the part is not to be lined, neaten them in one of the following ways.

A. For Thin Fabrics (Fig. 45)

Turn back each raw edge for $\frac{1}{8}$ inch or more and either run by hand or stitch by machine—of course, keeping clear of the material below.

D   (Dress)   97

B. For Medium Weight (Fig. 46)

Bind with narrow ribbon or bias binding. Fold the ribbon down the middle, place it over the raw edge, and fell down on each side. If the material will allow of it, you may run or machine through all three layers. When using a bias strip, place the right

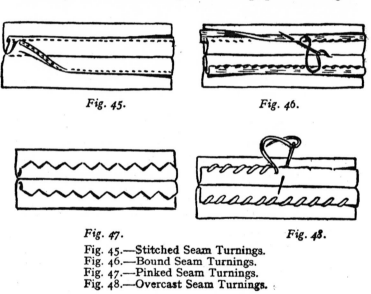

Fig. 45.

Fig. 46.

Fig. 47.

Fig. 48.

Fig. 45.—Stitched Seam Turnings.
Fig. 46.—Bound Seam Turnings.
Fig. 47.—Pinked Seam Turnings.
Fig. 48.—Overcast Seam Turnings.

side of it to right side of turning, edges level, run or machine the two together; turn the strip over to the wrong side, turn raw edge under, and fell over the first line of sewing. If the fabric is very thin, both raw edges of the strip may be turned in and folded to meet. It should then be placed over the raw turning and the five layers of material either run through by hand or machined.

C. For Firm Cloth (Fig. 47)

Pink the turnings, either with special pinking-shears or by making tiny snips, first to right and then to left, on the extreme edge, using small scissors.

D. Also for Firm Cloth (Fig. 48)

Overcast the raw edge lightly from left to right with soft cotton. On no account draw it tightly.

E. For Cloth Which Frays Easily

Work over the turnings loosely with loop stitch (see Fig. 34, p. 61).

Note.—When the seam is a curved one, snip the turnings, if wide and of loosely woven fabric, to within $\frac{1}{4}$ inch of the stitching; but if they are narrow and the fabric firm, to within $\frac{1}{8}$ inch. Then cut off the corners of the snips to form scallops (see Fig. 49).

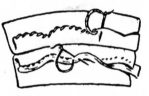

Fig. 49.—Stitched Seam.

STITCHED SEAM

For cloth. Make a plain seam as before, but after pressing and before neatening, stitch from the right side close to the seam at both sides, or, if preferred, just under $\frac{1}{4}$ inch from it. Press on the roller before neatening (see Figs. 114–5, p. 179).

LAPPED SEAM (Fig. 50)

For cloth. Make a plain seam, press the turnings double over the stitching (see Fig. 114), then fold both turnings back one way. (In a skirt they should all face the centre-front; on a coat they should face the centre-front and the centre-back from the sides. Shoulder seam turnings should face the back, but under-arm turnings should be left plain. In a coat sleeve the turnings of the outer seam should be laid on the upper sleeve, while

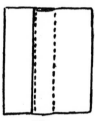

Fig. 50.
Lapped Seam.

the inner seam should be plain.) Tack the turnings back, press over a roller, then stitch ⅜ inch or so from the seam, through the turnings; or, if preferred close to the seam, or in both positions. (In the latter case, stitch close to the seam first to prevent puckering). Press over a roller and neaten the raw edges in one of the ways prescribed for a plain seam.

If the cloth is a heavy one, cut off the under-turning ⅛ inch or so from the stitching.

A rather different effect is produced if the first row of stitching is omitted. After tacking very closely, press both the turnings back one way and tack them; then stitch ⅛, ¼, or $\frac{3}{16}$ inch from the tacked seam. Press over a roller, then remove the tacking-threads.

SLOT SEAM (Fig. 51)

Tack as for a plain seam, but with smaller stitches than usual. Press turnings open over a roller, then tack a straight strip of material about 1 inch wide, either of the same or a different colour, behind the turnings. Press over a roller, then stitch on the right side from $\frac{1}{16}$ to ¼ inch at each side of the meeting edges. Remove the tacking and press again on the roller. Cut down the turnings and overcast them.

Note.—There is an adaptation of this seam which is a useful way of widening a skirt cut in several gores and found too tight. Untack the seams and turn back each gore on the fitting-lines; press the edges on the wrong side, then tack up the skirt according to the notches, but tacking each fold to a strip of material and leaving a space between the

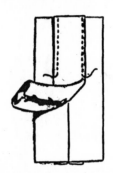

Fig. 51.—Slot Seam.   Fig. 52.—Strapped Seam.

two sufficiently wide to make up the deficiency. If none of the skirt material is available, a different one may be used; for instance, velvet or satin strips for a plain cloth, while if a striped fabric is in question the same may be used for the strips with the stripe running across.

STRAPPED SEAM (Fig. 52)

This comes into favour from time to time for tailored coats and skirts. First stitch and press a plain seam, allowing turnings at least $\frac{1}{2}$ inch wide. The strapping may be from $\frac{1}{2}$ to $\frac{3}{4}$ inch in width, according to fashion. Cut strips to twice this width exactly on the bias, join them up by the straight warp threads, and press the little seams. Fold over the raw edges to meet in the middle (right side of material outside) and draw them together with lacing stitch (Fig. 31). Press on the wrong side, then tack over the seams on both edges, using small stitches. When the seam is curved, one edge of the strapping must be stretched gently to fit. Now stitch on the right side as close to each edge as possible. When the cloth is very firm, the strapping may be single with raw edges. This requires very careful cutting, and in many cases it can be done best with a very sharp knife on a board.

FRENCH SEAM (Fig. 53)

Chiefly used for very thin fabrics or for washing garments. Its great merit is that the raw edges are enclosed neatly and there is no possibility of their fraying. It may be stitched either by machine or run by hand. Place the two layers of material with their *wrong* sides together and tack about ¼ to ⅜ inch outside the fitting-line, according to the nature of the fabric. Machine or run on this tacked line, cut off the turnings as close as possible outside the stitching, press over the stitching, stretching a little as you do so; turn the material to the other (wrong) side, re-tack on the fitting-line, and stitch over it. The drawback of this seam is that the first row of stitching is inclined to be tight, and therefore a little puckering may result, and to obviate this the first row may be run by hand and the second row machined. On this account this seam is not suitable for edges on the inside of a curve, for which the next seam is better.

FRENCH FELLED SEAM (Fig. 54)

Suitable for materials which are to be washed or which fray easily, as the turnings are enclosed. It is very quickly worked either by hand or machine, as there is only one row of stitching. Tack as for

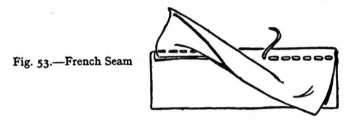

Fig. 53.—French Seam

a plain seam, then cut off the nearer turning to less than half the width of the other. If the edge is on an inside curve, make tiny snips on both turnings and, if possible, stretch them under an iron. Then fold the wider turning like a hem over the narrow

Fig. 54.—French Felled Seam.

one and tack it. If it is to be felled by hand, the fold must come just on the tacked fitting-line, but if to be machined, it must come a little below it—and the stitching must come on the exact fitting-line.

DARTS

A dart is a method of taking away a wedge-shaped piece of fullness to get a plain effect. It is like a tuck with the stitching slanting off to join the fold (see Fig. 55, A and B). Darts are found running downward round the waist of a skirt, upward round the waist of a bodice, downward in the middle of back or front shoulders; horizontally on the under-arm edge of a bodice front, and sometimes on the side edge of the front gores of a skirt;

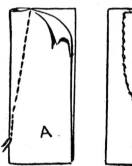
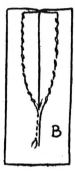

Fig. 55.—Dart, Stitched (A) and Neatened (B).

Fig. 56.—Darts in Back Neck.

diagonally on the front armhole, pointing toward the bust; upward from wrist to elbow on a one-piece sleeve, or horizontally at the under-elbow edge. Very tiny darts are also seen at the back neck when the edge is full and a plain effect is desired across the shoulders (see Fig. 56); they are sometimes seen also in the front neck.

A dart should never be cut before being stitched. It should be folded down the middle, pinned from the wide end downward, then tacked similarly to a fine point. It should also be stitched from the open end, and when the point is reached the stitching should be carried ½ inch or so farther down, just clinging on to the edge of the fold. In this way the unsightly poke which is sometimes seen is avoided.

Tie the threads firmly at the point of the dart, then press double like a seam, and if it is a very narrow dart you may then press it to one side; but if it is too large for this, or the fabric too thick, snip the dart across about 1 inch above the point, then split the upper part, press the turnings open, and neaten by overcasting, loop stitching, or binding.

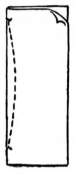

Fig. 57.
Closed Dart.

A Closed Dart (Fig. 57)

This is pointed at both ends, and it is used in the front and back of a frock —half above and half below the waist —and also at times, to improve the fit, running along the waist-line of the back of a frock. A closed dart, as a rule, should not be split, but should be pressed to one side.

HEMS

A hem consists of a twice-turned fold on the raw edge of anything, sewn down in a variety of ways to make it firm. It may be quite plain, or so decorative as to be a trimming in itself.

A Plain Hem

Always mark with chalk or a tacked line the position for the outside fold of the hem. Now on the wrong side make a narrow fold on the extreme edge, and tack it down so as to bring the outside fold on the chalked line. For anything but a very narrow hem the following plan is recommended. After marking for the outer fold turn back on this line from the *right* side and tack close to up the fold. You will get a better line this way, especially if the material is on a curve. If the edge is straight, you will find it quicker to pin on the right side not less than ½ inch below the fold, then to turn to the wrong side, and there to press the extreme edge with a merely warm

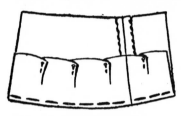

Fig. 58.—Removing Fullness in Curved Hem.

iron, placing a strip of the same material between the hem and the iron. After this measure the depth of the hem on the turnings, chalk lightly, turn up, and tack. In the case of a springy fabric it is best to tack this second fold singly, press it and then tack down. If the material is transparent, the folded-under part should be the same depth as the hem, so that the raw edge does not show through.

If the hem is on an outer curve, the turned-in edge will be fuller than the material beneath it. It may be gathered finely and drawn up to fit the outer material, or tiny pleats may be made and felled down on themselves (Fig. 58). The hem may be stitched on the right side by machine, or it may be slip hemmed (Fig. 28). Another method when the fabric is thin, is to machine this turned-down edge only, and then to slip hem it to the material below. The depth of a hem of this kind may be anything from ⅜ inch to 3 inches.

For Thick Material

When the fabric is too thick for any of these methods, proceed thus : After tacking the outer turn, cut off the turnings equal all round, bind the raw edge with bias binding, or stitch one edge of prussian binding to the single edge ; tack to the background and either fell or slip hem it into place (Fig. 59) or, after pressing, stitch once or twice from the right

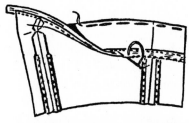 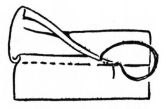

Fig. 59.—Skirt Hem in Thick Cloth.   Fig. 60.—French Hem.

side. If the edge is curved, the turned-up part will be full, so before binding it should be gathered or pleated to fit as described in the previous paragraph. If, however, the material is woollen, and only thin, the fullness, after being gathered, may be shrunk away with a damp cloth and a hot iron.

FRENCH HEM (Fig. 60)

This is really a hem, though it has the effect of a binding. It is a very decorative finish for a skirt of thin material, if the edge is either on the straight or exactly on the bias, but it is unsuitable for curves. Mark the line for the outside edge with tacking or chalk, then allow beyond this three times the depth you wish the hem to be, which in any case should not be more than ¼ inch. Now fold back the turning by the tacked line to the *right* side and run finely close to the fold. After this turn over to the wrong side and fold under the raw edge just over the line of running. Fell or slip hem this into place. You should pin this part down carefully, as it is important that it should be kept very even. On no account press the fold, as the appearance is spoiled if it is flattened.

ROLLED HEM

This is delightful for ninon, etc., and the stitch is identical with the whipping shown in Fig. 30 on p. 59. Leave just over ⅛ inch turning. Secure the silk at the right-hand end, then bring out the needle at the back. Begin to roll the edge toward you between the thumb and finger of the left hand, and as you do so put in the needle at the front just below the roll, bring out the point at the back, but do not draw the needle out of the material. Then work the needle over and over the roll toward the front, and as it gets full push the rolls off the eye end, never taking the whole of the needle out. Do not draw the thread tightly, or the edge will be puckered. This same stitch serves for a seam for very fine materials working over the double turnings ; and also for a whipped frill of muslin or lace, by drawing up the edge to the required fullness. For lace, however, the edge must not be rolled over, but the needle must be worked over and over the corded edge as described for the roll.

SCALLOPED HEM (Fig. 61)

This is very pretty on thin, unlined fabrics. Leave for turnings double the desired depth of hem. In no case should this be more than $\frac{3}{16}$ inch. Fold a plain hem and pin it with points upward—it is not necessary to tack it—and use fine, matching silk and a fine needle. Begin to slip hem the turned-down edge, and at intervals of not less than $\frac{1}{4}$ inch take a stitch right over the edge

Fig. 61.—Scalloped Hem.

and draw the silk tightly, continuing the slip hemming in between. When the fabric is transparent it is useless to try to slip hem it, and the fold should then be run or hemmed with tiny stitches.

CROSS STITCHED HEM

After working as described for a rolled hem, fasten the silk at the right hand and take single stitches over and over, crossing the first ones, and keeping them perfectly regular.

HEMSTITCHING

This makes a very effective trimming for linen and (sometimes) silk frocks. It is worked exactly the same as for household linen. [1]

FALSE HEM (Fig. 62)

This is sometimes called a facing. It is used to simulate a hem where the material is too thick to

[1] Full instructions for hemstitching and drawn-thread work are given in *Teach Yourself Embroidery*, pp. 136–43.

turn twice, or where the turnings are insufficient. It may be of the same material or a thinner one. (Old material may often be used.) If you wish to apply a false hem to a skirt of thick cloth where the edge is much curved, proceed in this way.

Turn back to the wrong side on the fitting-line and tack as close as possible to the edge, leaving about 1 inch turning. Where you turn up over a seam, notch the turnings exactly at the turn, to

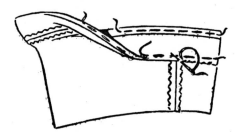

Fig. 62.—False Hem on Skirt.

avoid clumsiness (Fig. 59). Measure up from the fitting-line on the inside of the skirt the desired depth of hem and chalk a line. If the false hem is to be of the skirt material, take all the spare pieces and pin them round the lower edge of the skirt, fitting them up to one another and pinning the joins. The grain of the fabric is not very important if it is firm in texture, otherwise you should see that the grain of the pieces matches all round that of the skirt below. Cut them to shape round the lower edge of the skirt, then cut off the upper edge by the chalked line on the skirt. Now take off the pieces and seam them all together; press their turnings open, then lay the false hem on the wrong side of the skirt, wrong side downwards, and the edge level with that of the skirt. Pin together at intervals. Then, for a few inches at a time, remove the pins, lift up the false hem, and tack its edge to that of the skirt, right sides together. (Arrange that the seam comes about $\frac{1}{2}$ inch or so above the turn of the skirt.) Then finish the upper raw edge in one of the ways described for thick material on p. 107. If there are large pieces of spare material, you can cut sufficient strips exactly on the bias to go all round the skirt, and then, after stretching one edge slightly to fit the lower edge of the skirt, apply as just described.

OTHER FALSE HEMS OR FACINGS

False hems or facings are used in many other parts of garments—front or back openings, cuffs, neck edges, wrists of sleeves, collars, trimmings, etc. When the shape is irregular it is best to cut out the facing to the exact shape; but when it is simple, or only slightly curved, you can take a bias strip, pin it to the shorter edge, and fell it into place, then stretch the other edge to fit and fell this also.

CHAPTER X
SLEEVES

THOUGH sleeves may vary much from year to year in style, yet the principles of their making remain the same. The plain, two-piece type, known as the coat sleeve, is its plainest form, and is the basis upon which all others are built (Fig. 4). To look well, the coat sleeve should define the arm closely, but should allow for free movement, and there should be no wrinkles anywhere. The warp threads should run straight down from the top of the arm to the elbow on the upper sleeve and from the armhole to the elbow on the under. This rule is usually followed for this type of sleeve, whether used for a coat or a frock, but it should be noted that French dressmakers frequently cut it, when using any material without a nap, exactly on the bias—that is, both upper and under pieces are placed on the bias from top to elbow. This method produces a beautifully moulded effect, without wrinkles, and can be commended heartily. It does, of course, take rather more material than the ordinary method, and needs more care in planning out. In treating here of the various types of sleeves, it will be taken for granted, however, that they have been cut out in the customary way.

Some dressmakers complete the sleeves before any other part of a frock or bodice, as they consider that once these are made almost half the work is done. Be that as it may, it is a fact that a sleeveless frock is very quickly made.

OTHER TYPES OF SLEEVES

1 (Fig. 63). One-piece sleeve with dart running from elbow to wrist on the outside of the arm. Top may be plain or may have fullness arranged in gathers or pleats. In that case it is usual to pleat

Fig. 63.—One-piece, Darted Sleeve.

Fig. 64.—One-piece Sleeve with Elbow Fullness.

up a double strip of stiff muslin and sew it inside the sleeve on the top of the armhole to keep it extended.

2 (Fig. 64). One-piece sleeve with a little fullness on the elbow curve on the under edge. This fullness may be gathered, pleated, or suppressed by two or three small horizontal darts.

3. Full, unlined sleeve, such as those of the " bishop " type. This is cut in one piece, the top fullness is gathered into the armhole and that on the

lower edge is set into a plain cuff. There may or may not be a tight lining.

4. Shirt sleeve. Generally in one piece, with plain or slightly gathered top, and its lower edge set into a plain cuff. It is usually set into an armhole of easy fit, and sometimes a quite loose one, according to fashion.

5. Fancy sleeve with puffs, frills, etc. This usually has a tight-fitting foundation of thin net or silk.

PITCH

The correct " hang " of a sleeve depends upon its correct pitch. The front and back pitches (or

Fig. 65.—Point of Sleeve-inset on Armhole.

points of inset) are generally marked on the front and back of both armhole and sleeve by notches, and these must be carefully translated into chalk marks or large tacked crosses on the cut-out material. It sometimes happens, though, that these marks have been lost, in which case there is a rough-and-ready method of finding out where the inner seam of the sleeve should come on the armhole.

On the front armhole you see warp threads running down and weft threads running across; now, where these cross the material is exactly on the bias, and this comes exactly on the lower part of the front armhole, and this is where the inner seam of the sleeve should be put (see Fig. 65).

There are, however, certain types of one-piece sleeves in which the only seam is placed to the

under-arm seam of the bodice. You can usually
tell this type at once, as, when folded down the
middle, the two halves of the upper edge are almost
identical—probably the part going to the front of
the armhole is slightly flatter than the other. Sleeve
shown in Fig. 64 is of this type. Care should be
taken that the sleeves are put into their corresponding armholes. I remember a dressmaking student
who rather belligerently showed me her finished
frock, which she said fitted abominably—implying
by her manner that the fault was mine. . . . I
didn't think it was, and pointed out to her that she
had transposed the sleeves !

DON'T MAKE THE SLEEVE-HEAD TOO TIGHT

Making the sleeve-head too tight is a frequent
fault—it should always measure at least 2 inches
more than the armhole, even when apparently it is
to be set in plainly. The edge of the upper sleeve
must be gathered finely between the two points
indicated on the pattern; in the case of a two-piece
sleeve these are usually about $1\frac{1}{2}$ inch above each
seam, but the positions differ slightly in different
types of sleeves. The gathering-thread is then
drawn up and the fullness distributed evenly over
the top of the arm, a little more, if anything, coming
exactly on the top of the shoulder just in front of the
seam. When the sleeve-head is darted it is still
necessary to gather it, very finely, of course, and if
there is any appreciable fullness when the sleeve
has been sewn in this may be shrunk out.

SLEEVE LININGS

Sleeves may be lined or not, according to taste and fashion. In a plain frock, sleeve material and lining—usually a thin silk or net—will be made up together, but in a fancy sleeve there will generally be a tight lining, on which the outer sleeve will be mounted. In the case of a lined bishop sleeve, lining and material will be stitched up separately and the two joined together at the armhole and wrist. A tailored coat sleeve will usually be lined, lining and cloth being stitched up separately and the lining felled in; if unlined, the cloth turnings will be bound.

COAT-SHAPED SLEEVE SET IN A FROCK

The sleeve should be completely finished, pressed and turnings neatened (see pp. 80–82 for tacking up). It is then pinned into the armhole, tacked, and finally back stitched or machined in. In all these processes the work must be done from the inside of the sleeve—this is an invariable rule. If it were done from the outside of the armhole—that is, with the bodice nearest to you—puckers would form all round the outside of the armhole.

Take the sleeve and slip it inside its corresponding armhole—right side of sleeve to right side of armhole—then, holding the inside of the sleeve towards you, pin together the inset marks on sleeve and armhole, inserting the pins on the fitting-line and bringing them out below. Now turn the work round so that the under part of the armhole is at the top and the upper part below and, still holding the inside of the sleeve towards you, pin round the under part of the armhole plainly between the inset points, at intervals of 1 inch or so, the pins pointing downward as before. Then turn round again and arrange the slight fullness so that it is nicely graduated, with most of it on the top of the arm just in front of the shoulder seam (see Fig. 66). Tack in the sleeve very finely and firmly, and, after fitting, machine or back stitch it in from the inside of the sleeve—that is, with the bodice next to the machine and the sleeve next to the needle. If preferred,

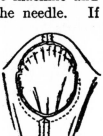

Fig. 66.—Setting Sleeve into Armhole

Fig. 67.—Lining a Coat Sleeve.

back stitching may be substituted for machining. Cut down the turnings as close as is safe, in accordance with the nature of the material—when firm, the turnings may be cut down to ¼ inch. Neaten them to match the other seams.

TAILORED COAT SLEEVE

The sleeve should be completely finished, and, if lined, the lining should be felled in round the wrist

and run to the cloth by its inner seam turning (see
Figs. 67, A and B). Pin and tack in as described in
the previous paragraph, keeping the lining of the
sleeve and coat free. If the under part of the sleeve
comes rather fuller than the armhole, make a small
pleat meeting the under-arm seam of the coat.
Stitch the seam as before described, shrink out the
fullness on the sleeve-head (Fig. 68), then press
the turnings open. Make a roll of wadding about

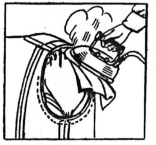

Fig. 68.—Shrinking Full-
ness in Sleeve Head.

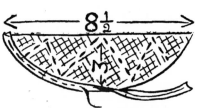

Fig. 69.—Sleeve Extender.

as thick as the forefinger and sew inside the turnings
of the upper armhole.

When the sleeve head has fullness which is
pleated or darted it must be extended by means
of a pad. The size and thickness of this depend
upon the amount of fullness and the effect which is
desired, so each case must be treated accordingly.
The diagram in Fig. 69 gives an average size. Cut
this on the bias in double canvas for each sleeve.
Stitch across by machine in zigzag lines, then bind
the raw edges with a strip of lining or sateen. If
two pieces of canvas do not provide sufficient

stiffness add another piece or a thin layer of wadding. Try on this pad when the sleeve is being fitted and make any needed alterations, then after the sleeve has been sewn into the armhole sew the straight edge of the pad to the seam turnings with the middle of the pad exactly on the top of the arm, and the curved edge projecting into the sleeve.

If the sleeve head is only slightly full a ready-made pad will probably be sufficient to give the required extension.

TIGHT-FITTING ONE-PIECE SLEEVE

The inner sleeve seam may be set about 2 inches in front of the under-arm seam, as in a coat-shaped sleeve, or it may be set in exactly to the under-arm seam. This depends upon the shape of the sleeve, so the inset points must be carefully noted. Pin these together and work on the principles just explained.

SHIRT SLEEVE SET INTO WIDE ARMHOLE

This sleeve is specially cut to fit a wide armhole, and is usually without fullness. Stitch and press the shoulder seams, but leave the under-arm seams open. Make the placket in the sleeve, but do not set on the cuff or stitch up the sides. Place the shirt on the table, wrong side upwards, and armhole towards you. Take the sleeve, wrong side upwards, and match the inset marks. Place the sleeve-head up to the armhole and pin the two together, keeping the material flat on the table and the turnings upwards. Then tack on the fitting-line, taking out the pins one by one (see Fig. 70).   If there is fullness on the sleeve, this should be gathered finely on the

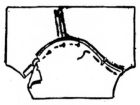

Fig. 70.—Pinning and Tacking In Shirt Sleeve.

fitting-line between the inset points and arranged evenly on the armhole.   Press the turnings on to the shirt; cut down the under turning to half the width of the upper, then turn in the upper, tack it, and stitch through on the inner edge of the fold from the right side.   Now stitch up the sides of the shirt and sleeve, pinning from the armhole in both directions, and finish with a French or French felled seam.   Set the lower edge into a cuff as described for another method on p. 140.

FULL SHIRT OR BISHOP SLEEVE

The placket should first be made, as described on p. 139.   The seam should next be stitched—either French or French felled—and the cuff set on as described on p. 140.   The top must then be gathered according to the notches on the pattern.   If there is much fullness, two rows of gathers are advisable. Take in the sleeve, but if a French seam is used, the sleeve must be *wrong* side out and be inserted in the *wrong* side of the armhole.   Stitch by machine close to the edge of the turnings, then turn to the wrong side and stitch in the usual way on the fitting-line. If the sleeve is set in with the ordinary plain seam, the turnings must be cut down and bound with a bias strip of the same material.

RAGLAN SLEEVE

In this there is no armhole seam, but the sleeve runs up into the neck and is joined to the front and back by slanting seams. Place front and back on the table with wrong side upwards, insert the sleeve between them in the same way with notches matching; then pin, tack, and stitch with either felled or lapped seams, usually. Tack under-arm and sleeve seams from the armhole downward, and stitch in the usual way.

SLEEVE WITH FULL HEAD

When sleeves with a full head are fashionable, the fullness is arranged in gathers, pleats, or darts. The position of these will be plainly marked on the pattern. One, two, or three rows of gathers may be made, according to the amount of fullness, and pleats may be single or box-pleats. Darts must be tapered off sharply and pressed. It is usual to extend the fullness with the help of a pleated frill of stiff muslin sewn inside the upper part of the armhole, or by means of a piece of canvas cut to the shape of the diagram in Fig. 69, p. 118. The size will vary according to the amount of extension required. Extra support for heavy materials may be given by one or two more layers of canvas stitched together by machine. The pad should be covered with sleeve material or thin silk or lining.

CHAPTER XI

FASTENINGS

An otherwise well-made garment may be spoilt entirely by badly made fastenings. If they are intended to be invisible, then make them really so by means of press studs, hooks and eyes, hooks and loops, etc., placing them in an inconspicuous seam or under folds or trimmings; but if they are to be visible, make them so perfectly that they become a trimming in themselves. Of this latter order are buttons and buttonholes (the latter either worked or bound), and buttons and loops. Zipp fasteners are now made so ornamental that they become a decorative feature. But whatever the form of fastenings, their positions should be spaced carefully with a tape-measure and marked either with chalk or tacking.

BUTTONS AND BUTTONHOLES

For a feminine garment the buttons are always on the left side of the opening and the buttonholes on the right, while the opposite is the rule for masculine dress. Need I say, " Buy your buttons before you make your buttonholes "? Mark position of buttons first on the left side, place right and left sides together, and insert pins through both at the button sites, then chalk over these on the right side as a guide for the buttonholes.

Buttons

Buttons are never sewn on single material, so that, if unlined, a strip of the same fabric should be tacked under the button site, and after the sewing-on the strip may be cut down and the raw edges neatened, keeping them quite free from the garment.

When the buttons are heavy, a small mother-of-pearl button should be held under the material and the stitches taken through both buttons. Flat buttons

Fig. 71.—Sewing on Buttons.

are sewn on with cross stitches taken over a pin (see Fig. 71). Buttonhole twist should be used on woollens, sewing-silk for silks and thin fabrics other than cottons and linens, where strong mercerised thread should be used. The number of crosses depends upon the strength of the thread. After they have been made, pass the needle to the right side under the button, wind the thread round several times, withdraw the pin, and finish off neatly and firmly (see Fig. 71). If you want to be specially neat, you can begin by making a few back stitches on the right side on the button site, and, after sewing on, finish off in the usual way.

TAILOR'S BUTTONHOLES (Fig. 72)

Measure and chalk positions for buttonholes to correspond with buttons. If there is to be a row of closely set buttonholes down the front or back of the bodice, for instance, tack the tape-measure to the edge of the opening and make chalk marks or insert pins at equal distances. Mark with a ruler on a coat. Sew buttons on first. On right side rule straight lines for the holes at right angles with the edge. The distance from the edge should allow

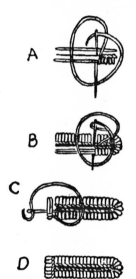

from $\frac{1}{8}$ to $\frac{1}{2}$ inch of material to show when the buttons are fastened. (This space varies with the size of the button.) The length of the slit should be: for a flat button its diameter plus $\frac{1}{16}$ inch, and more for a ball- or dome-shaped one. (In cloth or thick material extra length is necessary.) It is a good plan to experiment with a spare piece of material before deciding these points.

Buttonholes should always be made in double material, so, if the edge is single, another piece of the same material should be tacked beneath it, and afterwards the edge of this

Fig. 72.—Tailor's Buttonholes.

may be slip stitched to the outer fabric. In a coat there will be an interlining of linen or canvas. For cloth use special buttonhole twist and a shortish needle; for medium woollens, silk, etc., use sewing silk, and for linens and cottons mercerised thread.

Cutting the Slits

Cut each hole as you need it. If you use the

special buttonhole scissors, cut the slit from the front
edge, which the gap in the blades just fits over.
Make one cut only. If ordinary small scissors are
used, it is best to pierce a hole at the outside end of
the buttonhole line, then to insert the point of the
scissors and make one cut to the other end of the
line. Another method is to cut the slits over a piece
of cardboard, using a safety razor blade and a ruler.
If the material frays easily whip lightly over the edges
with *fine* silk. Fasten the thread at the right end of
the slit at the farther end from the edge and prepare
to work from right to left. Lay a strand of thread
along each side of the slit, passing the needle upward
and downward at both ends, then bring it out at the
right-hand end of the slit farthest away from the
edge of material (see Fig. 72A).

The Stitch

Take the thread which is coming from the slit,
carry it upward and to the left, then down and to
the right, thus forming a loop which you should
hold down with your left thumb. Insert the needle
under the cut edge and bring out just below the
strand and over the loop (Fig. 72A). Pull up the
needle sharply so that a knot is formed on the edge
of the slit. Repeat this to the end of the first side,
then work round in fan shape with five or seven
stitches (Fig. 72B), and continue to starting-point.
Here carry two strands across, then work over them
in loop stitch (Fig. 72C) from left to right, keeping
the corded edge to the buttonhole, and the stitches
free from the material (Fig. 72D).

DRESSMAKER'S BUTTONHOLES (Fig. 73)

Mark and cut slits as before described, then, without stranding, join on the thread at the end farthest from the edge of the material and prepare to work from left to right. Insert the needle from the back and bring out the point only a few threads below the cut; take the thread which is coming from the needle, pass it to the left of it, and bring it round under the point to the right side; take the needle and draw it through the loop, then pull up smartly and continue all round, spreading the stitches out at the first end in fan shape (Fig. 73A). At the other end complete the buttonhole with a bar as shown in Fig. 73B.

BOUND BUTTONHOLES (Fig. 74)

These may be in either single or double fabric. Mark the lines for them to correspond with the position of the buttons on the other side of the opening. Take a piece of matching material (or contrasting if wished) cut on the bias. This should be 3 inches deep and 2 inches wider than the length desired for the buttonhole. Mark the line for the buttonhole exactly in the middle of it. Place this piece right side downward on the right side of the other material with buttonhole lines matched. Tack the two together, then machine $\frac{1}{8}$ inch from the line all round it (Fig. 74A). Cut along the line (either with scissors, or with a penknife on a board), stopping $\frac{1}{16}$ inch from each end, then from there snip up to each corner, but be careful not to cut the stitching (Fig. 74B). Turn the material through the slit to the back; press the little seams open over a small roller, then fold so that the edges meet and form a little inverted pleat at each end. Turn in each raw edge of material and fell it down to the back threads of the main piece, if unlined (see Fig. 74C).

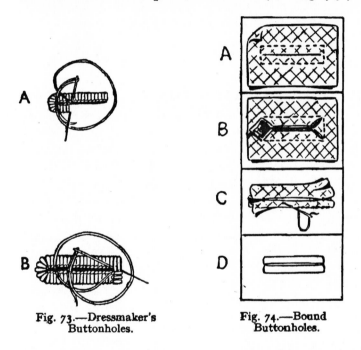

Fig. 73.—Dressmaker's Buttonholes.

Fig. 74.—Bound Buttonholes.

The finished effect is seen in Fig. 74D. When making several of these buttonholes beneath one another it is best to tack a long strip of material over the series, then, after stitching them, to cut across the strip between them.

If made in double material, the lining should be left free from the stitching, but after the buttonhole has been stitched the raw edges of the binding piece should be catch stitched (Fig. 35) to the back threads of the material and, after pressing, the lining should be turned in all round the buttonhole and slip hemmed to the binding.

BUTTONS AND CORD LOOPS (Fig. 75)

Fine cord is used for these loops, and they are generally attached to the extreme edge of the open-

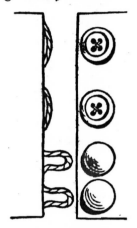

ing, with the buttons sewn on the fitting-line on the other side of it. The position of the buttons must be chalked, also that of the loops on the opposite edge. If the buttons are flat the loops will lie straight on the edge; but if ball- or dome-shaped the cord must be loose enough to slip over easily. Sew the end of the cord to the right-hand end of the inside edge. Allow

Fig. 75—.Buttons and Cord Loops.

cord for the loop and (running the thread between the two layers of material) sew in the next position. Carry it along plainly just under the edge, securing it with a few stitches, until the position for the next loop is reached. Then repeat to the end. Neaten the inside edge with a facing of silk or self-material, if necessary.

BUTTONS AND BUTTONHOLE LOOPS

These loops are made on the edge, or just under the edge, of an opening to pass over buttons on the other side in the same way as cord loops. The buttons are sewn on the fitting-line of the left side, leaving sufficient material outside them to avoid gaps when the loops are slipped over the buttons. Mark positions for buttons and sew on as before. Take buttonhole twist and join it to the edge of the right side of the opening with right side of material uppermost. Allow the width of the button on the

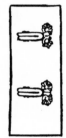

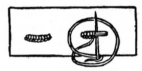

Fig. 76.—Buttonholed Loops.

Fig. 77.— Hooks Sewn on.

edge for the loop, pass the needle through the edge, leave the thread level or loose, as required to slip over the button, then pass back to the starting-point and repeat to make a foundation of three strands. Now work back over these in loop stitch as in Fig. 76 or working from right to left instead, if more convenient. After finishing the loop, if you have plenty of thread pass the needle through the edge until you come to the next position. Some people find it easier to work the stitch with the eye end of the needle, as shown above.

E   (Dress)

HOOKS AND LOOPS

Mark position of these on the two sides of the opening. Hooks should be sewn on so that their ends are invisible from the front, and the loops should be made on the fitting-line with a little extension of material left beyond it (known as a " wrap "). Sew on hooks as in Fig. 77 if they are to be neatened; if not, sew them on with loop stitch. The loops or bars are made on the left-hand side of the opening, similarly to the loops described in the previous paragraph, except that they are not on the extreme edge, and also they are very small— just large enough for the hook to fix into—and they are made in sewing silk (twist would be too thick), or mercerised cotton in the case of linen or cotton fabrics (see Fig. 76). These little bars are also used to strengthen the bottom of an opening or placket, and are worked across on the right side.

HOOKS AND EYES

These are generally used for edge-to-edge fasten- ings, such as come on a bodice lining. A turning of $1\frac{1}{4}$ inch should be left on each edge, turned back $\frac{1}{16}$ inch *outside* the fitting-lines, and tacked. Positions for hooks and eyes must be chalked or tacked on both edges with the aid of a tape-measure. The hooks should then be sewn on inside the right edge with their ends $\frac{1}{16}$ inch back. If sewing to lining only the stitches may go right through; but if there is material also, the stitches must be kept free from this (see Fig. 78A). After sewing on all the hooks fold up the turning (cut off any material close up to the hooks), turn in the edge, and fell right up to the ends of the hooks. Sew on the eyes on the other side in the same way, and neaten as before (Fig. 78B). If preferred, hooks and eyes may be sewn alternately on both sides. Sometimes the turned-back edges are machined close to the

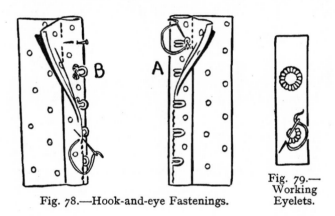

Fig. 78.—Hook-and-eye Fastenings.

Fig. 79.—
Working
Eyelets.

fold before the hooks and eyes are sewn on, to give extra strength.

HOOKS AND EYELETS

Prepare the two sides of the opening as for hooks and loops. The left side should be faced with a strip 1½ inch wide, if it is not already lined, as the eyelets cannot be made in single material, unless it is very strong. Mark position of hooks and eyelets on both sides, then sew on the hooks as for hooks and loops (see Fig. 77). Pierce each eyelet as required in position marked, using a stiletto. Secure the thread (silk for silk or woollens, and plain cotton or mercerised thread for linen or cotton fabrics) to the edge of the eyelet; then work round with an oversewing stitch from right to left (see **Fig.** 79). This is just like the stitch in Fig. 32, but is worked very lightly, only taking up sufficient depth to make firm stitches. After finishing one eyelet pass **the** needle through the lining and work the next one.

PRESS STUDS

The stud part must be sewn under the upper or right side of the opening and the socket on the under

or left side. Positions should be measured carefully and marked, so that when the studs are fastened the fitting-lines shall meet. Sew on with strong thread or silk with over-and-over stitches taken through the holes (Fig. 80).

Fig. 80.—Sewing on a Press Stud.

ZIPP FASTENERS

The fasteners are sold in various lengths, and are so ornamental that the metal is purposely allowed to show. If you are inserting a short one in the middle front or back of a bodice, tack the fastener roughly in place to the under side of the material first, then make a cut down the middle exactly over the middle of the fastener to within ⅛ inch of the bottom of the metal. From there make a tiny downward cut at each side in an inverted **V** shape. Take away the fastener, turn back each edge to the wrong side by half the width of the closed zipp, and turn down the little tongue at the bottom (Fig. 81A). Press

the folds, then tack the material to the closed
fastener and machine down each side, making it
very firm at the bottom (Figs. 81B and 81C). If the
fastener is to be inserted between two open edges,

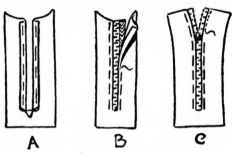

Fig. 81.—Inserting Zipp Fastener.

make four or five evenly spaced chalk marks at each
side as a guide. Turn back each side by half the
width of the closed fastener, press them back with an
iron, then tack them close up to the metal and
machine as before.

CHAPTER XII

PLACKETS AND OPENINGS

A PLACKET has two essential qualities—neatness and strength. A few years ago a third—invisibility —might have been added. But Fashion is now more sensible, and decrees that it may proclaim itself unblushingly, and at the same time often be a decorative feature.

PLACKET IN A TAILORED SKIRT (Fig. 82)

It is usually placed in the seam at the left of the

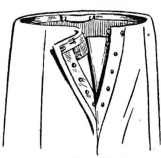

front gore. Its length should be just sufficient to allow the skirt to slip easily over the head— generally about one-sixth of the hip mea-sure. The right edge, of course, always over-laps the left. Turn back the right edge on the fitting-line, tack, and

Fig. 82.—Skirt Placket.

press it. (If the fabric is loosely woven, a straight strip of tailor's linen or thin canvas may be placed inside the fold and tacked in with it. This should be about 1½ inch wide.) A line of fine stitching close to the fold makes for neatness and strength, but is not essential. Face with a straight strip of material or Italian cloth, about 1½ inch wide when finished.

Left Side

Cut a strip of material 3 inches wide and $\frac{1}{2}$ inch longer than the placket. The warp threads should run down it. Place its right side to the outside of the left side of the opening, tack together, and machine on the fitting-line. Turn up the lower edge of the strip, then press both turnings of the seam away from the skirt. Fold the strip over and fell down on the wrong side of the skirt just over the line, if machining. Overcast the turned-in edges along the bottom of the strip. Press well, then measure the position for the press studs. They should be $1\frac{1}{2}$ inch apart and $\frac{1}{2}$ inch from the fitting-lines—inside them on the right edge and outside them on the left. If the material is not very firm, a length of prussian binding may be held underneath the fitting-line on the left side and the socket halves of the fasteners sewn to this. It is a good plan to sew a press stud at the very bottom of the placket, and, after fastening it, to strike it with a hammer so that it is permanently closed and the seam cannot tear. Instead of this, a small buttonholed bar may be made across the bottom of the placket.

Sometimes the whole front gore is faced with Italian cloth or sateen from the waist to just below the knees, and this not only makes a neat placket, but prevents the skirt bagging when the material is a loosely woven one. The warp threads should run down this piece, and at the lower edge it should be hemmed on to itself, while the turned-in side edges should be felled over the seam turnings and, at one side, over the placket.

IN A SKIRT OF THIN, FULL MATERIAL

A continuous wrap serves well here, and the placket need not be so long as in a tight skirt. Cut a strip of self-material on the warp threads 1½ inch wide and twice the length of the placket. Place this on one side of the opening, edges level and right sides together. Tack down one side, turn back and tack up the other, then machine all round. Press the turnings away from the skirt. Turn the strip over, turn in the edge, and fell it over the turnings; or else tack only, and machine through from the right side close to the seam, thus securing both sides of the wrap at once. Turn the wrap inside and fold back on the right edge, then at the bottom or fold of the strip, machine once straight across it. Sew on press studs at intervals of 2 inches.

UNDER-ARM PLACKET IN A FROCK (Fig. 83)

Leave the left under-arm seam undone for about one-fifth of the hip measure—half above the waist and half below it (Fig. 83A—wrong side). Face the front edge with a piece of narrow ribbon or a piece of frock material. Sew a double wrap 1 inch wide (when finished) to the left side, as described for a tailored skirt. Sew on press studs 1 inch or more apart so that they are invisible when the placket is fastened. For extra firmness sew a hook on the waist-line at the right side of the opening and make a loop on the left side (Fig. 83B—right side). A zipp fastener may be sewn in this placket as described on p. 133.

PLACKET IN CENTRE-FRONT OR CENTRE-BACK OF BODICE (Fig. 84)

Chalk a line exactly down the middle of front or back for the length required. Cut a lengthwise strip of self-material or of a contrast, 4 inches wide and 2 inches longer than the opening. Place this

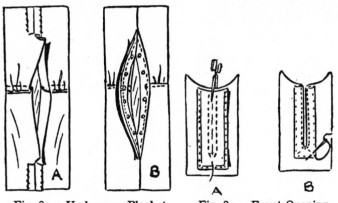

Fig. 83.—Under-arm Placket in Frock.

Fig. 84.—Front Opening in Frock.

strip right side downward on the right side of front or back of bodice, and tack down the middle through the line beneath it. Machine all round this line $\frac{1}{8}$ inch away from it (Fig. 84A). Cut down the line almost to the bottom, and here make tiny diagonal snips to each side. Press the turnings open over a roller, take the strip to the under side, tack into place, and machine all round close to the seam.

Bind the raw edges of the strip (as in A) or else turn them back and machine them (as in B), but in either case they must be kept free of the main piece of material. This placket may be fastened at the top only with a button and loop, or all the way down with a close row of buttons and loops, or with hooks and eyes to meet.

PLACKET WITH A ZIPP FASTENER

This is described on pp. 132–3.

WRIST OPENING OF TIGHT SLEEVE

Leave open the sleeve seam (if there are two seams, the outer one), for $1\frac{1}{2}$ or 2 inches. Turn back the edge of the upper sleeve (if there are two pieces, or its equivalent edge if there is only one) on the fitting-line and tack, but leave the turning of the other edge and bind it with narrow ribbon or a bias strip. Turn back the wrist edge on the fitting-line and face all round with a bias strip of silk. Fasten the opening with press studs, the stud part being on the faced edge $\frac{3}{8}$ inch in, and the sockets on the other the same distance *outside* the fitting-line. If preferred, hooks may be sewn on the edge which is to be faced, the ends just inside, and loops may be made on the other, on the fitting-line. Another method is to sew tiny buttons on the fitting-line of the bound edge and to make cord or buttonholed loops on the other. It is a good plan to make a buttonholed loop across the top of the opening.

WRIST OPENING OF SHIRT SLEEVE

This is made on the under side of the sleeve seam when worn, generally about 2½ or 3 inches from it, and the length from 3 to 3½ inches. The seam should be unstitched. For the edge of the narrower side of the opening cut a strip of material 1½ inch wide and ¼ inch longer than the slit. (The strip must be cut with the warp threads running down it.) Place right side of strip to the *wrong* side of the slit, run or machine the edges with ⅛-inch turnings; press the turnings on to the strip, then fold it over to the right side, make a turning ⅛ inch wide on it,

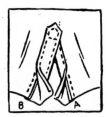

Fig. 85.—Opening in Shirt Sleeve.

and fold it over the little seam. Tack so that the fold is level with that on the wrong side, and machine close to the folded edge (Fig. 85A).

For the edge of the other side take a similar strip, but 1¾ inch wide and 1 inch longer than the slit. Stitch to the wrong side as before, starting at the bottom of the sleeve; press, fold over, and tack as before, then stitch close to both edges, but only as far as the top of the slit. Now point the top of the strip, lap the broader strip over the narrower one and tack the point into place. Stitch round the point and also straight across at the top of the opening (Fig. 85B), then join up the sides of the sleeve with a French or a French felled seam.

Setting on the Cuff

Gather the edge of the sleeve all round finely and draw up to fit the cuff. Fold the cuff wrong side out and stitch up the ends. Turn it right side out. Hold the wrong side of the gathered edge towards you and pin each end to those of one edge of the cuff (right sides together). If there are any inset

Fig. 86.—Finished Sleeve with Cuff.

marks on the edges, match them; in any case graduate the fullness so that there is very little at each side of the sleeve seam and most of it towards the ends of the cuff. Run together finely, then bring the other cuff edge over the turnings, turn it in, and fell lightly into place. Tack the cuff all round, press, then machine once or twice all round. Sew two buttons on the under edge of the cuff and make buttonholes to correspond on the upper edge (Fig. 86).

ANOTHER METHOD

For a not strictly tailored shirt sleeve, cut the slit as before, then cut a lengthwise strip 1¼ inch wide and twice the length of the opening. Sew this on as a continuous strip as described for a skirt placket on p. 136, but stitch first on the under side of each edge and then on the outside. Fold back this wrap on the edge which will be placed to the buttonhole end of the cuff, and set on the cuff as just described.

A Word of Caution

Plackets and openings should be just long enough to avoid strain, but no longer, or they will be too obtrusive. Careful sewing at the beginning of the opening is essential for strength.

In a Pleated Skirt

Here the placket should be arranged under a convenient pleat, possibly in a seam, or cut down the inner fold of the pleat. Press studs need not be so closely spaced as in a plain skirt.

When a Placket Wears Shabby

After much wear a placket in the left side-front of a plain skirt is apt to get shabby. Remedy this by covering the upper side with a shaped strapping of self-material (interlined with canvas), and treating the corresponding seam in the same way.

CHAPTER XIII

POCKETS, COLLARS, AND CUFFS

PATCH POCKET

For a Frock

CUT to the desired shape with 1 inch turning on the top and ½ inch on the other edges, and matching the grain of the part to which the pocket is to be sewn. Neaten the top with a stitched hem or trimming, line if desired, tack to the frock, and stitch round sides and lower edge. If preferred the pocket may be stitched all round and lined, and after being tacked into place the garment may be run to the back of the pocket on the sides and lower edge. Press at every stage of the work, and make the ends of the pocket very firm.

For a Coat

Cut as before described, stitch across the top (interline with linen or canvas if more firmness is required), line with coat lining, tack into place, and stitch round sides and lower edge. Cut a circle of canvas 1 inch in diameter and tack on the under side of the coat below each end of the top of the pocket. Then thread the ends of the machine silk in a needle and work over several stitches in stab stitch to make the pocket ends firm. Press well at every stage of the work.

JETTED OR PIPED POCKET (Fig. 87)

Suitable for a tailored coat. Chalk position of
opening on right side of garment, using a ruler.
Cut a piece of the same cloth with warp threads
running downward, 2 inches wider than the chalked

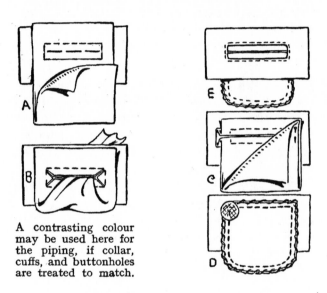

A contrasting colour
may be used here for
the piping, if collar,
cuffs, and buttonholes
are treated to match.

Fig. 87A, B, C, D and E.—Jetted or Piped Pocket.

line and twice the desired depth of the pocket plus
3 inches. Chalk a line on it to correspond with the
first one $1\frac{1}{2}$ inch below top of the strip on wrong side
of material. Place this piece right side downward
on the right side of the garment, with chalked lines
over one another, and tack through them. Stitch
along each side of the line $\frac{1}{8}$ inch away from it, and

down each end (Fig. 87A).   Then cut along the line
to within $\frac{1}{16}$ inch of each end, and from there make
tiny diagonal lines to the four corners (Fig. 87B).
Press these tiny seams over your smallest roller.
Push the pocket through the slit to the back, then
fold it so that the edges meet exactly (Fig. 87C).
Tack them with a small inverted pleat at each end
of the slit on the wrong side.   Stitch along on the
right side just below the seam of the lower edge of
the opening.   At the back turn up the long strip
over the opening to form a pocket, and tack the
double raw edges together all the way round.   Stitch
round the sides and lower edge (keeping the material
free from the garment (Fig. 87D) then stitch across
on the right side above the seam to match the lower
stitching (Fig. 87E).   Cut two small circles of linen or
canvas, and tack under each end of pocket.   Now
from right side back stitch across each end through
the linen, pushing needle up and down through the
layers of material.   These are called "stays" (Fig.
87D).   Bind or overcast the turnings.

FLAP POCKET (Fig. 88)

Chalk the line for the pocket opening with a ruler
on the right side of the cloth.   Cut out the flap to
match the garment in grain, interline it with linen
or soft canvas.   Stitch round sides and lower edges
once or twice if desired, but this is not essential.
Line with the coat lining.   Place this flap upside
down over the chalked line.   Tack just above this
chalked line and machine through it (Fig. 88A).
Cut out a pocket in lining.   This must be twice the

estimated depth of the pocket plus $1\frac{1}{2}$ inches, and 2 inches wider than the line. At top and bottom of this strip stitch a 2-inch-deep strip of cloth to the right side of the lining. Now place one end of the strip with the cloth side downward and its raw edge just up to the chalked line (Fig. 88A). Stitch less

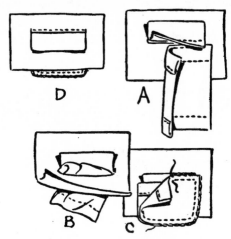

Fig. 88.—Flap Pocket.

than $\frac{1}{8}$ inch from the raw edge, then cut along the chalked line, either with scissors or a penknife, with the material laid on a board. Press open the turnings of each little seam over a small roller. Draw the pocket through to the back and fold it so that a little bind comes above the lower edge. Tack close to the seam, then stitch from the right side.

Now press the seam which joins on the flap with the turnings upward. At the back, fold up the pocket strip and lay the loose end over the top of the opening. Tack into place and stitch on the right side just above the seam (Fig. 88c). At the back, stitch down the sides of the strip and along the bottom (keeping them loose from the coat), trim off the edges, and if the coat is to be unlined, bind them all round; if not, overcast them. To strengthen the corners work stab stitch through circles of canvas. Press well at every stage of the work. The final effect is shown in Fig. 88D.

COLLARS

Unlined Turn-down Collar for Frock or Blouse

Cut it with straight warp threads running down the middle of the back. Neaten the lower edges by

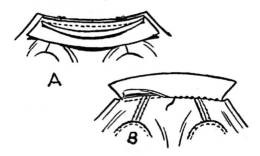

Fig. 89.—Setting on a Blouse Collar (double).

hemming, binding, or trimming. Place the collar on the outside of the garment, pin centre back of collar to that of neck, then from there pin to each end. Take a bias strip of the same material (or a thinner one), place over the turnings, and tack through the three layers, afterwards running or machining. Cut down the turning and fell the bias strip over them on the inside of the neck.

A Lined Collar

Stitch the two layers of material together on the wrong side (right sides of both facing), cut down the turnings, then turn the collar right side out and press the edges. Pin to the neck as before, but by the under layer only, then tack and afterwards run or machine together (Fig. 89A). Turn round so that the inside of the neck is towards you, turn in the raw edge of the upper collar, and fell it down over the turnings (see Fig. 89B).

Narrow, Stand-up Collar

Cut out an interlining of soft muslin or canvas on the bias and without turnings. Place on the material with the warp threads running down the middle of the back, and allow from $\frac{1}{4}$- to $\frac{1}{2}$-inch turnings all round. Pin the two together in a few places, then hold in the left hand with the material uppermost, turn back the edges over the canvas all round, and tack. Mitre the corners on the wrong side, then catch stitch (Fig. 35) the raw edges of the material to the canvas so that no stitches show on the right side. Hold the inside of the bodice towards you, place the collar behind the edge of the neck (wrong side facing you), pin middle of neck to that of collar, then from there pin to each end. Run the two layers together so that no stitches show on the right side. Cut out a lining in thin silk on the bias and fell into place all round the collar. (If collar is to fasten in the front, sew on two hooks on the inside of the right end and two eyes on the left, before sewing in the lining.)

Tailored Step-collar

The interlining for this collar must be cut from canvas which has been shrunk previously. Place the paper pattern on double canvas with the "break"—the little straight edge on the bottom of the collar which will be joined to the top of the lapel when the collar is sewn to the coat—on the straight warp thread as shown in Fig. 90. Pin the pattern to the canvas

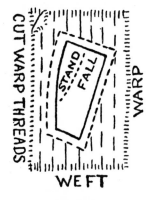

Fig. 90.—Cutting Underpart of Collar and Canvas Interlining.

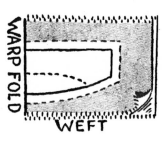

Fig. 91.—Cutting the Upper Collar.

and then cut out double with $\frac{1}{4}$-inch turning on the back edge *only*, cutting the canvas close up to the pattern on the other edges. (The turnings shown on the other edges in Fig. 90 are for cutting out in cloth only.) Cut out the cloth under part of the collar in the same way, but with $\frac{3}{8}$-inch turnings all round. For the cloth upper part place the back edge of the pattern to the warp fold, and if the cloth has a nap, place the pattern so that when the collar is worn the nap will run downward (Fig. 91). Cut out with ⅜-inch turnings all round.

Note.—Sometimes both the canvas and the cloth underpart are each cut in one piece, exactly on the bias—that is, with the centre-back of the pattern on a bias fold, without turning. The cloth upper collar may be cut in the same way if the material has no nap or decided pattern or weave.

The upper collar in a striped cloth may be cut out in one piece with the back edge to a warp fold, or it may be cut in the same way as the under collar, with a seam at the back, and the stripes forming inverted V's there. Checks look best on the straight without a seam.

Making the Collar

Overlap the back edges of the canvas for ½ inch and herringbone them together. Stitch up the back edges of the under collar and press open the turnings. Place the canvas on the wrong side of the cloth underpart with the seams together, then tack together once along the length. Now with fine silk make a line of fine running along the crease row (where the collar turns down). Hold the collar curved over the fingers of the left hand (canvas uppermost), and starting close to the crease row, cover the " fall " with pad stitch (Figs. 92 and 93). Leave about ⅛ inch of the canvas free all round. Use matching silk for this padding. While this is being done the canvas will begin to " roll "—that is, take on a rather convex appearance. Now make some straight rows of machining along the " stand " and cross them with zigzag lines (see Fig. 94), after which fold the collar (canvas outside) by the crease

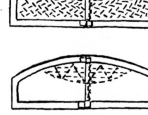

Fig. 92.—Padding a Coat Collar.

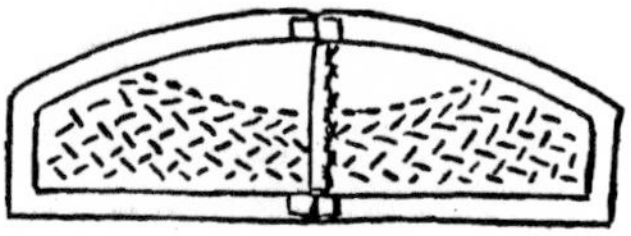

Fig. 93.—Padding the Fall.
Fig. 94.—Padding the Stand.

row, place on the ironing-board, and press the fold while holding the collar in the position shown in Fig.

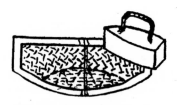

Fig. 95.—Pressing a Coat Collar.

Fig. 96.—Stretching the Fall Edge.

95. Then take up the collar, place the fall edge just on the edge of the ironing-board (canvas uppermost),

and work round it with the iron, stretching slightly as you do so. Do the same on the curved edge of the stand, but *not* on the little straight edges known as the break.

Take the other piece of cloth, place it right side downward on the ironing-board, and stretch the edges corresponding to those you stretched on the collar. Place the right side of it to the under side of the collar (right sides together) and tack round the lower edges of the fall and up each end. Then machine as close to the canvas as possible on these edges (in fact, rather under the edge). Cut off the turnings as close as is safe and press them open over a small roller. Now turn the collar right side out and press on the under side.

Setting on the Collar

Turn back the cloth turning on the stand edge of the collar and herringbone it to the canvas, then press it. Place the collar on the outside of the coat as it will be when worn. Pin the middle of the stand to the middle of the outside of the neck, then from there pin to each end, with points upward. See that the crease row of the collar meets that of the lapel. Fell the stand invisibly to the coat with matching silk, then press on the inside. If the front of the coat has a stay-tape (" bridle ") on the crease row of the lapel, bring up the loose end and sew it over the crease row of the collar. Now on the outside where the turnings of the collar meet those of the front facing (the break), turn in the edges of both and tack them to meet exactly.

Then take matching silk and draw them together with slip stitch (Fig. 97). Do this to the end of the front facing, then press. If desired, stitch round the edges of collar and fronts.

Fig. 97.—Slip Stitching together Facings of Coat Front and Collar.

CUFFS

There are three kinds of cuffs. The first is the straight band, into which the sleeve is gathered, like a shirt or blouse sleeve. The second is purely ornamental, is made separately, often over an interlining of canvas or muslin, and is then tacked into position outside the sleeve, after which the edges of wrist and cuff are generally slip stitched together. The third type is ornamental also, and is cut to extend over the hand and be sewn inside the wrist edge. It is generally interlined with canvas or muslin, then lined with silk. The wrist edges of the sleeve are catch stitched down on the inside, then the raw edge of the cuff is tacked inside the wrist, and the turnings of both are run together. After this the wrist is faced in the usual way with silk.

The Shirt Cuff

The making and setting-on of this are described in Chapter XII.

CHAPTER XIV

TRIMMINGS

TRIMMINGS may be divided roughly into three classes. First there are those made in the material itself and forming part of the main pieces, such as tucks, pleats, gathers, shirrings, gaugings, cordings, etc. Secondly, there are those made separately and sewn on, such as pipings, ruchings, kiltings, shell edgings, folds, strappings, etc. (sometimes, however, these two classes may overlap a little). Thirdly, those worked directly on the material, such as drawn-thread work, hemstitching, smocking, and various embroidery stitches which come into favour at intervals. Of course, in addition there are many ready-made trimmings, such as braid, passementerie, lace, frilling, cord, etc.

TUCKS

Tucks are either run by hand or stitched by machine, on the right or top side of them. They are easiest to make when running with the warp threads, though frequently they are made across the grain, and they are very effective on the bias—but it must be the true bias, as, if the fabric is even a little off the diagonal, the tucks will " wring ", or twist. In planning for tucks remember that you must allow twice the width of the tuck *extra*. The charm of tucks lies in their perfect regularity, so be sure that yours are evenly spaced. Sometimes they are made with only the width of the tuck between them, so that the fold of one touches the stitching of the next. At others the full width of the *unstitched* tuck is left, so that when all are stitched there is the width of the finished tuck between the fold of one and the stitching of the next; but it is seldom that they are spaced more widely than this.

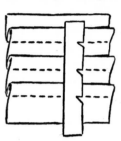

Fig. 98.—Measuring Tucks.

To ensure accuracy make a gauge on a strip of cardboard. Decide on the amount of the spacing—that is, the distance between one row of stitching and the next, or (which is the same) the distance between one fold and the next, and make several notches on the edge of the card at this interval. Take up and tack the first tuck on the material, measuring it with a ruler, then lay a notch on the stitching of this tuck and take up the next tuck at the next notch, and so on (Fig. 98). Run or machine these tucks from what will be their upper side when they are laid flat. Of course, most sewing-machines have a tucking attachment which simplifies the spacing and stitching considerably, and you will be wise to make yourself proficient in the use of it.

Tucks as a rule are not pressed, unless the material is very springy; even then only the extreme edge is pressed *very lightly* with a moderately warm iron. Another plan is to draw the back of the tucks (wrong side of material) over the face of an upturned, moderately hot iron as described on p. 181 for pressing velvet. When tucking a yoke, or anything of uneven shape, allow a good margin all round the pattern, and then, after tucking, trim the material to the desired shape.

Diamond Tucks

Evenly spaced tucks are made exactly on the diagonal; these are then crossed by others of the same spacing on the opposite diagonal, thus producing diamonds. They should be very narrow—varying from but a few threads in width to $\frac{1}{8}$ inch, not more.

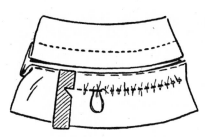

Fig. 99.—Making Curved Tucks.   Fig. 100.—Scalloped Tucks.

Curved Tucks (Fig. 99)

These are sometimes used on a circular skirt, and, being on a curve, the under side of each is wider than the upper. First measure and tack the position and depth of the tuck all round, then fold midway between the lines and tack close to the fold thus made. Now pin for the sewing-line from the under side, and afterwards tack the slight fullness into place evenly. Run or machine the tuck from the top, or outside.

Scalloped Tucks (Fig. 100)

Though very pretty, these are only suitable for thin fabrics, and should not be more than $\frac{1}{8}$ inch wide.

Make them in the ordinary way, but at equal distances—say every ¼ inch—take a stitch right over the edge of the tuck and draw it tightly, then continue the running. When there is a group of these tucks the over-stitches must come underneath one another in all the rows.

Pin Tucks

The name describes these, as they are but a few threads in width. They are frequently seen in the middle of the back neck of a bodice, about 3 inches in length, to take out any unwanted fullness. At other times they are purely decorative, being used for yokes, collars, etc., and sometimes they may cover the larger portion of a frock or skirt. Of course, they are only suitable for thin materials.

Shirred Tucks

Useful for very thin fabrics where a good deal of fullness has to be disposed of. Make several rows of pin tucks, then draw up the threads to produce the desired width and regulate the fullness.

Corded Tucks

There are two ways of making these. In the first, make the tucks in the usual method, just sufficiently wide to enclose the cord or thick wool. Then secure the end of this to a safety-pin and run it through the tuck, keeping the material quite smooth. In the second, enclose the cord or wool in a fold of the material and make a line of running close up to it. If the cord and running threads are drawn up, " corded shirring " is produced.

PLEATS

A pleat is simply a tuck which is not stitched, at least for not more than part of its length, for often in skirts pleats are stitched half-way down or more. They set best when on the straight warp thread, but with care they may be made successfully in most materials when slightly off the straight thread. Pleats should be measured very carefully to ensure a perfect " hang ", and it is a good plan to chalk or tack the outer fold of each as a guide. Pleats must always be arranged on a flat surface, and never over the knee. When they come down the middle of any part of a garment it is best to make them before tacking up the seams, so that the material can be laid flat. It is also advisable to press the under side of each fold with a piece of the same cloth between the iron and the pleat quite apart from the main part of the garment, before laying the fold in its desired position. The inside fold is often stitched down its length to give firmness.

Kilting

This is a succession of narrow pleats of equal size, the beginning of one touching the end of the previous one. The amount of material required is three times the width of the space to be occupied, and the lower edge should be hemmed and pressed. Supposing you are making 1-inch pleats, then chalk lines on the material 1 inch apart (Fig. 101A), carefully measuring them with a ruler. You may chalk on the right side if the marks will rub off easily; if they will not, you must chalk on the wrong side

and tack through the lines to the right side so that
the positions for the folds are plainly marked there.
Now make a fold on the right side exactly on each
third chalked line, and tack ⅛ inch from the fold.
Then press each fold on what will be the under-
side of each pleat. (See chapter on Pressing.)
This done, place the material right side upwards

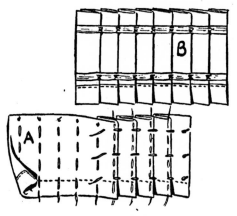

Fig. 101.—Kilting.

on the table with the tacked folds running horizontally. Now start at the edge farthest from you
and fold the first pleat upwards for 1 inch. Pin
across the pleat at intervals, and then tack from
right to left near the fold in a fresh colour of cotton.
Take the next fold and turn up 1 inch so that it comes
just up to the end of the previous pleat. Pin and
tack as before, and continue in this way until all the
pleats are made.

Now make lines of tacking **across** the pleats at

intervals of 5 inches or so, in the case of a skirt. Place the material wrong side upward on the ironing-board, lay a damp cloth over, and press according to the weight of the fabric. When the kilting is more than 6 or 7 inches in depth it must be taped on the wrong side by a piece of prussian binding laid across the pleats and caught to each one with two or three cross stitches (see Fig. 101B).

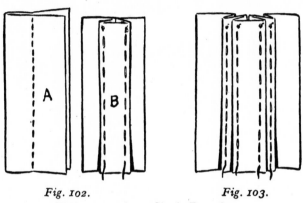

Fig. 102.   *Fig. 103.*

Fig. 102A and B.—Single Box-pleat.
Fig. 103.—Double Box-pleat.

Box-pleats (Single)

Each single box-pleat takes in *extra* material twice the width of the space it is to occupy; therefore, if the finished pleat is to be 2 inches wide, 4 inches must be allowed for it. Take up the amount allowed and tack it like a big tuck on the right side of the fabric for its full length (Fig. 102A). Now flatten this tuck so that the middle of it comes exactly over the tacking. Secure with a few pins across the pleat, then tack each fold, keeping it loose from the material below. Press the under side of the folds, then tack into place to the material below and remove the first lines of tacking (Fig. 102B). Press on the wrong side of the garment, after which you may stitch down the side of each pleat for some distance, if desired. In any case, do not remove the tacking of the pleats until the rest of the garment is complete. If it is a skirt, they must be untacked at the lower edge for a few inches until the hem is made and pressed, then the pleats may be re-tacked and pressed. If the pleats are not stitched down their sides, they may be taped at the back as described for kilting.

Box-pleats (Double)

Amount of extra fabric varies with different types. As shown in Fig. 103, there is a box-pleat in the middle with a single pleat laid at each side, facing away from the middle of the box-pleat. Suppose you wish the middle one to be 2 inches wide and each side one 1 inch, you will need 8 inches of extra material, this being twice the width of the space the pleats occupy. Find the middle of the piece and form a tuck there 2 inches wide (taking up 4 inches, of course); now make this into a box-pleat as described in the previous paragraph. Measure 1 inch from each fold of the box-pleat, tack a fresh fold and press it, then form an inch-wide pleat at each side, tack and press from the wrong side. Stitch for a few inches, as described for the single box-pleats, and tape at the back, if necessary.

Sometimes the side pleats are exactly under the middle one, so that the extra width required will be four times that of the space occupied.

Inverted Pleats

The making of these, when in a whole piece of material, is just like that of single box-pleats, but working on the wrong side of the material. When they occur in a skirt and come from the waist but

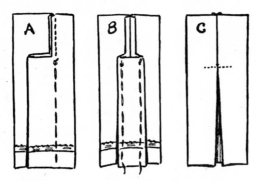

Fig. 104.—Inverted Pleat in Skirt Seam.

open a good way down—perhaps just below the knee, or lower—the upper part of the pleat must be stitched like a seam, and then, if the turnings are bulky, they may be cut away as shown in Fig. 104A. In some paper patterns this cutting away is always done. After the seam has been stitched and the tuck tacked as in Fig. 104A, flatten it as shown in 104B, press the edges, and then tack flat. After pressing, the result on the right side will be as in C. It is usual to secure the raw edges of the top of the pleats in some way—a straight line of stitching as in C,

F   (Dress)

or in the form of an inverted V. A Sprat's Head (otherwise known as an Arrowhead Tack) makes a smart finish. See Fig. 174, p. 354). This should be worked in buttonhole twist with the point exactly on the seam and the broad base worked through the pleat turnings to secure them.

Sometimes, however, the pleats occur in the lower part of a real seam—that is, between two distinct pieces of material. It looks very ugly when there is a seam up the middle of the pleat, as there would be if extensions for the pleat were made on each side of the opening; the best way is to leave 2 inches or more extension on both sides of the seam, then to take a piece of material the depth of the opening and twice the width of the extension (that is, 4 inches if the extension is 2 inches). The sides of this piece should be seamed to the sides of the extensions, and the pleats will form themselves. The folds should be tacked on the right side, pressed, and then secured at the top in one of the ways previously suggested.

FLOUNCES AND FRILLS

These are really the same thing, except that a flounce is deep and a frill is narrow. They may be either gathered, pleated, or circular.

Gathered

Gathered flounces are generally cut across the width—that is to say, with the warp threads running downward—but frills may be cut either across or down the material, and at times either of them may be cut on the bias, and they set well that way. But in whatever way they are cut, it is essential that the edges should be placed correctly on the material. A deep flounce requires more width than a short one. With thin fabrics, such as voile or muslin, three times the plain width is not too much, and it may be more for ninon and georgette and similar fabrics. The width for a frill depends entirely upon the fabric and upon the effect desired, and it is best to experiment with a spare piece of material to find out the exact quantity.

A flounce or frill may be either hemmed, whipped, or picot edged, and a deep flounce may have its lower edge bound or trimmed with a ruching, according to fashion. The upper edge may be set on with a heading or sewn on with raw edges, and these covered with a strapping of the same material or with trimming of some kind. Should a heading be used, a little more than twice its depth must be added for this. A flounce always hangs better if it has at least two rows of gathers, even if the upper one is on the extreme edge of the turnings and does not show. A gathered flounce or frill should always, before it is gathered, be divided into a certain number of equal portions, and the divisions marked with pins. The part to which it is to be sewn should be divided in the same way, then, when the gathers have been drawn up, the pins on flounce and garment must be placed together and the gathering threads adjusted. In this way the regularity of the fullness is ensured.

Pleated

The rules given for cutting a gathered flounce or frill apply equally here. The amount of material required depends upon the closeness of the pleats. Single pleats, or box-pleats, if set closely with no spaces between them, take three times the width of the part to which they are to be sewn. They may be sewn on by machine from $\frac{1}{8}$ to $\frac{1}{4}$ inch below a turned-down edge, or they may be sewn on raw edged and neatened with a strapping. Sometimes the skirt is cut off, and the lower edge turned up and stitched over the top of the flounce.

Circular Flounces

These are not always perfectly circular, but they are cut on a curve, so that while the top fits the foundation plainly, the lower edge is full. A flounce of this kind may be turned upside down and its raw edge run to the foundation, and, though not essential, a narrow trimming may be sewn over the join, if desired. Sometimes a circular flounce is sewn to a raw edge, in which case the skirt and flounce should be placed with right sides together and edges level; then they should be run or machined together. The turnings must be snipped at frequent intervals to prevent puckering, after which they may be turned upwards on to the skirt and a row of machining added just above the seam.

GODETS (Figs. 105a and 105b)

A godet is a wedge-shaped piece of material inserted into either a slit or seam to add width in a

decorative fashion. It is chiefly used in skirts of
fragile material, and may be of the same or contrasting fabric. The top is pointed and the sides
slope to give a width at the bottom of from 6 to
12 inches, or even more, according to the height of
the opening. The point of the godet should first
be pinned to the top of the opening, and from there
each side must then be pinned to those of the opening (Fig. 105A). Care is needed when the sides of

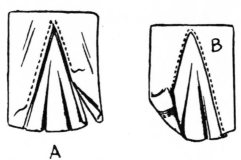

Fig. 105A and B.—Inserting Godet in Skirt.

the godet are on the bias, and it is often desirable
to hang the skirt after tacking, but before machining
in the godets, as the bias sides may drop, and can
then be adjusted before machining. Sometimes the
top of the godet is rounded and set into a rounded
opening, but the same rules for inserting still hold
good. Careful snipping of turnings will be needed
round the curve. When the material is suitable, the
turnings, after being pressed on to the skirt, may be
stitched through from the right side just outside the
seam (Fig. 105B).

GATHERS

These may find a place in any part of a garment where fullness is desired. They certainly set best when either on the straight thread (preferably weft) or on the exact bias, but they may come in any direction. Silk should always be used for the gathering of any material but linen and cotton. (The stitch is shown on p. 56, Fig. 25.) When several rows of evenly spaced gathers are used, they are known as "shirring". Gathers in dressmaking are never "stroked" as in plain sewing, but they may be coaxed into place gently with a coarse, blunt-pointed needle, though great care should be taken not to injure the fabric. Gathering may be done very quickly by machine. The stitch should be made as large as possible, then the single material should be stitched as usual. The top thread should first be drawn up as required, the fullness regulated, and after that the lower thread should be drawn up to fix the gathers.

SCALLOPS

These make a nice finish either to the edge of a skirt or to that of a flounce or other parts of a frock. If you are not working from a pattern, it is best to cut the shape of two scallops in cardboard with the aid of compasses, or a plate, and then to lay this guide on the right side of the material, and, after planning out carefully, to tack or chalk round the scallops, but do not cut out. Scallops are usually bound, so cut some bias strips $\frac{3}{4}$ inch wide, join them up on their straight edges, and press the turnings

open. Run the strip all round the scalloped line,
allowing it rather easy on the curved edge and
stretching it at the points. Then cut off the scallops
level with the edge of the bias strip (Fig. 106A), turn
this over, turn in the raw edge, and fell over the
first line of sewing, making a neat little pleat at
each point (Fig. 106B). When the material is transparent the strip should be double. Its raw edges

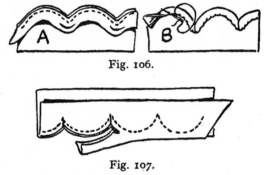

Fig. 106.

Fig. 107.

Fig. 106A and B.—Bound Scallops.
Fig. 107.—Faced Scallops.

should be placed together and run to the scallops,
after which the double edge can be felled down on
the other side.

Another method is as follows (Fig. 107). Cut a
bias strip of the desired material a little deeper than
the scallops are to be. Mark the scallop on the
wrong sides of this with the aid of the cardboard
or the paper pattern, but do not mark the edge of the
garment. Tack this bias strip on the edge of the
garment (right sides together) and run all round the
scalloped line. Cut out the scallops with ½-inch

turnings, turn the facing over to the wrong side, and tack, leaving only a tiny ridge of it showing. Cut off the facing to an even depth all round, turn in the edge, and slip hem it into place.

PIPINGS

These are usually applied to seams or round the edges of various parts, such as collars, cuffs, yokes, etc., and they make a very effective trimming, either in self-colour or a contrast. Cut out bias strips about ¾ inch wide. Join up their ends and

Fig. 108.—Inserting Piping in a Seam.

press the turnings open, then stretch the united strips over the edge of a smooth table. Shrink the piping cord by steeping it in hot water and drying it in a hot place; then place it on the wrong side of the strip, fold the raw edges over so that they meet, and run as close to the cord as possible (Fig. 108A). When inserting in a seam, hold the piping, turnings upwards, between the two pieces of material and tack all together close up to the cord, afterwards running or machining over the tacking (Fig. 108B).

When piping the edges of any part, the shape should be chalked or tacked very carefully. Place the piping on the right side of the edge and tack close up to the cord through the fitting-line. When you come to an outside corner or curve, ease the piping, but stretch it on an inner corner or curve. Now run finely close up to the cord, fold the turnings over to the wrong side, and neaten them in some way. If unlined, a bias strip may be joined in with the running, and after the turnings of the piping have been cut down, this bias strip may be felled over them to make all neat.

CORDED PUFFINGS (Fig. 109)

Cut bias strips $\frac{1}{2}$ inch wider than the finished width will be. The length required is twice that of the part it is to be sewn to. Join up the strips on their straight edges and press the turnings. Then turn down one edge $\frac{1}{4}$ inch to the wrong side, enclose piping cord in the fold, and run close up to the cord. Treat the other edge in the same way, then draw up the cord to the required amount and pull up the threads also to fix the fullness. (When a long length of trimming is to be made, it

Fig. 109.—Corded Puffing.

is best to do the running in sections, as it would be impossible to do it with one length of thread.) Pin the trimming into place, and then sew it on through the fullness.

RUCHINGS (Fig. 110)

A ruching may be either pleated or gathered, and in either single or double material, but it must always

F 2 (Dress)

be cut on the bias, unless ribbon is used.   For a box-pleated ruche, in single material, cut bias strips to the required width and three times the length of the part to which it is to be sewn.   Join up the strips by their straight edges, and press the turnings open. Place the cut edge on a board, open out the blades of the scissors a little, and fray out the edges of the strip with them.   Afterwards you may draw these edges between the thumb and first finger of both hands to improve the appearance.   Lay the strip

Fig. 110.—Box-pleated Ruche.

in single box-pleats and tack along the middle, then sew invisibly into place on the garment taking the stitches through the sides of the pleats.   Some-times the edges of the pleats are caught together in the middle.   If the material is very thin, more than three times the finished width should be allowed, then, after making the pleats, a gathering-thread should be run across the middle of them and drawn up as required.   As an alternative, the strip may be cut double the required width, plus $\frac{1}{4}$ inch for turnings.   The raw edges must be folded to overlap in the middle of the under side, then the pleats made as before.   Gathered ruches are made similarly in either single or double fabric, but they are simply gathered (in sections) along the middle of the strip. Ribbon, of course, needs no preparation.

KILTED FRILLING OR QUILLING

Cut strips either on the straight (either grain) or on the bias, and join them up. Fold down the middle, then lay in pleats, ¼ inch or less, which touch one another, tacking as you go. Place to the outside of the edge to be trimmed, raw edges level, run or machine the two together; turn the kilting to the inside with its raw edge projecting as much as desired, and neaten the turnings with a facing. If preferred, the frilling may be box-pleated.

BIAS FOLDS

These must be in firm material. Cut bias strips the required width and join up as usual. Turn over the raw edges to meet in the middle of the under side and draw them together with lacing stitch as in Fig. 31. Tack into place on the garment and slip stitch to it by the upper edge of the fold.

When the folds are required for ties, girdles, etc., cut the bias strips the required width, plus turnings. Stitch the raw edges together on the wrong side, then take a small safety-pin and secure it to one end of the strip with a loop of double thread. Insert the safety-pin in the same end of the strip and push it through (Figs. 111A and 111B).

A BIAS BIND

If the edge to be bound is much curved—as, for instance, a neck edge—run a fine gathering-thread round it to prevent stretching. Run the bias strip to the right side of the edge, turn it over, and fell on the wrong side over the turnings (Fig. 112A and 112B). When the fabric is very thin, cut the strip double, run the raw edges to the edge to be bound, then fell down the fold on the wrong side.

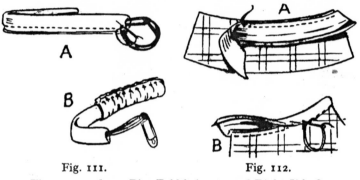

Fig. 111.   Fig. 112.

Fig. 111A and B.—Bias Fold being turned Right Side Out.
Fig. 112.—Sewing on a Bias Bind.

STRAPPING

Generally used in firm cloth or strong silk. Cut bias strips the required finished width, plus $\frac{3}{4}$-inch turning. Fold back both edges $\frac{1}{4}$ inch, tack, then press under a warm iron. Now tack into place and stitch through both edges by machine. When going round curves, the outside edge must be stretched gently. If the material is thin, cut bias strips of muslin or thin canvas without turnings, tack the material over them, and apply as before.

SHELL EDGING

Suitable for very thin silk materials. Cut bias strips twice the desired width (which should not be

more than ½ inch), plus ⅜ inch. Fold one edge
over the other in the middle of one side and gather
as shown in Fig.
113. Draw up
the gathering-
thread and sew
on the edging

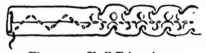

Fig. 113.—Shell Trimming.

through the gathers. The finished length of the
edging will be less than half the original length,
according to the amount of fullness required. Narrow ribbon may be used in this way, but single, of
course.

LACE

This, if in the form of medallions, should be tacked
into place on the right side of the material, then the
edges should be sewn finely, but strongly, to the
background with matching cotton. The material
behind the lace should then be cut away, leaving a
small turning to be loop stitched to prevent fraying.
If lace edging is to be applied as a frill, it should first
be divided into a number of equal sections, and
the edge to which it is to be sewn should be divided
into the same number. Draw up the edge thread
of the lace, regulate the fullness according to the
divisions, pin and tack to the material, and oversew
the two together. An attractive way of applying
lace edging plainly to material is to lay the straight
edge of the lace over the fabric on fairly stiff paper,
tack it into place (leaving a small turning on the
fabric), and then to work over the lace edge with

silk in satin stitch, afterwards cutting away the turning close up to the stitches.

There are two usual ways of applying insertion. (1) Place right side of insertion to that of material, with a tiny edge of the latter above the lace. Now roll this edge over the edge of the insertion and sew on with the whipping stitch shown in Fig. 30, p. 59. Flatten the join with the thumb nail or the thimble. (2) If the insertion is to be applied to a whole piece of material, tack it into place by both edges, cut away the material behind it with ⅛-inch turnings. Roll these back over the tacked lines like a hem or fold back just once, leaving a raw edge, then machine them from the right side. (See Fig. 150, p. 284.) When applying insertion to a curve, the inside edge of the lace should be drawn up to fit.

BRAIDING

This is done either in rows or according to a stamped pattern. Military braid varies from ¾ inch to 2 inches in width. It should be tacked into place on one or both edges, according to width, and then slip stitched to the background. Soutache braid may be sewn on with the special braiding attachment supplied with the sewing-machine, or it may be applied by hand in one of two ways. (1) The braiding design should be either ironed off from a transfer or chalked on the material. Pierce a hole in the cloth with a stiletto at the beginning of the design and push the end of the braid through to the wrong side, where it should be sewn to the back threads of the material. Carry the braid over the outline with the left thumb and forefinger and sew with fine silk, taking stab stitches up and down through the middle of the braid. (2) Begin in the same way, but stand the braid on edge and hold it upright. Bring up the needle to the right side, take a little horizontal stitch along the edge of the braid, then take a tiny fell stitch in the material, and make these two stitches alternately all along the design. When the end is reached, in either method finish off as you began—by pushing the end of the braid through a hole to the wrong side and securing it there.

PICOTING

This is really machine-hemstitching cut through the middle, and it is an excellent way of finishing the edges of thin materials such as crêpe-de-chine, silk, and georgette. Before sending to the shop, the seams must be stitched and the position of the picoting must be tacked. If frills are needed, a strip wide enough for two should be taken, and a line tacked through the middle; then, when this is cut, two picoted edges will result. When sending bias edges, these should be tacked to tissue paper, to prevent them from stretching.

CHAPTER XV

PRESSING, SHRINKING, AND STRETCHING

THOUGH it is difficult to cite any one process in dressmaking as more important than another, yet certainly pressing yields place to none. It is not a job which can be done hurriedly at the last moment, to give the garment a final hallmark, as it were, but it has to be carried out in instalments as the work proceeds. The iron, therefore, should always be at hand, and if an electric one is available, so much the better, especially if it is one of those in which the heat can be adjusted to suit all grades of material. The ordinary electric one, however, will serve for most fabrics, except for thick cloth, which calls for the regulation " goose " of 12 lb. or so. If you have made a coat of thick tweed, for instance, and have pressed it during the process with an ordinary electric or flat iron, and you are not quite satisfied with its finish, but you are not prepared to invest in a " goose ", a working tailor will give a final pressing for a small sum.

You will find your iron will be your constant friend in any job of dressmaking. For example, before cutting out at all, see that there are no creases in the fabric. First press it double on the wrong sides, using a not-too-hot iron with a side-to-side movement, and never allowing it to stand still. Then, after cutting out any part which has been placed to a fold, this must be pressed out before tacking up the seams, in the manner just described.

If the fold is very obstinate and the cloth thick, soak a piece of stay-tape in water, lay it along the wrong side of the fold, and press it over a roller, then remove the tape and press the cloth on a covered board until dry.

PRESS EDGES BEFORE STITCHING

Again, before stitching any hems or folds, press them first, and you will find the stitching will be more regular in consequence. Also, when turning hems, if you press the turns as you make them, before tacking them, you will find them much more even than if made without pressing. .In all cases the pressure and heat of the iron should be adjusted to the weight of the fabric. Thin materials need very little, as if they are pressed heavily and often, all the " nature " seems to be taken out of them, and they look lifeless and poor. Water is a great help in pressing obstinate fabrics, but it should be applied very sparingly, and never unless it has been tested previously on a spare piece of the material to see if it leaves a mark, as this may be difficult to remove. Never damp the garment itself, but always a spare piece of the same material, and lay this over the part to be pressed.

Of course, pressing can be overdone. Many amateurs seem to take as their motto " Strike while the iron's hot " ! But a much better one is—to parody a musical axiom—" Press as much as you need and as little as you can." What you press *on* is just as important as what you press *with*. For large surfaces you need a skirt-board or table, covered smoothly with at least three layers of blanket or cloth. Over this should come an adjustable cover of washed calico. One made from an old sheet will serve, and it is essential that it should be kept clean by frequent washing. The skirt-board may be one of those mounted on a stand, or it may be rested on two pieces of furniture. In either case· it should be very firm.

PADDED ROLLERS

For skirt and other long seams padded rollers are needed, and they should be longer than the seam, to avoid creasing the material. A long blind-roller makes an excellent foundation. A piece of blanket or cloth should be rolled round this several times and sewn on, and a removable cover of calico should also be provided. For sleeves and other short seams shorter rollers are required—an old-fashioned round ruler or rolling-pin will serve—while for very tiny seams or folds in collars or trimmings a thick pencil will be admirable. All these should be wrapped as described before. If you have a good assortment of rollers, they will save much time which would otherwise be lost in improvising what is needed. A tailor's cushion of oval shape (see Fig. 1, p. 13) is also essential for pressing darts, curved seams, armhole seams, etc., and for shrinking various parts in a tailored coat.

A covered sleeve-board is very useful, but not essential if you have a short roller and a tailor's cushion. One can be bought for about a shilling. For pressing velvet and other pile fabrics a special wire brush is often used by professionals, but it can be dispensed with.

PRESSING SEAMS

Lay the seam on the skirt-board just as it comes from the machine, with turnings away from you. Take a strip of the same material, lay it over the

Fig. 114.

Fig. 115.

Fig. 114.—Pressing Seam Turnings Double.
Fig. 115.—Pressing Seam Turnings Open.

stitching, and press from one end of the seam to the other, stretching slightly as you do so, as the stitching is always liable to contract the material a little. The iron must not be pushed along the fabric as in ironing lingerie, but it should be pressed down, kept there a little time, then lifted and put down again on the next bit of unpressed seam, and so on for the whole length. This is called " pressing double " (Fig. 114). After each seam has been treated in this way, place the roller under one of them (turnings outside) and rest its end on two pieces of furniture of equal height. Then open the turnings, place the piece of spare material over, and press the turnings open with the same movement as before (see Fig. 115). If the cloth is obstinate, the pressing cloth may be damped, before pressing, or a piece of kitchen soap may be rubbed on the under side of each turning.

Press all skirt, coat, or frock seams in the same direction, usually from the top downward, and if the fabric has a nap, it is essential that it should be pressed with this, and not against it, which would roughen the material. If the seams are curved at all, the turnings should be snipped across to within $\frac{1}{4}$ inch of the stitching at intervals of $1\frac{1}{2}$ inch or more, and then scalloped out at the snips so that the seam will not pucker. You will note the advantage of using a roller for seams, as the pressure of the iron comes only on the seam itself, and the turnings fall away at the sides, thus avoiding their impression on the right side of the garment.

For Thin Fabrics

Here work similarly, but with lighter pressure and a cool iron, and on no account use water, especially in the case of silk. Above all, stretching must be avoided. Silks, especially artificial ones, need great care in pressing, and the iron should first be tested on a spare piece, as heat frequently causes a change of colour. Instead of pressing, when the fabric and colour are delicate, hold the seam about 2 inches from an upturned iron with a wet cloth across it (turnings facing it), afterwards pressing the turnings gently with the fingers or with the folded blades of the scissors. Chiffon, net, and similar fabrics should be pressed between tissue paper. Pressing with a cool, light iron without water is sufficient for most cottons, but thick linens may need a slightly damp cloth.

Note.—Whenever a piece of shiny surface has been accidentally damped, take a spare piece and with the right side of it gently rub the damp spot on the right side, using a circular motion, until the fabric is dry and the gloss is restored.

Velvet, Other Pile Fabrics, Crêpes, etc.

Never press these flat. Instead, stand an iron on end and place a wet cloth over the face of it. Draw the seam turnings across this (holding their ends between scraps of the same fabric to prevent finger marks) and allow the steam to come through the

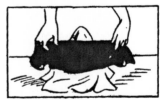

Fig. 116.—Steaming Velvet.

material (Fig. 116). For long seams, however, a better method is for a second person to hold one end while you hold the other with the left hand (turnings upwards) and apply the iron with the right (Fig. 117).

If no second person is available, one end of the seam may be pinned to a table.

TO REMOVE SHINE FROM WOOLLENS

Wring out a piece of wet cambric and place it over the shiny mark, then press very lightly and quickly with a hot iron. Pull off the cambric at once, thus raising the surface of the material. Now press on a padded board on the wrong side. If the spot is

Fig. 117.—Pressing Seams in Velvet.

obstinate, the surface may be brushed (the way of the nap, if there is one) and then pressed as before. Impressions of an iron may be removed in the same way.

LIGHT CREASES

Do not be in a hurry to apply the iron to these. Hanging up the garment in a warm or steamy atmosphere will often remove them much more satisfactorily.

DARTS

Cut the dart down the middle to within $\frac{3}{4}$ inch of the point, here snip across almost to the stitching. Now press over the stitching as described for a seam, then cut down the fold of the dart and press the turnings open over a roller. In thin materials, however, it is often inadvisable to open the dart, and it is better to press it back on to the garment unopened, but using the iron over the stitching only, so that the shape of the turnings is not impressed on the right side.

ARMHOLE SEAMS

Frock or Blouse

Lay the seam over the end of a tailor's cushion, and press the turnings on to the sleeve.

Coat

Place the seam over the cushion, lay a wet piece of cloth over the slight fullness on the top of the arm-hole, press the iron on it until the steam rises, then remove the wet cloth and replace with a dry one, and press until all fullness is shrunk away (Fig. 68, p. 118). A second application of the wet cloth is sometimes necessary. Then open the turnings and press them open, one going on to the sleeve and the other on to the coat. Of course, the lining of both coat and sleeve (if there is one) must be kept well out of the way while this is being done. When the sleeve-head is cut full and arranged in gathers or pleats, no shrinking is of course necessary, but the seam should be pressed with a damp cloth and the turnings pressed open as before. Sometimes, however, in the case of large box-pleats and much fullness, it is better to press the turnings of these on to the sleeve, and open the turnings of the under part of the armhole only.

PLEATS

Pleats should first be tacked closely along each fold, keeping them detached from the material below. Press each fold on its under side and withdraw the tacking as you do so in order that the cotton shall make no impression. When all pleats have been done like this, lay them in place, tack them, and press from the inside of the garment, but be sure to avoid the tacking-threads. It is best to press pleats on a skirt-board instead of on a table.

TUCKS

If the material is very springy or thick, press each tuck on the under side of its fold, away from the main material, then draw the back of the stitching of the tucks (wrong side of material) across the face of an upturned iron, barely touching it.

SMOCKING

Treat this in the same way as velvet.

SHRINKING CLOTH

Unless cloth is guaranteed shrunk when bought, it must be shrunk before it is cut out. If bought unshrunk, extra length will be required, generally 3 or 4 inches for each yard—but the salesman's advice should be taken on this matter. This is the method of shrinking.

Take a piece of washed, unbleached calico the full width of the cloth and half its length. Soak this in water and wring it out. Place the cloth on the bare table with its wrong side upward and open out to its full width. Place the calico on it and smooth out carefully, so that it is free from wrinkles. Snip the selvedges of the cloth every 2 or 3 inches. Fold up the remainder of the cloth over the calico, so that the former is double with the wet calico between. Now roll up the three layers very tightly, wrap up in a newspaper, and leave overnight. Then unroll the material gradually over an ironing-board and press on the wrong side until dry. Move the iron about with a gliding, ironing movement, and do not lift it as in pressing seams; at the same time avoid keeping it in one position, or its impression will show on the right side.

SHRINKING TAILOR'S CANVAS

This must never be used before being shrunk, otherwise it will pucker and shrink after the first shower of rain to which the garment in which it is used is exposed, and the appearance of lapels or fronts will be quite spoiled. Lay the canvas on an uncovered deal table and wet it thoroughly with a sponge or rag dipped in water, then rub all over with a piece of kitchen soap. Take a very hot iron—one of the flat variety will be best, as the process may damage the face of an electric one. Iron all over very quickly until the canvas is quite dry.

SHRINKING FULLNESS AT POINT OF DART

This may occur in a cloth coat or skirt. Take fine matching silk and run a circle through the back threads large enough to enclose the fullness. Be sure that the stitches do not show on the right side. Draw up the silk a little, then place the cloth right side downward on a tailor's cushion, cover with a wet piece of the same cloth, lay a hot iron over it, lift quickly, and allow the steam to escape. Repeat the process as often as is necessary, then press until dry, and rub on the right side with a dry piece of the same cloth. (If the cloth has a nap, rub down it, not against it.)

SHRINKING ON FITTING-LINES OF A COAT

When making a tailored coat there are various parts where shrinking will improve its fit. These will be marked on the pattern as a rule, for different styles all need different treatment. The usual positions are : Front of armhole near front inset of sleeve, downward in the middle of the back and under-arm pieces just above and below the waist-line, elbow fullness on the upper sleeve, and fullness on the sleeve-head of the same. Except for the last, it is best to shrink the two corresponding pieces at the same time, before they are separated, and then they will be shrunk the same amount. When the shrinking is to be done on the edges of the pieces, place them on the skirt-board (wrong sides upward and downward), push up the edges as if gathered, place a wet cloth over them, and press with a hot iron. Repeat this process two or three times, if necessary, then press on both sides (wrong side only of each piece) until dry. If preferred, you can gather finely on the fitting-line. When the shrinking occurs down the middle of a piece, fold downward, push up

as before on the edge of the fold, and work similarly.
Then lay the pieces straight and press on the wrong
side of both until dry. Shrinking a sleeve-head is
described on p. 183.

STRETCHING

Sometimes parts of a garment have been shrunk
accidentally or the seams have become puckered,
either by faulty stitching or by exposure to rain. It
is often possible to overcome these defects by stretching under the iron. Place the shrunk part right
side downward on an ironing-board (if corresponding parts have been shrunk they should be placed
with their right sides together), damp thoroughly
with a piece of the same fabric, then apply a hot
iron and press the shrunk part, at the same time
stretching it gently in the required direction. Do this
until the desired result is achieved. To stretch a
puckered seam, place it on a roller with turnings
upwards, damp them with a piece of the fabric, and
press a few inches at a time, stretching gently.

Various parts of a tailored coat should be stretched
—viz., front shoulder and a few inches on the neck
and armhole next to the shoulder, and also the top
of outer edge of under sleeve for 2 inches. Stretch
these double. Lay them on the ironing-board with
the turnings away from you. Hold the left end of
the edge with the left first finger and thumb and
stretch it while you are working along the edge with
the right hand. Turn over and stretch the other
piece. The stretching of the stand and fall edges of
a step-collar is described on pp. 150–1.

TIPS

1. All pressing to be done on wrong side, except in rare cases.

2. No water to be applied until it has been tested on the fabric.

3. Press all hems and edges before stitching.

4. Press seam turnings before neatening them.

5. Stretch while pressing all seams on which one side, if not both, is on the straight thread of the material.

6. Press all seams and edges with a piece of material (the same as the garment, if possible) between the iron and the hem.

7. Do not use water on silk or delicate fabrics, and test the iron on a spare piece before applying.

8. Heat and weight of iron should be in accordance with the nature of the material.

9. Press velvet and pile fabrics by drawing the wrong side across the face of an upturned hot iron which has been covered with a wet cloth.

CHAPTER XVI
SKIRTS

THE basic principles of skirt-making show little alteration however much the styles may alter. Thus seams must run straight from waist to hem; the straight warp threads must run down the centre-front and centre-back; if tight fitting round the hips, there should yet be sufficient ease to allow for sitting; the waist edge, even for a tight-fitting skirt, must be 2 or 3 inches wider than the band, this surplus being imperceptibly eased on to it, etc. While observing these rules, it is still possible to make minor adaptations to keep abreast of prevailing modes. Thus from time to time there is a vogue for skirts cut on the bias, etc. (see pp. 67–8).

PLAIN GORED SKIRT

Here is the method of making a plain gored skirt, similar to that shown in the layout in Fig. 38 on p. 68; though for the purposes of this chapter we will take it that it has been cut out in the usual way with the warp threads running downward. Remember that pressing must be done at all stages of the work. Seams must be pressed after stitching, and hems must be pressed before and after, and edges and folds before ornamental stitching. This will be taken for granted, and not referred to again in this chapter.

Test and adapt pattern (see pp. 38–9). Shrink material if necessary (see pp. 184–5). Cut out (see pp. 63–6) and tack up (see pp. 76–8). Take sufficient petersham to fit the waist plus $3\frac{1}{4}$ inches, thus allowing a wrap of $1\frac{1}{2}$ inch at the left end, 1 inch for a hem at the right end, and $\frac{3}{4}$ inch for one at the left end. Make these hems and sew on a temporary hook and bar. Tack up the lower edge on the fitting-line. Make first fitting as described on pp. 90–3. Remove skirt from band, being careful to mark fitting positions on both; fold down front and back, and transfer any alterations from the fitted to the unfitted side by pinning through on the new lines and then chalking over them on both sides. Re-tack seams, then stitch in one of the ways suggested in Chapter IX, press them (see pp. 179–80) and neaten in one of the ways described in Chapter IX. Make the placket as directed on pp. 134–5, then gather finely with double silk on the waist-line and mount the skirt.

Mounting a Skirt

The petersham band will be hemmed at both ends, with centre-front, centre-back, and other fitting positions marked to correspond with others on the skirt. There are two chief methods of mounting.

1. For normal waist-line. Place the skirt outside the band, pin corresponding positions together on the lower edge of the petersham. Regulate the gathering evenly, then tack very finely, remove pins, and cut down the turnings. Cover them with prussian binding and stitch on both edges. Sew two hooks just inside the right end and sew two bars (or make two loops) on the fitting-line of the left end.

If liked, another hook and bar (or loop) may be put a little behind the other. Mark the centre-front with a large cross in coloured silk and sew a flat hanger of prussian binding about 3 inches long inside the lower edge of the band in the middle of the back.

2. For raised waist-line. Pin and tack the waist edge of the skirt just inside the top of the band, according to the fitting positions marked on both skirt and band. Then stitch binding over the cut-down turnings on both edges, keeping the skirt itself quite free. Finish as described in the previous paragraph. (Fig. 82, p. 134 shows the finished effect.)

An alternative way of treating a raised waist-line is as follows. Turn down the skirt on the fitting-line, tack, press, and stitch it close to the edge. Tack into place on the outside of the band, pin and tack to it in accordance with position marks, and with the edge of the band a little below that of the skirt, then fell the band to the skirt very firmly. Finish as before.

The Lower Edge

This must be finished in one of the ways described on pp. 105–7, 109–11.

Second Fitting

This should be unnecessary if the first has been done with care. But if there is doubt, make it after the skirt has been tacked into position on the band and the lower edge has been finished, except the final felling or stitching.

SKIRT WITH CORSELET TOP

The corselet top, or belt, must first be cut out in tailor's canvas according to directions given with the pattern; usually it is cut with warp threads running downward to prevent stretching. A covered bone must be sewn to each seam (see pp. 210–11), then the inside of the belt must be lined with thin silk and the fastenings made with hooks and bars usually, at the left under-arm seam. The skirt should be made in the usual way and mounted on the belt in the alternative method for a raised waist-line described on p. 191.

SKIRTS WITH PLEATS

Pleats must be tacked only, for the first fitting. If bulky, the superfluous turnings may be cut away at the back near the stitching and the raw edges overcast. When the cloth is heavy, it may be necessary to support the top edges of any pleats which start some way down the skirt with a length of prussian binding attached to the waist-band. (Read pp. 157–62 in Chapter XIV, which describe the different kinds of pleats.) When pleats are made in the seam, starting somewhere below the knee, the top must be secured in some way. They may be stitched across once or twice from the right side, a tab or strapping may be applied, or Sprats' Heads may be worked in buttonhole twist (see Fig. 174, p. 354).

SKIRT WITH YOKE

The yoke may be round, pointed, or of fancy shape. It is usually made separately from the lower part, then the lower edge of the yoke is turned up and pressed, and tacked and stitched over the lower part, unless this is gathered; when, if preferred, it may be set on with a heading outside the yoke and sewn by hand through the gathers.

SKIRT WITH FLOUNCES

If these are gathered, they may be set on outside the skirt with a heading, or the extreme edge may be gathered and covered with a fold or other trimming. If preferred, the top part of the skirt may be cut off to meet the flounce, and the two parts tacked and stitched edge to edge, the turnings being (1) opened, pressed, and neatened singly, (2) pressed upwards and stitched close to the seam on the right side, (3) pressed downward and neatened double. The second and third methods apply particularly to a shaped flounce which is the same width on the top as the skirt edge.

SKIRT WITH GODETS

These may be set either into a seam or inserted into a slit or a shaped opening. In any case the method is the same (see Fig. 105 A and B, p. 165). They are a very effective means of widening the lower edge of a narrow skirt while retaining a tight-fitting upper part. They may be of the same material as the skirt or of a different one.

CIRCULAR OR UMBRELLA SKIRT

This may be cut in three ways : (1) Centre-front of skirt placed to straight warp fold, then widths joined on to the selvedges at each side to procure the

G (Dress)

requisite width. This brings the back seam on the bias. (2) When the material looks the same viewed both warp and weft ways, it may be opened out to its full width and the fold pressed out, then re-folded *across* the warp threads and the centre-front of the pattern placed to the fold. Small extensions will be probably needed on the selvedges. (3) Centre-front and centre-back both placed on the bias, with a seam at both places. The placket is generally made in the back seam as invisibly as possible, but if preferred it may be in the front seam by means of an ornamental zipp fastener (for making a placket like this see p. 133). How to fit a circular skirt is described on pp. 92–94. It is best to let a skirt of this kind hang a few days after it is mounted and before the lower edge is stitched. For a cloth skirt the best finish will be a false hem, either shaped or on the bias (see Fig. 62, pp. 110–11), but for a thin fabric a $\frac{1}{2}$-inch hem machined from the right side would be suitable, or the edge could be picoted.

SKIRT MOUNTED ON PETTICOAT BODICE

This is in fashion from time to time to wear with jumpers and tunics. The skirt is made in the usual way in its first stages, except that it is not fitted into the waist—indeed, it is generally cut off a few inches below the waist-line, and as the bodice usually fastens down the back, no skirt placket is required. The bodice can be made in sateen, cambric, silk, or net, and will have large armholes, a low neck, and a very loose fit round the waist. The bottom of the bodice should be placed edge to edge with the top edge of the skirt (right sides facing), and the two machined together. The turnings may be pressed upward on to the bodice, trimmed off a little, and then covered with a strip of bias binding, this being either felled on or machined along both edges.

To Remedy a Tiresome Fault

If you have a skirt with raised waist-line, which drops at the back, you can remedy this fault quickly by adding an inch-wide piece of petersham at the lower edge of the back of the band, and gradually sloping this off to nothing at the sides.

CHAPTER XVII

SHIRTS, BLOUSES, COATEES, BOLEROS, ETC.

THE orthodox shirt blouse must be cut and made with precision and a tailored finish. Let us take the regulation type, which is never really out of date, though its details may vary. The pattern will be cut with front, back, back yoke, sleeve, cuff, and collar, but there may be, in addition, a front pleat and a narrow neck-band. The material may be silk, flannel, linen, cotton, etc. In cutting out the usual rules (explained in Chapter VI) as regards grain will be followed; but the cuffs will be cut with the warp threads running round them, and these threads will run across the back yoke if the material is quite plain in weave (that is, if it looks the same viewed either down its length or across it) or else striped, and the same rule holds good if there is a neck-band. Cuffs will be cut double with a fold on the lower edge, and back yoke and neck-band will be cut double (to provide a lining), with no seam down the back. Turnings will be $\frac{1}{2}$ inch everywhere unless directed otherwise.

MAKING A SHIRT-BLOUSE

Note.—Pressing must be done at every stage of the work, after each seam has been stitched, before and after hems, and before ornamental stitching on folds and edges. This will be taken for granted, and will not be referred to again in this chapter.

FRONT FASTENINGS

First tackle the front fastenings, as they are easier to do now than later.   There are several methods, and here are two of the simplest.

First Method

Right front is cut with an extension of 1 inch or so beyond the fitting-line, and there is a separate strip about 2 inches wide to be added.   Place strip with its right side to wrong side of front edge (edges level), tack and stitch together.   Turn strip to right side and fold over so that the seam comes just under the edge on the wrong side.   Tack into place, then turn back the other edge of the strip and tack it to the front.   Stitch close to the edge on both sides of the strip, and again, if liked, as directed for the yoke.

Left front.   Stitch a hem $\frac{1}{4}$ inch *inside* the fitting-line, to provide double material on which to sew buttons.   Sew buttons on the fitting-line.   The number is generally three or four.   If there is no neck-band there will be one button close up to the neck, another about 2 inches above the waist-line, and two others equally spaced between them; but if there is a neck-band, one will come on this with the other three as before.

Buttonholes.   Mark position for buttonholes on the strip by measuring against the left side, then make them running downward in the middle of the strip, in the same way as described for dressmaker's buttonholes on p. 126, but with both ends barred.

Second Method

Right front is cut with an extension of 4 inches or so (this allowing for a pleat 1¾ inch wide), plus ¾ inch turning. Turn back ¼ inch on the edge and hem down on the wrong side ½ inch outside the fitting-line, then flatten the hem so that the middle of it comes exactly over the fitting-line and the hemmed edge on the under side is *outside* the fitting-line. Tack and stitch down each side.

Left front. Treat this as described in the former method.

Buttonholes. As in the former method.

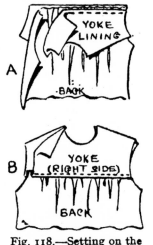

Fig. 118.—Setting on the Yoke to the Back.

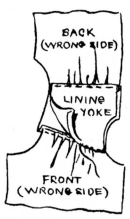

Fig. 119.—Applying Yoke Lining to the Front.

Setting on the Yoke

If the back has fullness on its upper edge, gather, pleat, or tuck this as directed. Place right side of this edge to right side of the bottom of the back yoke (raw edges level), regulate any gathers, and tack the two together on the fitting-line. Place the lower edge of yoke lining right side downward over the other turnings (edges level) and tack along the previous line of tacking, then machine through the three layers (Fig. 118A). Turn out with wrong sides of yoke and lining together and tack along the bottom just above the edge (Fig. 118B). If there is fullness on the front shoulders, arrange this to match that on the back, then tack these to the shoulder edges of the yoke as directed for the back. Stitch the two layers together, then press the turnings up on to the yoke, fold back the shoulder edges of its lining, and tack them over the yoke turnings (Fig. 119). Stitch along the back and shoulder edges of yoke close to the fold and also just under $\frac{1}{4}$ inch away from it if desired.

Collar

Gather the neck edge very finely to prevent its stretching. If there is no neck-band, make the collar and set it on as described on pp. 146-7, at the same time neatening the little extensions on both fronts by turning in the edges and machining along with the collar, which should be stitched like the other edges. If there is a neck-band, work thus. Place collar and lining with right sides together, stitch along bottom and ends, cut down turnings, turn right side out. Place the raw edges between the two upper edges of the neck-band (right sides together) and pin all together at centre-back. Machine from end to end and down front edges.

Place collar on the blouse as it will be when worn, with outside of blouse towards you. Lift up the lining neck-band and pin together the centre-back of neck-band and that of back neck, then from there pin to each end, arranging ends of collar to meet in the middle of front pleat. Tack finely, then turn to the inside of the neck, fold under the turning of the neck-band lining, and tack it over the other turnings. Then on the right side stitch once all round the edges of the neck-band. Sew the button on the left end and make the buttonhole (horizontal) on the right end.

Sleeves

There are two main types, which are set in quite differently.

1. Sleeve set into wide armhole (see Fig. 70). This is set in before the under-arm seam is stitched, then the ends of the armhole seam are put together and the under-arm and sleeve seams pinned from there. It is next tacked and stitched from one end to the other, either as a French or French felled seam. After this the sleeve is set into a cuff, which should be stitched to match the other edges, and button and buttonhole fastenings are made.

2. This is a one-piece sleeve with cuff, with slight or much fullness on the top, according to fashion, with the seam set about 2 inches in front of the under-arm seam. Make and set in as described on p. 120.

Finishing Off

Cut a lengthwise strip of material from 4 to 6 inches long and 1 inch wide. Turn down upper and

under edges about $\frac{1}{8}$ inch and turn back each end
$\frac{1}{4}$ inch. Take into place in the middle of the back
exactly on the waist-line and run a tape through
long enough to tie in the centre-front. Sew the tape
securely in the middle of the slot. Hem the lower
edge.

Fitting

If the pattern has been tested and careful measurements taken, no fitting should be necessary; if,
however, there is any doubt, there may be a fitting
when everything is finished but the setting-in of the
sleeves and the sewing-on of the collar, these being
merely tacked.

SHIRT WITH OPEN NECK

There is another style of shirt in which the fronts
are double-breasted and turn back to form revers,
the collar being of the tailored " step " type. The
back may be set into a yoke as in the previous shirt,
or there may be whole back and no fullness on the
front shoulders, while the sleeves may be of either
kind described on pp. 119–20. There will be a facing
for each front, and one (otherwise called a lining) for
the collar, which will be cut with the warp threads
running from end to end and no seam down the centre-
back. The under-collar must be stitched to the shirt
and the facing to the front facings. Set on the yoke,
if there is one; if not, then stitch up the shoulders
with lapped seams (see Fig. 50, p. 100). Take one
part of the collar, lay it on the outside of the shirt,
right side downward, and pin middle of collar edge
to middle of back edge, then from there pin to each

end of the collar, right on to the revers.   Now stitch.
Take the collar facing, find out from measuring by
the revers on the shirt exactly where the ends of the
collar come on them, and pin the collar facing to the
front facings in the same position, then tack and
stitch.   Turn back the side (not front) edge of each
facing $\frac{1}{4}$ inch on to the wrong side and stitch $\frac{1}{8}$ inch
from the turn.   Now place right side of front and
collar facing to right side of shirt and tack together
round the outside edges and along the bottom of the
fronts.   Stitch on the fitting-lines, cut down the
turnings and turn right side out (this process of setting
on collar and facings needs great care in fitting
together the two parts exactly, and turnings must be
snipped here and there to make them set well).   Tack
all round and stitch once near the edge, from the
bottom of one front right round to the bottom of the
other.   Turn up the lower edge of the collar facing
on the back neck and fell it over the turnings.

Front Fastenings

Sew buttons on left front in positions marked on
pattern, make buttonholes in the right front.
Bound ones as described on pp. 127–8 are usually
preferred, unless the material is thick enough to be
clumsy, when the worked ones should be used.

Sleeves

Sleeves may be of either of the types described on
pp. 119–20, and the general finish will be the same.

OTHER BLOUSES

The " fancy " blouse, as distinct from the plain
shirt, may be simple or.elaborate, according to the

mode of the moment. Its treatment, however, and general finish are much more dainty; thin, fragile materials call for light stitchery and as little handling as possible. A good deal of hand-work may be employed in the way of trimmings. A blouse, as a rule, is unlined, though in the case of elaborate styles a lining of net is often an advantage. In general style a blouse is often similar to the bodice of a frock, but it may be finished off at the waist edge in a variety of ways, of which the following are the most usual. (1) Carried 4 inches below the waist, hemmed, and the fullness kept in place with a tape run through a slot at the back (this is when the skirt is to be worn over the blouse). (2) Cut off at the waist-line and the fullness gathered into a plain band or shaped basque.

JUMPER-BLOUSES

There is now no sharp dividing-line between the jumper and the blouse, but a blouse which comes below the waist and is set into a rather loosely fitting hand often goes by the name of jumper-blouse as it combines some of the features of both.

JACKET-BLOUSES

Jacket-blouses are cut on plain lines and are semi- or close-fitting, ending below the waist with a basque cut round or pointed, after the style of a Victorian jacket-bodice. The rules given for fitting a bodice with few seams apply here (see pp. 87–90), though the fit should be a little looser. The front fastenings may be of buttons and buttonholes, buttons and loops, zipp fasteners, etc. The seams may be plain ones, with the turnings pressed open and neatened, or they may be lapped to give a more tailored effect. All edges must be neatly faced or hemmed. If a lining is desired, as in the case of taffeta or any non-washing silk, a lining of Jap silk may be made separately and felled in.

COATEES AND BOLEROS

These give endless scope for trimming if a plain fabric is used, while if a handsome brocade or lamé is employed, perfect plainness, except perhaps in the matter of the collar, is desirable. The seams are generally plain ones with the turnings pressed open, and a lining of thin silk is desirable. This should be made separately and felled in round the edges, the only seams which are stitched in with the outer material being those at the armholes. When required for extra warmth, an interlining of wadding or domette may be tacked to the lining before it is sewn in.

CHAPTER XVIII

FROCKS

THERE are mainly two types of frocks: (1) that in which the upper (or bodice) part is cut in one with the lower (or skirt) part; (2) that in which they are made independently and joined at the waist. These again have many subdivisions—(a) the "tub" frock, made simply in inexpensive cottons; (b) the plainly cut, fairly heavy woollen frock, with almost a tailored effect; (c) the "little" frock, for afternoon or semi-evening wear, usually carried out in soft material, with a certain amount of trimming; (d) the evening frock, which calls for dainty or fragile fabrics, or else handsome ones, although at times wool, and even cotton, has a vogue. But in all these varieties the main lines of making are the same, and here is the general outline of work.

Note.—All frocks must be pressed at every stage of the work. Seams should be pressed after stitching but before neatening; hems, folds, and edges both before and after stitching. The weight of the iron, the amount of pressure, and the degree of heat, must all be regulated by the nature of the fabric (see Chapter XV on Pressing). This will be taken for granted throughout this chapter, and will not be referred to again.

Outline of Work

Test and adapt pattern (see Chapter III). Shrink material if necessary (see pp. 184–85), then cut out (for rules see Chap. VI). Tack up all lengthwise seams and the shoulder seams—no others (see pp. 78–80). Tack up one sleeve only, the right if you are fitting another person or a dress-form, and the left if you are fitting yourself. Lower edge should be tacked up on the fitting-line; if there is a waist seam this may be pinned; trimmings may be tacked or partially made; collar and cuffs should be cut out in muslin or canvas. Unless the frock is loose enough to slip over the head, one seam must be left open—in a bodice, front, back, or under-arm seam; in a skirt either the centre-back or that nearest the centre-front. Now the frock is ready for the first fitting.

First Fitting

Put on the frock with the turnings outside. Only one side of the frock, and one sleeve, should be fitted—the right if you are fitting another person or the dress-form, the left if you are fitting yourself. Fit according to the principles given for frock, bodice with under-arm and shoulder seams only, skirts, and sleeves. These will be found in Chapter VIII, which should be read carefully before fitting is attempted. Make any alterations to seams with pins; mark positions for trimmings, collar and cuffs, etc., with pins or chalk. Mark positions for any front or back fastenings, or for placket. Verify the armhole and neck-curves, and inset points of sleeves. Correct skirt length, if necessary.

Remove the frock from the figure; if it is necessary to unpick any seams to do so, withdraw the pins from one side only and keep them in the other. (If the seam has been altered at all, and one turning is wider than the other, the new fitting-line should be chalked over the pins on both pieces before unpinning the seam). Now fold the frock down the middle of the front and back so that corresponding seams come together, and pin the corrections through both sides. Chalk over the pinned line on both sides with a fresh colour of chalk, to avoid confusion. Then re-tack all corrections with a fresh colour of cotton (see Figs. 43–4, pp. 95–6). Make pencil notes of any special points to be observed.

Stitch all seams, except armhole ones, and neaten them (see pp. 97–103). The seams will generally be plain ones for cloth or medium-weight woollens, and French or French felled seams for thin or fragile fabrics, or for cotton. Make any fastenings or side placket. (For fastenings see Chap. XI.) The usual placket for a frock is shown on p. 137, or, if preferred, a zipp fastener may be used (for sewing-in see pp. 132–3). Sew on collar and trimmings; finish the lower edge (except for the final felling or stitching) in one of the ways suggested on pp. 105–11. Make sleeves completely and tack them in.

Second Fitting

Little or no alteration should be required. Any necessary adjustment may be made to setting-in of sleeves, waist seam, lower edge, etc.

Final Touches

Stitch in sleeves (see Chapter X), and neaten the seams. Finish the hem. Give a final pressing if necessary. Sew a hanger in each armhole. See that all inside edges are neat and all ends of thread made fast.

When There is One Fitting Only

This should be sufficient when the pattern has been carefully adapted. Stitch up and neaten all seams except under-arm and shoulder, armhole, and waist (if there is one). Tack under-arm and shoulder seams on the right, or outside, of the frock, and pin any waist seam. Tack up the lower edge. Make the sleeves, except for the final neatening of the wrists. Do not tack in the sleeves. Make fastenings and placket. Pin or tack on collar and trimmings. Fit the frock according to the rules given in Chapter VIII. Pin on sleeve to the outside of the armhole and carefully mark any alterations in the armhole curve. Remove frock, unpick corrected under-arm and shoulder seams, and chalk or pin corrections.

Correct the other side as before described. Re-tack seams, stitch, and neaten them, stitch any waist seam, complete the hem; set in the sleeves. Complete the frock as before described.

TUB FROCKS

Simple styles which will wash and iron easily should be selected, and the material should be guaranteed unshrinkable and of fast colour, otherwise the labour of making is wasted. Pleats are best avoided, unless made on the straight, or stitched on the edge for most of their length. Bias seams should be taboo, and the lower edge of the skirt should be as much on the straight thread as possible. All raw edges should be covered inside, as they would fray in washing.

PLAIN WOOLLEN FROCK

Exquisite neatness, and precision in sewing are called for here. With firm materials edges may be lightly overcast. Hooks, bars, etc., must all be of appropriate size to their position on the frock.

THE "LITTLE" FROCK

When using light materials, stitchery should be as light as possible, though at the same time firm, and frock should be handled and fitted as little as possible. If very fragile, a light bodice lining of net may be used (see Chapter IV on Linings).

EVENING FROCKS

The rules laid down in the preceding paragraph are applicable here, and should be observed even more stringently. Rich or fragile materials demand very delicate handling. Hands should be kept cool, using rice powder or toilet vinegar, if necessary. Materials should be kept under tissue paper when not in actual use, and white cloths should be everywhere to avoid soiling. Sewing silks, trimmings, and accessories must all be carefully matched, and the neatenings always correspond with the quality of the material. For instance, sateen facings instead of silk; prussian binding instead of narrow silk ribbon; bars instead of buttonholed loops—all these in use on an evening frock of expensive fabric offend the person of good taste and betray the amateurish outlook.

Frequently there is an underslip of crêpe-de-chine or taffeta (see Chapter IV on Linings), and if not, the bodice may be supported with a lining of net.

BONED BODICES

The sleeveless, strapless, off-the-shoulder evening frock calls for trim fitting and boned seams. Best lute ribbon should be used and best whalebone. Mark the desired height of the bones on the seams. On the front they should be just high enough to support the bust, but not to touch it. On the back they should reach a rather higher level than on the front—an inch or so higher.

Boning a Seam

Mark with pins the space on the seam which the bone is to occupy and cut the whalebone this length, rounding off the corners. Take lute ribbon (for best work) or prussian binding, turn down 1 inch and seam up the sides. Then pin the top to the position marked for the top of the bone and begin to run the ribbon or binding to the seam, easing it a little, and much more when it reaches the waist-line; below that the easing may gradually stop. Cut off the binding $\frac{3}{4}$ inch below the position for the end of the bone, then run the other edge. Insert the whalebone and push up very tightly, turn up the lower end of the binding and sew securely. You will find a hole pierced in the bone about 1 inch below the top. Take some coloured silk and knot it. Pass the needle up through the under side of the bone, and at the same time pull up the end of the binding a little, so that it is not pressing against the bone, then pass the needle back over the top of the bone, through the binding. Add two more stitches at each side of this one, slanting outwards from the first one, and secure the silk at the back.

The whalebone may be bought in bundles in convenient lengths. It is possible to buy ready-covered bones of whalebone substitutes, and these may be sewn to the seams instead of following the other method described, but they are not used in the best work.

CHAPTER XIX
A SIMPLE TAILORED COAT

THE amateur may attempt the making of tailored coats, but if she is wise she will choose only loose- or semi-fitting styles and avoid tight-fitting ones—at any rate until she has had a fair amount of practice. The extra trouble involved in learning the correct tailor methods is well worth while, for even the most ordinary coat will look much better for their use.

PREPARATION

Let us take the making of a simple cloth coat, three-quarter or full length, loose and double-breasted, with two-piece sleeve with a plain head, and step-collar (the collar usually seen on a man's coat), the lining being of satin or crêpe-de-chine. Assemble all your materials and tools—cloth, lining, canvas interlining, stay-tape, buttons, buttonhole twist, machine silk, strong black cotton, tacking-cotton in two colours, cutting-out shears, button-hole scissors, needles and pins, wadding, spare pieces of cloth for pressing, heavy iron (or tailor's goose), tailor's cushion, ironing-board, sleeve-board or roller, kitchen soap, tailor's chalk in two or three colours, water, clean rags, etc. If the cloth is not guaranteed unshrinkable, it must be shrunk as described in Chapter XV, also the canvas and stay-tape. The lining *must not* be shrunk, and **water** must not be applied to it.

TESTING THE PATTERN

Test the pattern and make any necessary alterations in it.   If it has turnings, pin these together at
under-arm and shoulder, edges of front and back,
then put the pattern on the figure.   If there are no
turnings, it must be pinned to the frock.   Observe
the general hang first.   Does the coat hang well from
the shoulders?   If the front sags, lift it at the
shoulder; if it pokes out at the lower edge, drop it
from the shoulder, and similarly with the back.
Then what about the width?   If too wide round
the bust, take in the under-arm seam; or if too tight,
let it out there.   If too wide on the shoulder, make a
dart running downward in the middle as far as required.   This may be done on both back and front.
Test the collar and the position of buttonholes and
pockets.   Test the sleeve and make any necessary
adaptations as shown in Figs. 14, 15 and 16.

CUTTING OUT

The cloth will be at least 54 inches wide, so leave it
in its original fold.   Now plan out the pattern in
accordance with the principles given in Chapter VI.
The front edge of the coat must be placed to the
straight warp threads (generally near the selvedge),
and the middle of the back must be placed to the fold.
Upper and under sleeve must be arranged so that the
warp threads run straight from the top to the elbow.
The front facing must be cut with the warp threads
running down the straight edge (if short of material,
a join may be made across about half-way down, or
lower).   The middle of the collar must come to a

warp fold, and an upper and a lower piece are needed. Pocket pieces must match the front of the coat in grain. If the cloth has no nap, the pieces may be turned either up or down to make them fit in well; but if it has a nap, this must smooth downward on all parts. If no turnings are allowed on the pattern, allow the following, marking them with chalk : 2 inches on the lower edge of front and back; ¾ inch on under-arm and shoulder seams; 1½ inch on lower edge of sleeves; ½ inch on all other parts. Chalk all fitting-lines or mark them with tailor tacking (Fig. 23). Stretch front shoulders in double material—first on one wrong side and then on the other, as explained on p. 187. Also stretch 2 inches on the front of the armhole and the front neck at each side of the shoulder (see Chapter XV).

Fig. 120.—Canvasing Coat Front.

CANVASING THE FRONTS

Cut out the shrunk canvas by the front pattern, having its straight warp threads running down the front edges, and no turnings except 1 inch on the shoulder. The canvas should be 3 or 4 inches wide on the shoulder, and then curve off down the side of the lapel until it is 4 or 5 inches, after which it should remain this width to the lower edge. (In any case, the facing must always be ½ inch, at least, wider than the canvas.)   Pin each piece of canvas to the wrong side of a front, then fix with rows of diagonal tacking with the materials flat on the table as you work (Fig. 22).   Make snips in the shoulder and down the curved side.

PADDING THE LAPEL

Take a piece of shrunk stay-tape 2 inches longer than the " crease row "—that is, the line where the lapel turns back—place it over the crease row and run through tape, canvas, and cloth finely.   When the cloth is very fine, however, it is sufficient to make a line of fine running in double silk.   Now pad the lapel (see stitch in Fig. 92, p. 150).   Begin close to the crease row and work a row of the stitch beside it, then fill up the lapel with parallel rows, holding the work curved slightly over the fingers of the left hand meanwhile.   This causes the lapel to " roll " a little, and thus to avoid that " sticking-out " appearance which is so ugly, and the sign of unskilled work.   A margin of $\frac{1}{4}$ inch of canvas should be left unworked all round the outside edges of the lapel.   The stitches should be made with matching sewing-silk, and should not show through to the right side of the cloth. Place the lapel on the covered ironing-board with the cloth downward.   Damp the canvas, then rub it over with kitchen soap and press well.   Fold back by the crease row and press the fold well.   (When the cloth is very thick, a piece of stay-tape may be sewn all round the lapel and the front edge.)   Trim the canvas neatly all round.

FACING THE FRONTS

A pattern for the front facings is usually supplied, but if not, cut them by the front pattern, the same shape as the canvas interlining, but at least $\frac{1}{2}$ inch wider on the curved edge, and with the same turnings

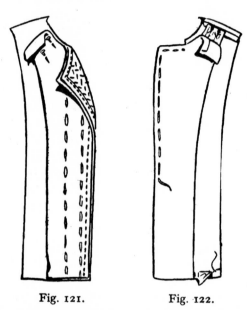

Fig. 121.   Fig. 122.

Fig. 121.—Front Facing Tacked and Stitched.
Fig. 122.—Front Facing Turned Right Side Out.

as the coat front on the other edges. They should, of course, match the fronts in grain. Place the facing right side downward on the right or outside of the front, pin together several times, then tack together all round the lapel and down the front edge (see Fig. 121). Now machine as close to the canvas

as possible on the top of the lapel and down the front.
Try the collar pattern against the lapel to find out
where to start.   A little adjustment is needed at the
crease row in order that when the lapel is turned back
the seam will be just under the edge both on the
front and on the lapel, and so quite invisible on the
right side.   Press the turnings open over the edge of
the sleeve-board or over a narrow roller, and trim
them off as closely as is safe.   Turn out the facing
and tack round the edges, leaving it easy over the
lapel so that it will lie back comfortably (Fig. 122).
Place the folded lapel downward on the covered
board and press well with a piece of cloth between the
iron and the coat.

POCKETS

If there are pockets make them now in one of the
ways described in Chapter XIII.   When the coat is
to be unlined, or half lined, the pockets will show on
the inside, so they must be made entirely of cloth
instead of being merely faced with it, as described.

BUTTONS AND BUTTONHOLES

Buy the buttons, sew on (as described on p. 123)
then mark the positions of buttonholes and either
work in buttonhole stitch or bind them as described
on pp. 123–28.   For large buttons from $\frac{1}{4}$ to $\frac{1}{2}$ inch
of the edge of the right front should show beyond
them when they are fastened.

SEAMS

Now stitch seams—either plain or lapped, for
preference (see Chapter on Seams).   Press them on

a padded roller, and if the coat is to be unlined, bind
the turnings with prussian binding or with bias
strips of satin or Italian cloth. Note that neither
the turnings of the facings nor the canvas are to
be included in the shoulder seams, but after these
have been pressed the turnings of facings and canvas
should be laid simply over the seam turnings.

COLLAR

The making of a " step-collar " (the kind used on
a man's coat) is described fully on pp. 148–51. After
it has been made and pressed, it may be set on to
the coat in accordance with the instructions on pp.
151–2, or, if not quite certain of the fit, it may be
merely tacked on for the second fitting.   If the coat
is to be lined, bring down the raw edge of the outside
of the collar over the neck turnings on the inside of
the coat and herringbone them into place; but if to
be unlined, turn in the raw edge and fell it over the
turnings.   Press well.

ORNAMENTAL STITCHING

If there is to be ornamental stitching round the
collar and front edges it should be done now.   There
may be one or two rows, according to current fashion.
Edges of pockets and cuffs of sleeves should match
the rest of stitching. Flaps or welts of pockets
should be stitched before being inserted, and cuffs of
sleeves should be stitched across about 3 inches
above the turned-up wrist after stitching the inner
seam, but before stitching the outer, as described on
p. 248 in Chapter XX.

BUILT-UP SHOULDERS

When built-up shoulders are in fashion this is the method to be employed :

Special pads for this purpose may be bought, and then they should be pinned in for the fitting before the lining is sewn in, but they cannot be adjusted finally until the sleeves have been sewn in and the armhole seams pressed open. The pads vary a little

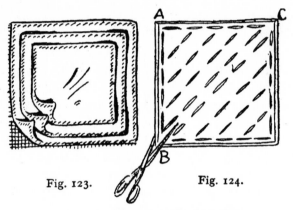

Fig. 123.

Fig. 124.

Fig. 123.—Preparing Shoulder Pads.
Fig. 124.—Cutting the Pad.

in shape, but can be adapted to requirements by thinning them down or spreading them out with the points of the opened scissors. If you prefer to make your own this is how to do so. Take a piece of canvas about 6½ inches square—rather more if the coat is a thick overcoat—and place on it a layer of wadding the same size. Cover this with two or three more layers, each one being ¾ inch smaller all round than the previous one. The object is to build up the middle of the square. More layers may be added if desired. Add a (thin) final layer the same size as the canvas and cover with a piece of muslin or thin cotton (see Fig. 123).

Now take a coarse needle and linen thread and make two rows of up-and-down stitches diagonally from one corner to another, with a space $\frac{3}{4}$ inch wide between the rows. You must push the needle up and down through all the layers and not draw the stitches tightly. Now add more rows of tacking as shown in Fig. 124 and finally make a row of tacking all round. When this has been done cut diagonally between the middle two rows to make two triangles. As thick wadding may be difficult to cut through you can obviate this by cutting each layer across after you have laid it in place, and then there will be only the foundation and the muslin layer to be cut. In fitting in the pad put the point A to the shoulder seam and let the edge B–C project slightly into the armhole. If the pad is too large you can make it smaller as suggested in the previous paragraph for a ready-made pad; while, on the other hand, if the pad is too thin, more layers of wadding may be laid on the inside of the shoulder and tacked lightly to the back of the cloth with stitches invisible on the right side. In some cases wadding may be needed to fill in a hollow in the front shoulder between the arm and the front neck.

Further Padding

Some figures fall in round the armholes, and in such a case a thin layer of wadding may be added

there. In Figs. 125A and 125B you see the usual
position for such padding, but the area may be
smaller, or may be extended, just as required. It
should be tacked first round the armhole, and then
gradually thinned away round the other edge, using

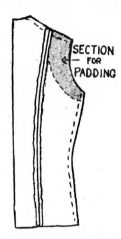

Fig. 125A.—Inside of Back
of Coat Showing Section
for Padding.

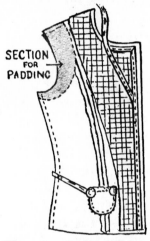

Fig. 125B.—Inside of Front of
Coat after Canvasing and
Inserting Pocket.

the points of the opened scissors to fray it out. The
wadding should then be caught with tacking stitches
to the back threads of the cloth, so that it may be
kept in place permanently. Note that this padding-
up of hollows may be done independently of any
fashion for built-up shoulders, and its use depends
solely upon the figure.

LINING THE COAT

Cut out the lining by the coat pattern, but with
these differences : leave enough to make a $\frac{3}{4}$-inch

pleat at the middle of the back neck and the same in the middle of each front shoulder, with a smaller one at the front armhole about half-way down the chest. At the front edge the lining should just overlap the facing with ½ inch to turn in, and no turning is needed on the lower edge. Stitch the back and fronts together at the under-arm edges and press the turnings open. Turn up the lower edge of the coat, tack it and press. If thick cloth, catch stitch it to the back threads of the coat material; or else soap the under side of the turned-up edge before pressing it upward. Turn in the edge of the front facing and slip stitch it to the turned-up edge.

Place the coat on the ironing-board or a table, with the wrong side upward, then lay the lining over it with the wrong side downward. First pin together down the middle of the back, then make the pleat in the back neck, turn in the neck edge, and pin all round. Replace all these pins by tacking, then turn back the fronts on to the back and run the turnings of the coat under-arm seams to those of the lining, leaving 3 inches free at the top and bottom. Now pin and tack the lining fronts in place, making pleats at the front of each armhole and in each front shoulder. Turn in the edge of each back shoulder and tack over the lining front shoulder. Turn up the lower edge. Now fell all these edges with matching silk, taking two stitches over one another at frequent intervals for strength.

Sometimes a coat is lined to the waist only. In such a case the seam turnings below the waist must be bound, and the raw turned-up edge must be bound with a bias strip of the lining, and then this edge must be slip stitched to the back threads of the cloth. Instead of the binding a piece of prussian binding may be machined to the turned-up edge (quite free of the outside material), and then this slip stitched as before. The lower edge of the lining should be hemmed by machine, and if desired a piece of cloth 2 inches deep, with its lower edge " pinked " may be placed under the turned-up hem of the lining and stitched with it.

SLEEVES

Tack up the sleeves as described on pp. 80–2. Stitch the seams, snip the turnings at intervals of 2 inches or so, and more closely at the elbow curve on the inner seam. Press open over a short roller or a sleeve-board. If the coat seams are lapped, then the outer sleeve seams must match, both the turnings being folded on to the upper sleeve. When there is slight fullness on the elbow of the upper sleeve, this must be gathered very finely, and after the seam is stitched the fullness must be shrunk away on the tailor's cushion. Gather the top of the upper sleeve *very finely* with matching silk on the fitting-line from seam to seam. Then draw up to fit the armhole and shrink out the fullness over a tailor's cushion (see Fig. 68, p. 118). Turn back each wrist over a bias strip of canvas 3 inches deep. Herringbone the cloth turnings to this, then use the same stitch to catch the other edge to the back threads of the cloth. Press over a roller or sleeve-board. If there are to be one or two rows of stitching about 3 inches above the wrist, the inner seam only should be stitched, the canvas tacked into place, the stitching done, and then the sleeve finished as before.

LINING A SLEEVE

If the coat is to be unlined, the sleeve seams must be bound like the coat seams and a 3 inch-deep facing of lining sewn inside the wrist, but if it is to be lined, the sleeve linings must now be set in. (Occasionally, however, the sleeves may be lined even if the rest of the coat is not.) Cut the sleeve lining to the shape and size of the cloth, except that on the wrist edge there should be no turning. Stitch up on the fitting-lines, then snip and press open the turnings. Keep both lining and cloth sleeves inside out. Place the lining under sleeve on the cloth under sleeve and tack the two together by the turnings of both seams, stopping short 2 inches from the top and bottom (see Fig. 67A, p. 117). Put the right hand inside the lining sleeve from the top, take hold of the wrist edges, and draw the sleeve lining right side out. Turn in the wrist edges of the lining and fell them over the cloth turnings (see Fig. 67B, p. 117).

SETTING-IN THE SLEEVE

Tack the sleeve into the armhole according to the inset marks—cloth only, as described on pp. 116–19, stitch in by machine with the sleeve uppermost—that is, next to the machine needle. Press the turnings open over a tailor's cushion. Make a roll of wadding as thick as your little finger and sew it to the turnings just inside the top of the sleeve. If the coat is lined, bring the armhole lining turnings over the turnings of the armhole seam and tack them into place. Then turn in the top edge of the sleeve lining all round, gather the edge of the upper sleeve, and fell these turnings over those of the coat lining. If there is no lining, the turnings must be bound after being pressed and the wadding must be covered with satin or sateen.

FINISHING OFF

Give a final pressing, then sew a flat hanger 2 inches long in the middle of the back neck. It is also advisable to take 1½ yard of inch-wide ribbon, double it, and sew the fold to the lining at the right under-arm seam at the arm-hole level. Then at the waist level on the edge of the left front make a buttonholed loop, through which one end of the ribbon will pass, to be tied to the other in a bow, thus keeping the left front from dropping.

FITTING

The experienced worker who is sure of her pattern, and also familiar with the figure of the future wearer of the coat, may find one fitting sufficient; otherwise two are advisable. When there is to be one fitting only, fronts should be canvased and faced, fastenings made, pockets set in, shoulder and under-arm seams tacked, sleeves tacked up, and collar cut out in canvas. Put the coat on the figure wrong side out, and fit one side of the figure only. Make any alterations at under-arm and shoulder seams. Note neck edge. If loose, it may be gathered and the fullness shrunk away, and any fullness round the armhole may be treated in the same way (see Chapter XV on Pressing and Shrinking). Remove the coat,

H   (Dress)

correct the unfitted side by the fitted one, and re-tack the corrections in a fresh colour of cotton. Replace the coat right side outwards. Pin on the canvas collar, then fit one sleeve, first on the wrong side and then on the right. Pin the top of the sleeve to the outside of the armhole, and be careful to make a good armhole curve with pins or chalk. Make a note of any special points which need care. After removing the coat from the figure, take out the sleeve, tack the inset marks on both coat and sleeve, and there may be more than two, if they will be helpful. Tack the armhole curve; also, if the top of the sleeve has been altered at all, chalk in the new fitting-line. Tack the neck-line for the sewing on of the collar and you may make corresponding marks on neck-line and collar to help the sewing on after the collar has been made. The coat may now be finished as has been described previously.

When there is a second fitting, this should take place at the following stage of the work : the coat and sleeves should (separately) be finished completely —collar sewn on, lining sewn in—but the sleeves should be merely tacked in (cloth only). If, however, the worker has any doubts about the accuracy of the fit, it is best to have the collar simply tacked on and the lining only tacked in.

PRESSING

It is impossible to overstress the necessity for the constant use of a heavy iron or tailor's goose at every stage of the work, and the Chapter on Pressing (Chapter XV) should be studied carefully.

CHAPTER XX

A TAILORED SUIT

THE reader who has made a loose-fitting coat according to the instructions given in the preceding chapter may now feel inclined to attempt the making of a suit, consisting of a short, tight-fitting coat, and a skirt with front and back panels and right and left side-pieces. A coat of this kind, while it

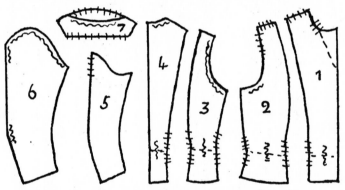

Fig. 126.—Where to Stretch and Shrink the Coat Pieces.

entails most of the processes of the former one, requires more precision in fitting and a somewhat higher standard of technique in making up. In a suit the coat is the first consideration, and when its style has been decided, the skirt must be designed to continue the lines of the coat. For instance, the coat we are considering is single-breasted, of hip

length, and has the usual step-collar.   The back has
no middle seam, but there are side-backs with a seam
running from the middle of each shoulder to the

Required for Medium
Size : 3 to 3¼ yards
cloth 54 inches wide ;
2 to 2¼ yards maro-
cain or other lining
38 inches wide for
coat.

Fig. 127.—A Tailored Suit.

lower edge, while the seams of the back-panel of the skirt continue the run of the last-named coat seams. The front has corresponding seams from the shoulders, while the front panel of the skirt carries on the lines of the coat seams. When a skirt has side seams these should continue the run of the under-arm seams of the coat. I do not say that these rules may never be disregarded, for from time to time fashion may ignore them; but they are sound foundation principles and make for harmony in design. There is, however, great variety in the cut of these short, single-breasted coats, and frequently they have a whole back, narrow under-arm pieces, and whole fronts darted at the waist, and perhaps also at the shoulders. Often, too, these coats are collarless. Back and front yokes are also seen, and there are many other deviations from the standard model.

To return to the coat we are specially considering : The sleeves are in the usual two pieces, with moderate fullness at the head, which is darted to produce the square-shouldered effect. There are hip pockets, and there could be a breast pocket in the left front if desired. The skirt has inverted pleats in side-front and side-back seams, starting from 8 to 10 inches above the lower edge. The suit pattern consists of eleven pieces (see Fig. 128) :

Coat. 1 front, 2 front facing, 3 side-front, 4 back (half), 5 side-back , 6 and 7 upper and under sleeves, 8 collar (half).

Skirt. 9 front panel (half), 10 back panel (half), 11 side piece.

Light-weight tweed, fine suiting, or hopsack would be a good choice for a beginner, as these are all easy to manipulate, have no nap, and are therefore reversible. Silk or crêpe-de-chine will be required for the coat lining.

PREPARATION

Look at the paragraph under the above heading on p. 212, where a list of essential tools for the making of a coat is given. Besides cloth, $\frac{3}{4}$ yard of tailor's canvas will be needed for the coat, $\frac{1}{4}$ yard of tailor's linen, 2 yards of stay-tape, $\frac{1}{2}$ yard of wadding, a pair of shoulder pads, four bone buttons for the front fastenings, and four smaller ones for the sleeves. For the skirt, petersham belting, bar-loops and hooks, press studs or zipp fastener, and prussian binding will be required.

TESTING THE PATTERN

Pin the parts of the coat pattern on your figure or dress form to see if the principal measurements are right—front and back lengths from neck to waist, width round bust, length of sleeve. If these are satisfactory, or almost so, you can go ahead and any needful alterations can be made in the fitting— due allowance for these being made on the turnings. If, however, the length between the armhole and the waist is wrong the pattern should be lengthened or shortened as required. (See diagrams on p. 35.) If the back or front is too wide or too narrow across the shoulders or chest, take in or let out at the seam running downward from the shoulder; while if too large or too small round the bust, the necessary alteration may be made at the under-arm seam as well. But it is really unlikely that anything more than very slight alteration will be needed if the pattern has been bought by the correct bust size. If the sleeve is not correct in width or length, adjust it as shown on p. 37, Fig. 14, and on p. 38, Figs. 15 and 16. Test the skirt according to the principles given on pp. 38 and 39.

PLANNING OUT THE PATTERN

Of course you have bought a well-cut pattern —any other is not worth buying—so it will be accompanied by a layout for cutting, and if your material corresponds in width to that in the layout, you may follow it exactly. If it does not, or you prefer to make your own layout, remember the following rules for a coat of this kind; as carried out in Fig. 128.

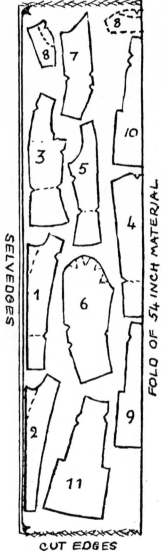

Fig. 128.—Layout of the Suit.

Lower part of front edge (from crease row of lapel to lower edge) should be parallel to the selvedges; back should be placed with its centre-back edge to the fold and its waist-line on the straight weft thread; waist-line of side-back should also be on the straight weft thread; the pattern of the side-front should be folded straight across the bust (on a level with the armhole) and this fold should be placed exactly on the weft thread; upper and under sleeves should be arranged with the top and bottom of the inner curve on the same warp thread. The collar should be cut twice—once for the under with the "break" on the warp thread (see Fig. 90, p. 148), and again for the upper with the back edge to a warp fold) (see Fig. 91, p. 148). When, however, the cloth is very firm and will not stretch, the upper may be cut like the under, or if it has no nap it may be cut exactly on the bias. The front facing should be placed with the grain matching that of the front.

In planning the skirt—and this should be done along with the coat—the centre-front and centre-back edges of the panels should be placed to a fold, and the front edge of the side-piece should be laid on a straight warp thread. *Note, however, that variations in the cut of a skirt may make differences in its layout, and the instructions given with the pattern should be followed.*

Turnings

After planning out the different parts with the turnings given below, each piece should be pinned to the double cloth according to the principles laid down for marking the turnings and cutting out on pp. 70–2. Turnings for the suit are as follows :

Coat :

Neck, armholes, and front edge, $\frac{1}{2}$ inch.

Centre-back, close up to fold, without turning.

Under-arm and shoulder seams, $1\frac{1}{2}$ inches.

Other downward seams, $\frac{3}{4}$ inch.

Lower edge of coat, $1\frac{3}{4}$ inches.

Front facing, as front, except for inner side, which should have $\frac{1}{2}$ inch.

Under collar, $\frac{3}{8}$ inch all round.

Upper collar, back to fold and $\frac{3}{8}$ inch on other edges.

Sleeve :

Sides, $\frac{3}{4}$ inch.

Top, $\frac{1}{2}$ inch.

Lower edge, $1\frac{1}{4}$ inches.

Skirt :

Centre-front and centre-back, close up to the fold, without turnings.

All seams, $\frac{3}{4}$ inch.

Waist edge, $\frac{1}{2}$ inch.

Lower edge, 2 to 3 inches, according to fashion.

CUTTING OUT THE COAT LINING

Before cutting out the lining any alterations which have been made in the pattern should be clearly marked. As the lining should always be larger than the cloth in both length and width, the following differences in cutting should be noted.

First of all the shape of the front facing should be marked on the front pattern, as the front lining will only extend as far as the facing. In this coat the remaining portion of the front would be so small that it is best to cut it in one with the side-front in the following way : Place the side-front up to the front with the waist-lines level and a space of 1 inch between the pieces at the shoulder and not less than ½ inch between at the bust-line. (Exact measurements for these spaces cannot be given, as the downward lines of these two pieces will vary in different patterns, but the essential thing is to allow a little ease at the bust and a pleat not less than ½ inch wide at the shoulder.) Turn back the front pattern by the line of the facing and cut the lining here with ¾-inch turning; allow the same on the under-arm, shoulder, and lower edge, and ½ inch on the armhole. Chalk closely round the edges of the pattern, and do not forget the facing lines of the front and side-front from the bust-line downward, as these will form a dart.

Place the centre-back edge of the back pattern up to a fold, then draw it ½ inch away from it at the neck, and slant this off to nothing at the lower edge of the pattern. On the side edge of the back allow for a pleat ½ inch wide at the shoulder, slanting off to nothing about 5 inches below; but outside this the usual ¾-inch turning must be allowed, also the same on shoulder, neck, and lower edge. Cut out the side-back with the corresponding pleat allowance on the shoulder, ½ inch on the armhole, and ¾ inch on the other edges.

Cut out the sleeve lining in the same way as the cloth, with ¾-inch turning on the sides and top but none on the wrist edge. (If there is a cuff opening no extra turning should be allowed here.

All fitting-lines should be marked carefully with chalk, or else the pattern may be kept pinned to the lining, and after the first fitting of the coat any alterations which have been made in the cloth may be transferred to the lining. In tacking up the lining, do so ⅛ inch *outside* the fitting-lines on the downward seams, as this will give the required " ease " in width. Leave the under-arm seams and the shoulders untacked. Tack up the lining sleeves as you tack up the cloth, but also ⅛ inch outside the fitting-lines.

In the lining fronts leave the fullness on the shoulder to be made into a pleat when sewing into the coat, but tack up the space between the front and the side-front from the bust-line to the lower edge in the form of a dart, taking the stitches ⅛ inch outside the lines so that the dart is made smaller and the lining left wider than the cloth.

THE SKIRT

The making of a skirt has been described in Chapter XVI, so no further instructions will be given here. Particular attention should be given to the paragraph headed Skirts with Pleats on p. 192.

STRETCHING AND SHRINKING THE COAT

Do not separate the cloth pieces of the coat, as, before going further, certain parts must be stretched and others shrunk in order to mould the cloth to the figure.

Stretching

Read the instructions for stretching a tailored coat on p. 187. But more stretching is required on a tight-fitting coat than on a loose-fitting one. On the coat we are now considering the parts to be stretched are : All downward seams for about 2 inches above and below the waist-line (and at each side of waist darts when these are used); on the front neck for 2 inches just beyond the crease row; the front shoulder; front of armhole for about 3 inches below the shoulder; at the top of the outer edge of the under sleeve for 2 inches. (The " stand " and " fall " of the collar must also be stretched, but not at this stage.) The positions for stretching are shown by short lines taken across the fitting-lines in Fig. 126, p. 227.

When the cloth is a firm one the edges to be stretched should be damped, first on one piece and then on the other without separating them, as the stretching should be done with the pieces double, to achieve an equal effect on both. Remember that it is only the *edges* which are to be stretched, and when the pieces are laid on the table afterward these edges should be slightly frilly.

Shrinking

For a tight-fitting coat such as this the parts to be shrunk are : Between the seams in back, side-back, front and side-front for 2 inches above and below waist-line; round back neck and back arm-hole, up front armhole on side-front for 2½ inches; at the elbow of upper sleeve for about 2½ inches, or between the marks given on the pattern; and at the top of the upper sleeve on the outer edge for 2 inches. The sleeve head should also be shrunk, but later. Read the instructions given for shrinking on p. 186. When pressing after shrinking be careful not to stretch what has just been shrunk, and, to avoid this, it is best to press on a tailor's cushion. Take notice that the pieces which have been treated should not be handled immediately, but should be put on one side until they are quite dry, and meanwhile some other part of the work should be proceeded with. The parts to be shrunk are indicated by wavy lines in the diagram on p. 227 (Fig. 126).

TACKING UP

Tack up the coat according to the principles given in Chapter VII, in readiness for the first fitting. If you are sure of the fit of the fronts you may canvas them before tacking up (as described on pp. 214-5); but, as figures vary very much in the shape of the shoulder, this is not advisable for a first attempt—later on you will become familiar with any personal peculiarity and make allowance for it in cutting out and tacking up.

In tacking up the coat, work, as usual, from the back. All the pieces will, of course, have had the fitting-lines marked out with chalk or tailor's tacking. Tack up the seams in the back, then those in the fronts, next the under-arm seams, and finally the shoulders. Be very careful to keep the waist-line continuous on all the parts, and to pin each seam before tacking, starting from the waist-line and working up and down from there. All tacking on downward seams must be done in the same direction, and shoulders must be tacked from the neck end. Be sure that the seams running from the shoulder match there. If there is any excess on the front shoulder, it should not be cut away until after the first fitting. (The appropriate parts of Chapter VII will be helpful here, especially from its beginning up to the end of the paragraph headed Balance Marks, and also the paragraph headed Tight-Fitting Bodice.)

Tack up the left sleeve only, according to instructions given on pp. 80–82; but as this will be fitted with wrong side out, it will be placed on the right arm. The first fitting is usually made with the coat and sleeve wrong side out and the right side of the figure only is fitted; but if there is any variation in the right and left sides of the figure, the garment should be right side out and both sides should be fitted. The under-arm seams and shoulders in this case would not be tacked, but pinned up closely on the right side.

THE FIRST FITTING

Place the coat on the figure if this is normal, and prepare to fit the right side only. Draw the front edges together and pin down the centre-front fitting-line—usually 1 or 1½ inches in from the front edge—from the crease row (where the lapel turns back) to the lower edge. First see that the coat fits

in well at the waist. This was considered when the
pattern was tested before the cloth was cut out, so
that there should be no difficulty now; but, in case
there should be, this is the way to set matters right.
Unpick the shoulder seam, then drop the coat if it
is short, or if it is too long lift it up at the shoulder.
Then smooth the back upward and pin to the frock
a few inches below the back neck. Now turn to
the front, smooth it upward and pin below the
shoulder. Re-pin the shoulder seam, unless the
width of back or front needs attention.

Here remember that, as the coat is only tacked,
the machined seams will be much tighter; also
that the fit should always be easy round the bust.
Another thing to bear in mind is that when the
lining is inserted the coat will be still tighter. So
do not fit too tightly. Try to make any needed
alterations in width at the under-arm seam, though
the seams running from the shoulder may be taken
in or let out a little if really necessary; but great
care should be taken not to spoil their line in any
way. Avoid a narrow-chested appearance, and
if the front shoulder is rather hollow do not take
in the seam over-much, but pad it up with graduated
layers of wadding.

Note the fit of the front neck just under the lapel.
If the lapel sags downward, a small vertical dart
should be made either in the lapel or just beyond
the crease row. If the fullness is only very slight,
a fine gathering thread should be run with silk on
the fitting-line and the fullness shrunk away.
Remember that the shoulders in this coat are to be

built up, so do not fit the seam too tightly at the armhole end. If you have pads ready, put one in place now (they can be bought cheaply from any working tailor, or from haberdashery counters, and save a good deal of time in making). If a pad is not available, use sheet wadding temporarily to get the right effect.

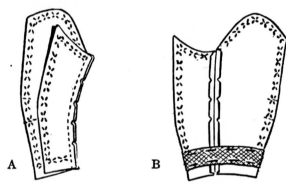

Fig. 129.

A—Inner Seam of Coat Sleeve Stitched.
B—Canvas Tacked to Wrist of Sleeve.

These remarks also apply to the back of the coat, as some figures fall in slightly at the back armhole and a little padding here is often a great improvement. In Fig. 125 A and B are indicated the parts where padding is often needed, and the area may be larger or smaller as required. In using wadding care should always be taken to thin off the outside edges with the opened blades of the scissors, and to make each layer rather smaller than the previous one so that there is no ridge visible on the right side.

The Collar

Cut out the canvas interlining as described in Chapter XIII for Tailored Step-Collar. Overlap the back edges for $\frac{1}{2}$ inch and join with herringbone or catch stitch. Pin the middle of the lower edge of the collar (known as the " stand ") to the middle of the outside of the back neck, seeing that it fits up snugly. From there pin round on the neck-line at each side till the " break " of the collar reaches the lapel. Make sure that the two edges meet exactly, as there should be no overlapping of the canvas. Now turn down the collar on the crease row, the end of which should meet the crease row of the lapel.

The Sleeve

Slip the sleeve over the arm. See that it hangs straight downward with the inner seam out of sight at the armhole and in a line with the thumb at the wrist, with no inclination to slant towards the top of the wrist. Pin the highest point of the sleeve to the top of the shoulder, then pin the top of the inner seam to the inset point on front armhole, and match the outer seam to the inset point at the back. It is seldom that these inset points have to be altered, but if there is any discrepancy it may be caused by the under sleeve being rather too wide at the top. If the fullness is small, make a pleat in the middle of the under sleeve so that it will come exactly under the arm when worn; otherwise the outer seam must be unpicked from the top towards the elbow and the excess taken off the under sleeve gradually to preserve an even line. Now pin the under sleeve to the armhole between the points of inset, and then adjust the sleeve head. The top of the upper sleeve should always be gathered finely with silk on the fitting-line, even if there are darts. This should then be drawn up to the width round the armhole. The gathering should be graduated so that most of the fullness comes on the top of the shoulder and with none at all for about 1½ inches above the seams.

Should the inner seam be correctly placed at the armhole and yet seem too far forward at the wrist, unpick it there for a few inches and re-pin to correct it by taking a little off the under sleeve and letting out the upper. See that the elbow fits snugly into the place provided for it, and if necessary adjust the slight fullness there on the upper sleeve. Note that the sleeve will appear shorter when stitched in, and will also shorten a little in wear.

Remove the coat and sleeve from the figure and immediately indicate in chalk of a special colour anything which needs alteration or particular care. Also make a note of such matters on paper. Transfer all alterations from the fitted half of the coat to the unfitted one, either with chalk or tailor's tacking, as described on pp. 95–96. Remove the collar and at the same time chalk its position on the coat; trim the collar edges if required. Make balance marks with chalk on the coat and collar to ensure correct setting on later. Do any further shrinking required.

THE FRONTS

Stitch up the seams and press the turnings open over a tailor's cushion. Make the hip pockets as directed for jetted pockets on pp. 143–44. Depth of pocket should be from 3½ to 4 inches, and width of opening as marked on pattern. If your material is either a loosely woven one or a thick tweed you may make the " jets " or bindings of fine cloth matching one of the colours in the tweed. Where there is a breast pocket make it in the same way on the left front only; but its depth should not be more than 3½ inches and the width should be less than that of the hip pockets. (Before putting in lining take a double strip of tailor's linen and attach to the pocket and side seam as shown in Fig. 125B, p. 221).

Canvasing the Fronts

Read the directions on pp. 214–15 for this process and follow with very slight differences. When the pattern for the front facing is given, as it is here on the layout, the canvas interlining may be cut to the exact shape of the pattern, except that it should be slightly smaller on the inside edge and the only turnings should be on the shoulder, where 1 inch should be left. This turning, however, should never be caught in with the shoulder seam, but should be laid over the pressed turnings after the seam has been stitched in the cloth. (Directions for shrinking canvas are given on p. 185.)

Padding the Lapels

Pad the lapels as described on p. 215. Note that

in ready-mades and dressmaker's work the padding is not always done so thoroughly when the material is a light one and not required for hard wear; or if there is to be machine stitching round the front edges, which will keep the canvas in place.

Facing the Fronts

Follow the instructions given on pp. 216–17. When this has been done trim off the lower edges of canvas and square the front corners carefully. Turn up the lower edge of cloth onto the canvas and also for 2 or 3 inches beyond it. Tack carefully, then press. Turn in the lower edge of the facing quite close to the turned-up edge of the front, tack and press; then fell very finely into place; also turn back the side edge of the facing at the bottom for an inch or so and fell to the cloth turn-up. Press well. Now, if desired, make a row of stitching round the lapel and down the front edge. On the right front start just below the lapel on the outside of the front, stitch from there down the front and along the botttom for the width of the facing, keeping close to the edge. This done, turn the front upside down, and on the right side *of the lapel* begin where you started the stitching before and stitch round the lapel to where the collar will meet it, and when cutting the threads leave a few inches for neatening later. Stitch to correspond on the left front, but here you must start at the end of the facing on the lower edge and work up to the bottom of the lapel; then turn to the *right side of the lapel* and, starting where the lapel will meet the collar, stitch round it to meet the front stitching. On both fronts the ends of silk must be threaded in a needle, the stitching made neat, and the ends hidden in the thickness of the cloth. (Note that after the collar has been sewn on, the stitching round the collar and lapel must be joined up in the same way.)

BUTTONS AND BUTTONHOLES

See that the centre-front fitting-line is marked on both fronts, and arrange that these lines come over one another when the fronts are fastened.

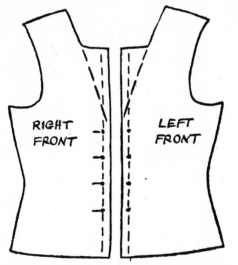

Fig. 130.—Marking for Buttons and Buttonholes.

There are four buttons, and one must always come on the waist-line, and the top one just below the bottom of the lapel; one should come half-way between the top button and that at the waist, and one below the latter—all evenly spaced. The same principle holds good whatever the number of buttons—one just below the lapel and one on the waist-line, and the rest spaced evenly above and below them. Mark the button sites with chalk and ruler on the left centre-front line (see Fig. 130, p. 245). Now on the right front mark the corresponding positions for the buttonholes. Place the fronts with wrong sides together and edges of lapels and fronts matching. Pin together, then pass a pin straight through every button site and bring out the point on the centre-front line of the right front. Mark with chalk the positions of the pin points, then separate the fronts. Rule with chalk a line for each buttonhole at right angles with the front edge. The length of each slit should be the diameter of the button, plus $\frac{1}{16}$ inch when the button is flat and up to $\frac{1}{4}$ inch when dome-shaped. The distance of the end of the buttonhole from the edge of the coat depends on the diameter of the button; from $\frac{1}{8}$ to $\frac{1}{2}$ inch of the coat edge should be visible beyond the buttons when they are fastened, so careful experiments should be made with the buttons before the buttonholes are cut.

Now make the buttonholes as described for tailor's buttonholes on pp. 123–5, and shown in Fig. 72, p. 124. If bound buttonholes are preferred read the instructions on pp. 126–8. Of course, the binding should be applied to the cloth and canvas only, and afterwards slits should be cut in the facing and the raw edges of these turned in and felled onto the binding.

Note.—*When the canvas is coarse or stiff it is difficult to make either worked or bound buttonholes through it. A small oblong piece of canvas should be cut away under the position for the slit, and this should be replaced by a larger piece of tailor's linen tacked under it.*

STITCHING THE SEAMS

Now stitch the seams—in this case they are plain ones. Other seams suitable for coats are described on pp. 99–101. Stitch the seams in this order: (Centre-back seam when there is one) back to side-backs; fronts to side-fronts; under-arms; shoulders; inner sleeves; outer sleeves. All downward seams must be stitched in the same direction, and if the material has a nap they must be stitched *down* the nap and not against it. Remember, in stitching the shoulders, to leave the canvas interlining and the facing of the front out of the seam. Press the seams as described on pp. 179–80. Then turn up the lower edge of the coat (if the cloth is thick cut a wedge-shaped piece out of each turning where it comes on the fold), tack close to the fold on the right side. Press on the wrong side, then catch stitch the raw edges to the back threads of the cloth, and be sure not to draw the stitches tightly.

THE SLEEVES

Make up these as described on pp. 223–4, with small deviations caused by the openings on the cuffs and the darts in the sleeve heads. Leave open the lower end of the outer seam for the depth of the extra turning allowed on the pattern for the opening.

Stitch the darts to the exact length marked on the pattern, to give the desired square effect. Cut them open to within ½ inch of the point and press them open over a tailor's cushion. Unless this is already done, gather the upper sleeve on the fitting-line all round very finely with silk, then draw up to the same size as the armhole. Press the gathered edge over a tailor's cushion and shrink away the fullness.

In this sleeve there is no stitching on the cuff as there is none on the outside edges of collar and fronts; if there were, the outer seam should not have been stitched, but should now be untacked from the wrist as far as the elbow—though some workers prefer to untack the whole outer seam.

Buttoned Cuffs

When the sleeves are to be buttoned at the cuff, cut the turnings wider at the bottom of the outer seam for about 3 inches above the wrist fitting-line (see Fig. 131, p. 249. These extensions are generally allowed on the pattern). The *extra* turning should be at least ½ inch wider than the button. (Buttons should match those on the coat, but should be smaller.) Tack a piece of tailor's canvas 3 inches deep on the wrong side of the cuff. The canvas should be on the bias, and should, of course, have been shrunk previously. The bottom edge should come just on the wrist-line and the strip should extend to the fitting-line on the upper sleeve, but should go to within ⅜ inch of the end of the turning on the under sleeve. (When the cloth is either

thick or loosely woven the end of the turning on
the under sleeve may be cut off and bound with a

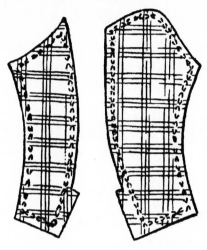

Fig. 131.—Sleeves with Extensions for Wrist Opening.

bias strip of lining.) Turn up the lower edge of
the sleeve and catch stitch the raw edges to the
canvas (Fig. 132). Turn back the turning on the

Fig. 132.—Canvasing Wrist
of Sleeve.

Fig. 133.—Inside of
Wrist of Sleeve.

upper sleeve edge of the opening by the fitting-line and mitre it at the corner; tack and press, then catch stitch the edges to the canvas (Fig. 133). Make two buttonholes on this side of the opening—they should match those on the front, either worked or bound. Mark the position of the buttons on the under sleeve. The bottom one should come about 1 inch above the lower edge, and the next one 1 inch above it. Press the buttonholes, neaten the under side of the opening, either by turning in the raw edge and felling the lining over it later or binding the raw edge with a strip of lining (Fig. 134). If there is stitching round the fronts and collar, a line (or lines) of stitching to match must now be made across the cuff, ruling a chalk line 3 inches above the wrist as a guide. Now stitch up the outer seam and press open the turnings over a padded roller. At the top of the opening make a very small button-holed bar across the seam (see Fig. 76, p. 129). Sew on the buttons before the lining has been inserted.

Fig. 134.—Opening of Sleeve Cuff.

Note.—There is no hard and fast rule about the number of buttons on the cuff, or their distance apart. Their number may be two, three, or four, and they may be closer together with no space between them, and the lowest button may be close to the edge of the cuff. Also there may be no real opening, but one may be simulated by leaving ¼ inch extra turning for 3 inches above the turn-up

of the wrist, and then stitching the turnings together
½ inch outside the fitting-lines. The seam should be
pressed with a fold continuing the run of the seam,

and the required number
of buttons should be
sewn through the sleeve
and turnings close up to
the fold.

MAKING THE COLLAR

Make the collar as
described for a Tailored
Step-Collar on pp. 148–
51. Then, if you are sure
that it fits, set it on as
described on pp. 151–2

Fig. 135.—Collar Sewn on but
Upper Collar Unfinished.

(Figs. 135 and 136). If not, tack it in place and
leave the final sewing until after the second fitting.

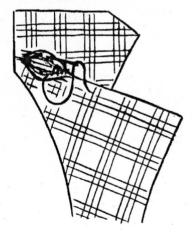

Fig. 136.—Slip-Stitching Collar to Lapel.

BUILDING UP THE SHOULDERS

Now build up the shoulders with wadding to the required height, after padding round the back and front armholes if needed.   It is a saving of time to use the special shoulder pads for square shoulders. These should only be tacked in at the moment, until after the sleeves are sewn in.   (See pp. 219–21).

LINING THE COAT AND SLEEVES

The coat and sleeves should be lined and the collar sewn on before the sleeves are stitched in, and before the final fitting.   Transfer to the lining any alterations which were made in the cloth at the first fitting.

Coat Lining

Stitch the side-backs to the back, and the side-fronts to the fronts—except, as in this particular coat, where these two are cut in one—$\frac{3}{8}$ inch outside the fitting-lines to give the necessary ease.   Do not tack the under-arms or shoulders.   Snip the turnings at intervals and press them open over a padded roller.   Place the coat wrong side uppermost on a table, with the neck to the right hand. Make a pleat $\frac{1}{2}$ inch wide in the back lining at the neck, then pin to the neck of the coat.   Tack the lining to the cloth down the middle of the back, starting 2 inches below the neck, and easing it in length at the waist.   Lift the lining and tack the turnings of the side-back lining seam which is the farther from you, to those of the cloth, making a pleat at the top and easing the lining at the waist as before. Now do the same with the other side-back seam. Leave the lining easy in width and tack it to the cloth about 2 inches from the under-arm seam. Tack the lining to the cloth about 2 inches below the neck and shoulders, and round the back armholes about ½ inch inside the fitting-line.

Lay the front lining over the cloth front—wrong sides together—turn in the front edge of the lining for ½ inch, and tack it over the edge of the facing, easing it slightly all the way down. Make the pleat at the shoulder over the cloth seam, and tack lightly to the seam all the way down from the right side of the lining, leaving it easy both in width and length. (If the front and side-front are cut separately in the lining, tack the turnings of the lining seam to those of the cloth in the same way as in the back.) Tack to the cloth down the under-arm and round front armhole as at the back.

Sleeve Linings

Stitch up both seams. Should there be a cuff fastening, leave the outer seam open at the bottom to allow for it. Snip the turnings and press them open. Turn down the top edge of the upper lining sleeve for ½ inch and gather finely between the seams, but do not fasten off the thread. (Look at Fig. 137A, B, and c as you read the next few lines.) Turn both cloth sleeve (A) and lining (B) wrong side out. Place the cloth sleeve on the table with the under sleeve uppermost and lay the lining over it with the under sleeve facing it (c). Tack the turnings of the inner seam of both together, then do the same with the outer seam, beginning 2 inches from the top and ending the same distance from the wrist,

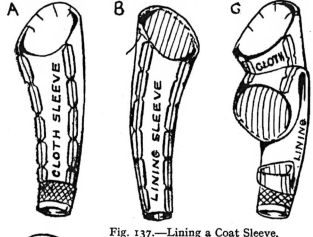

Fig. 137.—Lining a Coat Sleeve.

Fig. 138.—Felling in the Lining at the Wrist.

unless there is a cuff opening, when you should stop 1 inch above it. Put the right hand inside the lining sleeve and grasp the edge of the wrist, then draw the lining over and right side out. Turn in the lining at the wrist and fell to the cloth turnings. (If there is a cuff opening fell the lining to the buttonhole side just beyond the buttonholes, and on the other side fell the lining close up to the edge. See Fig. 138.) Turn the sleeve right side out.

SEWING ON THE BUTTONS

Sew on the buttons with buttonhole silk if the buttons are pierced, otherwise button thread will serve. Take twice the length of silk you think you will need and use it double. Make two small back stitches on the button site on the right side of the cloth; then, if the button has two holes, pass the needle up through one and bring out the needle on the upper side. Place a bodkin over the button and take a stitch over it and down through the other hole to the inside of the coat. Pass the needle back to the outside and make three more stitches, but pass it through the button only in the last stitch and bring it out between the button and the cloth. Withdraw the bodkin and twist the silk three or four times round the stitches to make a strong " neck ". (See Fig. 71, p. 123.) Finish off with one or two back stitches at the back of the button. When there are four holes, the stitches may consist either of two sets of parallel stitches or of a cross.

A shank button is sewn on with button thread used double, and four or five stitches must be taken through the shank quite tightly, then the thread should be finished off as before. When the material is not very strong a small flat bone or pearl button should be placed beneath the button site and the stitches taken through this.

TACKING IN THE SLEEVE

Turn the sleeve right side out; slip it through its corresponding armhole, then pin from the inside (cloth only) first to the front inset and then to the back. Now turn the coat round, and (still with inside of sleeve towards you) pin round the inside of the sleeve to the under part of the armhole between the insets, keeping the lining of both coat and sleeve free. Pin in the upper sleeve, inserting the pins vertically, and regulating any fullness. Take matching silk and tack in the sleeve very finely, still keeping the lining free. If the shoulders are not built up a roll of wadding should be prepared.

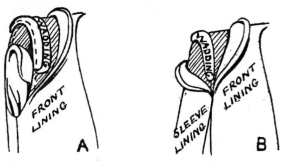

Fig. 139.—Inserting Wadding Roll in Sleeve Head.

(Fig. 139 A and B). Take a piece of wadding about 8 inches long and 3 inches wide. Fold it down its length with one raw edge beyond the other. Pin it outside the sleeve head from about 4½ inches below the shoulder seam at the front to 3½ inches below at the back. If the shoulders are built up with a ready-made pad, this should project into the armhole a little, and the roll will be unnecessary. Tack in both sleeves.

THE FINAL FITTING

Now put on the coat and make any final adjustments. If the collar has not been sewn on it will be tacked into place. If more padding is needed it may be added, or if too thick it may be thinned off; but it is unlikely that any serious alteration will be needed if the previous work has been done carefully. Turn in the edge of the side-back lining at the under-arm seam over that of the side-front and fell into place, with the usual ease at the waist-line. It is best to leave the neck and shoulders free until the sleeves have been stitched in. Turn up the lining at the lower edge of the coat and fell it over the turned-up cloth.

STITCHING IN THE SLEEVES

Take out any pad or roll which may have been pinned in. Make any needed corrections in the armhole seam, then stitch in (cloth only) by machine from the inside of the sleeve. Press the turnings open over a tailor's cushion as described on p. 183 and illustrated in Fig. 68, p. 118. Set in the roll of wadding or the pad. (See Fig. 139 A and B.) Now fell the lining over the collar, turn in the back shoulders and fell them over the front ones. Draw the sleeve lining over the lining turning at the armhole seam and fell to it all round. Give a final pressing to the coat, then sew a hanger of double lining or of galloon 2 inches long to the middle of the back neck, on a level with the lining.

I (Dress)

CHAPTER XXI

LINGERIE

THOUGH the making of lingerie is not, technically speaking, dressmaking, the well-dressed woman will naturally see that her invisible garments are as dainty and shapely as her visible ones. However smart and becoming in themselves her frocks may be, their effect can be spoiled completely by being worn over badly-fitting lingerie. Paper patterns for underwear are modelled with as much care as those for upper garments, and should be selected quite as thoughtfully. Also, just as much care should be taken in their fitting and making, although the actual workmanship is simpler than in dressmaking, and a smaller equipment is needed.

MATERIALS

These should be light in weight and dainty in weave, though at the same time strong in texture and dye, in order to withstand the rigours of the laundry—unless, as so many women do, you wash your own lingerie; and even then some strain is unavoidable. So, when buying your materials, test them by pulling gently in both directions, and be sure that they are guaranteed fadeless, and also, in the case of woollens, unshrinkable. For " best " wear at its most luxurious there are georgette and ninon; when something less ephemeral is desired,

silk, crêpe-de-chine, satin and rayon are available.
(A good satin wears remarkably well, and is not
really extravagant when its cost is balanced against
its good qualities. Many a bridal gown of shimmer-
ing ivory satin has ended its career twenty years
later as " nighties " and " knicks " !) For everyday
wear lawns and cottons, either white or coloured,
plain or patterned, are suitable, and may be most
attractive. Broadly speaking, at the present time
coloured fabrics are more favoured than white ones,
though there are still many fastidious women who
are faithful to fine white linen lawn trimmed with
a little satin stitch embroidery or *broderie anglaise*,
and perhaps a few real lace medallions. Others with
similar tastes, though lighter purse, may use fine
nainsook for everyday at least, with good crêpe-de-
chine for slips and knickers. (Passée frocks of
satin and crêpe-de-chine, either plain or patterned,
can always be cut down into these garments.)

STITCHES

All stitching should be firm, in order to resist the
strain of wear and washing; yet at the same time
it should be as light as is consistent with strength,
for clumsy stitching and coarse thread will prevent
the effect of daintiness which is so desirable. Therefore strong but fine thread should be used in sewing,
and both it and the size of the needles should be in
keeping with the nature of the fabric. For all
materials other than cottons fine sewing silk is
unsurpassed, as it is more elastic than cotton, and
therefore will not break so easily under strain. For

white lawn or nainsook the thread may be no. 100, the needle no. 10 or 12, and the machine needle no. 11 or 12; for the same materials coloured mercerised matching cotton should be used, no. 40 or 50, with the same needles as before. For finer materials threads and needles should be proportionately finer, and, of course, sewing cotton or silk should always match in colour.

Some people consider hand sewing essential to the best class of work; but really, if the machining is done well and with a small stitch, there is no reason why the seams, at least, should not be done by machine, thus saving time and labour. Open seams, even with neatened turnings, are taboo; for, besides being untidy, they will not stand the strain of repeated washing. The seams most in use for thin fabrics are the French seam and the French fell, and in both of these the raw edges are enclosed. Run-and-fell seams are used only for the firmer materials, for which either of the previously mentioned seams would be too bulky.

FRENCH SEAM

How to make this is shown in Fig. 53, p. 103, and its making is described on p. 102. Each line of stitching should be pressed, and stretched slightly during the process (to counteract the tightening caused by the stitching) under a warm iron, before doing the next one. Remember in hand stitching to make every ninth or tenth stitch a back stitch for firmness.

FRENCH FELLED SEAM

This is even quicker to make than the previous seam, as it has only one row of stitching. It is illustrated in Fig. 54, p. 103, and described on the same page.

RUN-AND-FELL SEAM

Tack the two edges together on the fitting-lines on the wrong side, then stitch on the fitting-lines by machine from the side which will be on the top when the seam is finished, or from the under side if hand running is used. Cut off the under turning to $\frac{1}{8}$ inch, or more if the material is a fraying one; then turn down the upper turning over the lower one as narrowly as possible, folding in the raw edge, and tack close to the fold. Stitch by machine close to the fold, or fell by hand. (See Fig. 27, p. 58.) Note that in side and shoulder seams the front of the garment should be felled onto the back.

BEADED SEAM

This looks very charming for thin fabrics, using silk beading for silk, or " near " silk, and cotton for cotton or linen. Beading generally has a strip of plain material with raw edge at each side. Lay the beading right side downward on the right side of the material with the corded edge close up to the fitting-line, then run the two together close up to the corded edge. (See Fig. 140, p. 262.) Cut off the turning of the material a few threads beyond the sewing, and cut off the turning of the beading a little wider. Now roll the beading turning over the material edge towards you, and while doing so apply whipping stitch, working this over and over towards you and pushing off the little rolls from the eye of the needle so that this is never taken really out until the seam is finished. (See Fig 151, p. 285.) If the beading has no turning, tack it up

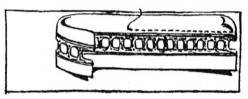

Fig. 140.—Applying Beading for Seam.

to the fitting-line as before described, then cut off the material turning and roll this over the beading edge with whipping stitch. Treat the other side of the seam in the same way, then press lightly with a warm iron. Lace beading, which has corded edges, may be applied similarly.

HEMSTITCHED SEAM
(by machine)

This can be done at any sewing-machine shop very cheaply, and is most satisfactory for very thin fabrics. Prepare the seams by laying one edge over the other and tacking through the fitting-lines, and the work will be returned to you with the hemstitching exactly over the tacking. (See Fig. 141A, p. 263.) Cut away the turning close up to the stitching on both sides, then press on the wrong side, stretching slightly at the same time. (Fig. 141B.) Be sure to tack with matching thread (silk or cotton, as the case may be), as the tacking-thread will be caught in with the machining, and cannot be removed. (It is usual to have any hems stitched to match, and how to prepare these will be described later.)

RULES FOR HEMS

The depth of hems varies with their positions. On the bottom of a petticoat-slip or nightdress,

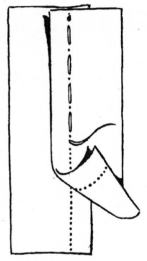

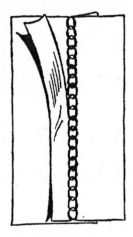

Fig. 141A.—Preparing Hemstitched Seam.

Fig. 141B.—Finishing Hemstitched Seam.

for instance, from ¼ to 2 inches is correct, and other edges in proportion—according to fashion and the kind of material. As a rule the lower edge of these two garments is on the straight, or only very slightly curved, so that the tacking of the hem is an easy matter. In any case, the bottom of the hem should be turned first from the right side—one gets a better line that way—and tacked finely, close to the edge. Then on the wrong side the depth of the hem should be measured on the turning either with ruler, tape, or a notched card, and the turned-in edge tacked into place. If the edge is on a slight curve the resultant fullness on the upper edge should either be gathered finely or laid in small pleats to fit. The hem should be pressed lightly before being felled by hand with small stitches, taking up merely a thread of the outer material, with a double stitch at intervals on the turned-in edge for safety. If the hem is machined, it should be done from the right side as near the turned-in edge as possible, so that careful tacking is needed as a guide.

When a plain hem is used on transparent fabric, the turned-in part should be the full depth of the hem, so that it is three-fold.

A deep hem on a garment cut on the bias is not possible, and the lower edge may be finished with one not more than $\frac{1}{4}$ inch wide, or with one of the hems described later.

IMITATION HEMSTITCHED HEM
(by hand)

This may be worked on ninon or any soft, fine fabric without drawing threads. Tack a hem from $\frac{1}{8}$ to $\frac{1}{4}$ inch wide. Take rather thick thread and a coarse, blunt needle. Join on at the left end of the hem, then put the needle under the fold and bring out $\frac{1}{16}$ inch above. * Insert the needle in the single fabric close up to the fold and slightly to the right, so that the stitch produced is slanting; bring out the needle about $\frac{1}{12}$ inch to the left in the single fabric (making a perfectly straight stitch on the right side of the material), then pass the needle under the fold again and bring out $\frac{1}{12}$ inch from where the first stitch came out, and on the same level. Repeat from *. Pull the thread rather tightly

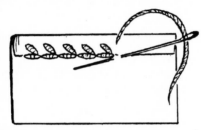

Fig. 142.—Imitation Hemstitched Hem.

so that rather large holes are made in the single material. (See Fig. 142.) Press on the wrong side.

HEMSTITCHED HEM
(by machine)

Tack the hem carefully, as for an ordinary plain hem, with the tacking as near the turned-in edge as possible, and using thread of the same colour as material, for the reason given in the instructions for a hemstitched seam. The finished stitch is the same as for the seam. When the fabric is transparent it is best not to turn in the raw edge of the hem, but to tack an even line $\frac{3}{8}$ inch below the raw edge. The hemstitching will come exactly over this tacking, and the raw turning must be cut away above it. Press on the wrong side and stretch slightly.

ROLLED HEM

This is only suitable for very thin materials, but it has a very decorative effect. The whipping stitch is shown in Fig. 30, p. 58, and the making of the hem is described on p. 108. It should be worked on the wrong side with rather coarser thread than is used for the rest of the sewing.

CROSS STITCHED HEM

This also is for thin fabrics, and a fairly thick thread should be employed. (It is illustrated in Fig. 143.) Tack the narrowest hem possible, join on the silk or other thread (which should be rather

Fig. 143.—Cross Stitched Hem.

coarse) at the right end, on the wrong side of the material. Then work over and over the hem with coarse but evenly-spaced stitches, bringing out the needle close up to the turned-in edge. When you get to the left end work back from left to right over the first set of stitches, crossing each perfectly. Do not pull the stitches tightly.

SCALLOPED HEM

This is only suitable for crêpe-de-chine and other thin materials. It is shown in Fig. 61, p. 109, and is described on the same page.

OTHER EDGE FINISHINGS

There are other edge finishings which cannot exactly be called hems, as they are more in the nature of trimmings.

BOUND EDGES

Either self material or one of contrasting colour or pattern may be used, but the strips must be exactly on the bias, and should be cut according to the directions given on pp. 68–9 (see Fig. 39, p. 69), and then sewn on in the way described on pp. 171–2. (If preferred, bias binding sold by the yard may be used.) When the material is very thin, the strips should be double—the double raw edges first being run onto the right side, and the fold being felled or slip hemmed to the garment on the wrong side just over the line of running, so that the stitches do not show on the right side.

Note that when the material is a stretchy one the joined-up strips should be stretched over the table edge before being sewn on, and especially if the edge being bound is on the inside of a curve, as on a round neck edge.

SCALLOPED EDGES

These are most attractive, and may be made in two ways: (a) bound with bias strips or (b) faced on the inside. For (a) see Fig. 106, p. 167, and the instructions on the same page; and for (b) see Fig. 107, p. 167, and the instructions on pp. 167–8. Note that when using (b) for lingerie the facing should be felled neatly instead of being slip hemmed, as the latter method is not firm enough to stand washing.

If liked, a fancy stitch such as chain stitch may be worked on the right side over the felled stitches.

BUTTONHOLED SCALLOPS

These are quite suitable for a thin material if it is firm and does not fray easily, otherwise the result does not repay the time spent on the work, and the scallops pull out of shape in washing. A very thin fabric, even though firm, may be faced on the wrong side with material cut to the shape of the edge and about 1 inch deeper than the scallops. The outer

Fig. 144.—Buttonholed Scalloping.

edges should be tacked level, leaving as much as possible outside the scallops to give a good " hold " for working, and the other edge of the facing should be turned in and felled neatly. A transfer may be used to mark the scallops, or their shape may be cut in brown paper round a coin—four or five in a row—and then the scallops may be drawn on the material round this pattern. When going round a curve, either outer or inner, some adjustment of the paper will be needed, either cutting or pleating it above or below the scallops so that their shape is not altered.

First run finely along the outlines of the scallops, then fill in the spaces between with running stitches. When working with silk, the padding may be done with matching cotton for economy. This running, besides rounding out the covering stitches, prevents the material splitting between the scallops. Now work over the padding with loop stitch (usually, though not correctly, known as buttonhole stitch), as shown in Fig. 144, p. 268, taking the stitches from left to right. Press the scallops on the wrong side over a padded surface, then with a sharp-pointed pair of scissors cut away the material outside the scallops from the back, being most careful not to cut the stitches.

FACED EDGES

When the edges are on the curve, hems are difficult, and facings are often substituted. If a different colour is used, they can be most decorative, as the second colour may be allowed to peep just $\frac{1}{12}$ inch or $\frac{1}{8}$ inch beyond the edge of the garment. Cut out the facing strips in the way described for bound edges, but when the edges are irregular it is best not to stretch the strips before applying them. Instead, when sewing the strip to an inner curve—for instance, a round neck curve—ease the strip very slightly, then turn the strip over and tack the edges level, stretching the other edge of the strip to allow it to fit the material below. If the edge of the facing is to project a little, then the strip must not be eased. When you are setting a facing on the outside of a curve, stretch the edge a little as you run it on, then, after turning the strip over onto the wrong side, you may need to ease it a little on the lower edge, or even to make tiny pleats here and there, to make the facing fit the diminishing width. But when the edge to be faced is very much curved or very irregular is is best to tack a piece of material to the right side of it, the two matching in grain, and with right sides together; then, after running round the outside edges, the facing should be turned to the inside of the garment and cut to an even depth before turning in and felling the raw edge.

APPLIED NET EDGES

First Method

For this it is necessary that the outside edges of the net should be straight, although the depth of the strip need not necessarily be equal all round. It is best to draw on paper the shape of the garment, and then mark on this the shape the net edge is to take. For instance, the garment edge may be applied to net in scallops in the following way. Stamp or draw the scallops on the material, and allow enough net to be fourfold and to go under the scallops with $\frac{1}{2}$ inch to spare. Fold the net once, then again, and make the fold meet the cut edges— it is now fourfold. Place the double fold to the outside edge marked on the paper and tack finely to the paper. Now lay the scalloped edge over the net, allowing as much net as you like beyond the scallops. Tack the material to the net and the paper, then run round the scalloped outlines through both material and net, using embroidery cotton or silk in accordance with the materials. Work the scallops as described for buttonholed scallops in Fig. 144.

Second Method

Here also the edge of the net should be on the straight thread, although the edge to which it is to be applied may be quite straight or very slightly curved. The finished width of the net should not be more than $\frac{3}{4}$ inch. Fold the net as before to make it fourfold, but when folding the second time let the raw edges project $\frac{1}{8}$ inch beyond the fold, then turn them in and tack them level with the folded edge. Draw the shape of the garment edge on to brown paper, and from this measure the width of the net strip and draw a second line. Now tack the net to the paper, and when going round a curve stretch the net edge very slightly. Tack the other edge also. (This stretching should only be slight, as otherwise, when washed, the net will go to its original shape and the effect will be spoiled. If the curve is very marked, tiny pleats should be made and sewn to the neck.)

CHAPTER XXII

LINGERIE (*continued*)

EMBROIDERY

ALL the stitches needed for embroidering any material you may choose for your lingerie are described fully in *Teach Yourself Embroidery*, but it is well to remember that adaptation to the nature of the fabric is often necessary. For instance, when working on fine lawn, the embroidery thread must be fine and the stitches tight and well padded; while when using silk or crêpe-de-chine, a fairly coarse embroidery silk may be employed, and the designs may be freer in style, and not worked so finely. Though here, again, one must always consider future washings, and therefore not use stitches which may be disarranged easily either during this process or in the subsequent ironing.

FAGGOTING

Faggoting gives scope for originality in the trimming of lingerie—yokes, cuffs, neck edges, etc. It consists in joining together strips of material, ribbon, or lace insertion by means of fancy stitches, of which there is a great variety from which to choose.

First draw out on stiffish paper the shape you require the faggoting to be, but leave a few inches of spare paper all round. Now draw out the design on the paper. This may consist simply of bands following the shape of the outside edge of the paper, or it may be an arrangement of bands twisting and turning, leaving somewhat irregular spaces. But the width of the bands, varying from ¼ inch or less to ½ inch, should be the same throughout the design.

In Fig. 145, below, you see a simple design for neck or sleeve edges; and, though the edge bands are shown on the straight, they may be adapted easily to a slight curve by stretching one edge of the

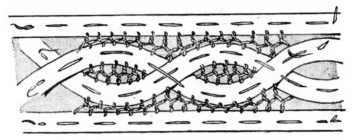

Fig. 145.—Simple Border in Faggoting.

strip as you tack it into place. The bands here consist of bias strips of crêpe-de-chine ⅜ inch wide, although the width is just a matter of taste. Cut out the strips as previously described, making them twice the desired finished width plus ¼ inch for turnings. Join up the strips on their straight edges, press the turnings open, then fold the long strip with right side inside and raw edges meeting. Machine these raw edges together with ⅛-inch turnings. Now attach a bodkin (or small safety-pin) to the seam at one end of the strip, leaving about 3 inches of double thread when joined on. Turn the bodkin back and insert it in the casing.

Push it along until you have turned out the strip completely and the bodkin emerges at the other end. (A similar method of turning a bias fold is illustrated on p. 172 in Figs. III A and B, though there a large safety-pin is used for a wider fold.) Now arrange the seam to come in the middle of what will be the under side, and press lightly with a warm iron on this side.

Tack the band to the paper in the position you have drawn out for it. One row of rather fine tacking-stitches is sufficient for a narrow band, but when wider than ⅜ inch, and when going round curves, both edges must be tacked. In this case the outer edge of the strip must be stretched slightly, and on the inner edge it may sometimes be necessary, though not always, to gather finely and draw up the thread to fit the curve. Sometimes it is better to make a tiny pleat instead of gathering, especially for a sharply-pointed corner. Now work across the spaces with the stitch D shown in Fig. 146, p. 276, though any one of the stitches shown in this Fig. may be used.

The thread used should be (for silk materials) twisted silk of the kind made specially for embroidering lingerie; for mercerised goods or plain cotton, tightly-twisted mercerised threads serve very well. A firm start should be made for the connecting stitch with a few tiny back stitches on the under side of the strip, and great care should be taken not to draw the stitches tightly, as even when they do not appear tight while the strips are on the paper they may do so when the strips are removed, so this fact should be borne in mind. As a rule the work is removed after all the strips have been joined, and is then neatened at the back and pressed; but at other times it is advisable to keep it tacked to the paper and attach the faggoting to the garment in that position. One's own discretion must be used as to which is the better plan in any particular case.

Faggoting Stitches

Four very useful connecting stitches are shown in Fig. 146, though it is an easy matter to find or invent others equally suitable.

A. Join on the thread at the right hand at the back of the lower strip. Bring out the needle at the front just below the folded edge. * Insert the needle in the upper strip, from the point exactly opposite where the thread came out on the lower strip; draw out the needle to leave a rather loose stitch, then pass it under the stitch thus made three times, and bring out in the lower strip close to where the thread came out, but slightly to the right. Draw up the thread, but not tightly, then insert the needle where it just came out and pass it along the inside of the fold from $\frac{1}{4}$ to $\frac{1}{2}$ inch to the left (according to the width of the strips), then repeat from *.

B. Join on the thread at the right hand in the lower strip, * take the thread straight across to the upper strip, and pass the needle to the back; bring out again in the same edge about $\frac{1}{8}$ inch to the left. Take a straight stitch across to the lower strip and

insert in the edge ⅛ inch from the first stitch. Pass
the needle along the back and bring out ⅛ inch to
the left. Repeat from *. Bear in mind that these
straight stitches must be decidedly loose and must

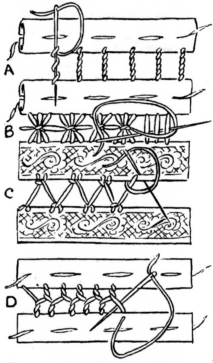

Fig. 146.—Some Faggoting Stitches.

be spaced perfectly evenly. When the whole
length has been done carry the needle to the middle
of the end stitch and fasten there, then turn the
work so that the stitches are horizontal. Hold
the thread coming from the fastening under the left

thumb just below the first three stitches. Insert the needle to the left of the thread above the top stitch and pass the point under the three stitches, bringing it out over the thread which is held under the thumb. Draw up the thread tightly to form a knot. Then repeat over groups of three stitches. Here again do not draw the thread tightly between the knots, or the finished effect will be ruined.

C. Work this with the strips running downward. Join on the thread at the top of the left strip, and bring out on the upper side about $\frac{1}{16}$ inch from the edge if a fabric strip is being used, or just inside the corded edge if insertion is employed. Hold the thread under the left thumb about $\frac{3}{4}$ inch below where it came out, insert the needle in the same edge about $\frac{1}{16}$ inch below where the thread came out, and bring out through the loop of thread. Carry the thread across slantingly to the other strip, and insert the needle about $\frac{3}{16}$ inch below the level of the stitch on the other side, and here make two little loops, as shown. Then carry the thread to the left strip at the same slant as before and repeat the two little loop stitches. Repeat as required. The beauty of this stitch lies in the regular slanting of the crossing threads.

D. Work this with the strips running across. Join thread to the left end of the upper strip, bringing out the needle on the upper side. * Carry the thread across to the lower strip about $\frac{1}{8}$ inch farther on to the right, pass the needle under it and bring out on the upper side. Pass the needle under the crossing thread from right to left, then insert under the upper edge about ¼ inch from where the first stitch was inserted, and bring out on the upper side. Pass the needle under the crossing thread from right to left as before, then repeat from *, keeping the stitches spread regularly.

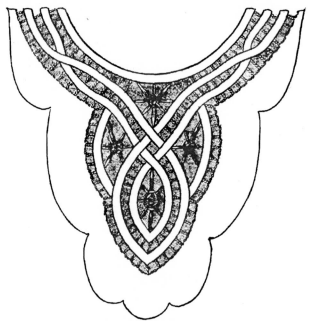

Fig. 147.—Dainty for Nightdress or Petticoat.

A More Elaborate Design (Fig. 147)

This makes a charming trimming for the front neck of a nightdress or petticoat-slip of crêpe-de-chine or satin. The strips are ⅜ inch wide when finished, and are prepared in the usual way. The spaces are irregular in shape, and the connecting stitches must be adapted to suit them, being made longer and shorter, closer together or wider apart, as required. The joining stitch is that shown in Fig. 146 A, and when a large space occurs it is filled in with a spider web.

After the stitchery has all been done, the work should be pressed lightly on the back through the paper. The edge of the garment should next be cut to shape and prepared for attaching. It should be noted that allowance should be made for a space of from $\frac{3}{16}$ to $\frac{1}{4}$ inch between garment and trimming, and also that even when the garment appears to be set on plainly to the trimming, as in this case, yet really it should be allowed with a very slight fullness, or, when set on, it will appear skimpy. The garment edge should be hemmed very finely, or rolled and whipped. The edge should then be tacked to the paper, leaving the required space between it and the edge of the trimming.

In cases where a full edge is to be attached to the faggoting it should be rolled and whipped and drawn up to fit the faggoting with the required space left, and then tacked on carefully. After the connecting stitches have been worked (either the same as in the example or any other preferred), the faggoting should be removed from the paper and the under side made neat. All ends of thread should be fastened off, crossed bands should be made firm, and any raw edges turned in and felled neatly into place. Then the trimming should be pressed lightly on the wrong side.

Pinched Strips (Fig. 148)

These are very decorative, but bands must not be more than $\frac{3}{8}$ inch in width before being " pinched ". After cutting and joining up the strips in the usual way, press them so that the join comes at one side. Join on the thread (usually the same as will be used for the faggoting) at the right end of the band; pass

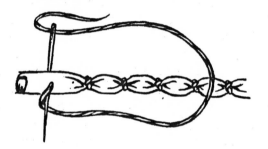

Fig. 148.—Making a Pinched Strip.

the needle and thread along the inside of the band and * bring out in the middle of it on the upper side, about $\frac{1}{2}$ inch to the left. Then put the needle behind the band from the top and bring it out below the edge; hold the thread coming from the hole under the left thumb and carry it under the point of the needle from left to right. Now with the right hand draw up the thread tightly through the loop. Put back the needle through the knot thus made, pass it along the inside of the band, and repeat from *. Note that the knots should be drawn tightly, but the thread between them should be left easy.

APPLIQUÉ

Appliqué makes charming trimmings, which are at the same time durable, on crêpe-de-chine and other materials of fine, even weave, especially when two pale shades are used together—for instance, pink on blue, or mauve on pink, etc. The designs should be simple and have smooth, not serrated,

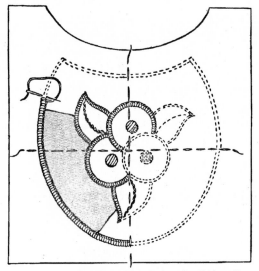

Fig. 149.—Appliqué Trimming for Lingerie.

edges, as the former are better for washing and wear. The usual methods of appliqué are described in *Teach Yourself Embroidery*, but it is well to remember that for lingerie the stitches should be small, even, and set closely together—preferably buttonhole stitch or padded satin stitch. But there is another method which may be described here, which, while not strictly appliqué, produces a similar effect.

In Fig. 149, p. 281, you see a trimming which could be used for front neck of petticoat-slip or nightdress or for nightdress sleeves or the sides of knickers. A motif of the same material as the garment rests upon a background of similar material, but in another colour, or of white or cream net, and is enclosed in a line of buttonhole stitch to form a circle, shield, or other suitable shape. You can easily draw such a design yourself, using a penny as a guide for the three circular flowers, and drawing the leaves freehand; or, if you prefer it, it is easy to buy a similar transfer. If you use one of these, iron it off on to the garment in the desired position; but if you draw your own design, outline it with a fine pencil on tracing paper, then lay a piece of carbon paper in the correct position for the design and place the tracing paper over the carbon. Trace the outlines with a hard, firm pencil, and be most careful that your fingers do not press over the carbon, or irremovable marks will be made. (In the case of new carbon papers, some of the colouring matter should first be removed with a soft rag or tissue paper.)

If you are using the same material, but of a different colour, for the background, cut a piece large enough to cover the outside edges of the space and with a spare 2 inches all round it. Be sure to match the garment material in weave. If you are using net, cut it in the same way, but double. Whichever you use, place it *under* the design on the garment, allowing an equal margin all round the

outside line. Tack to the garment first from top
to bottom, then from side to side, then tack again
at each side of the first line at a distance of 1 inch;
then again twice across, equally spaced. Finally
run together round the outside line rather finely.

Now work round the outlines of all parts of the
motif in tight buttonhole stitch over one or two
lines of fine running in the embroidery thread,
keeping the corded edge to the outside. Be careful
to take all stitches right through both layers of
material. Use fine corded silk for silk materials or
twisted cotton for cotton goods. (This should match
the material of the garment in colour.) When all
this has been done work round the enclosing line in
the same way, but with the corded edge of the
stitch on the inside. Work the ribs of the leaves
in outline stitch, and the roundels in the middle of
the flowers in padded satin stitch. Then take a
pair of fine-pointed scissors and cut away the
material (upper only) between the motif and the
enclosing buttonholing, as in Fig. 149. Press lightly
on the wrong side.

LACE TRIMMINGS

These may be in the form of medallions, motifs,
edging, insertion, etc. In any case, choose strong
lace which will last as long as the garment, otherwise
much labour is expended in renewing the trimmings
while the garment itself is still in good condition.
How to apply medallions, edging, and insertion is
described on pp. 173–4 under the heading Lace.
You will find an illustration of the second method of

applying insertion in Fig. 150 A and B. Here note that at the crossing of the insertion the under piece is cut away and the raw edges are turned back and run to the upper piece, but when the lace is very fine this is not necessary.

There are also very attractive machine-made laces of artificial silk on net in white, ecru, and

Fig. 150A and B.—Applying Insertion.

A   B
Right Side.   *Wrong Side.*

colours. They include yokes, motifs, neck and sleeve trimmings, etc., and are suitable for use on any of the silk (real or artificial) fabrics sold for lingerie. To attach them, lay the garment, right side upward, on a flat surface and place the lace over it, also right side upward. Pin together in many places, then tack carefully, and be sure not to get either lace or garment tight upon the other. Take silk matching the lace in colour, and work tiny stitches from the material over the edge of the lace. These stitches should be very close together and as small as possible. After this has been done turn to the back and cut off the turnings to ⅛ inch or less. Oversew the raw edges, or loop stitch them, to prevent fraying, or, if preferred, turn them under and fell very finely to the lace.

EMBROIDERY EDGINGS AND INSERTIONS

When the edging is narrow and is to be set onto the garment plainly—for instance, on the edge of the round neck of a nightgown—it is usual to place a beading between the edging and the garment.

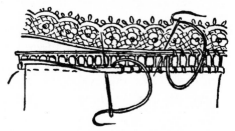

Fig. 151.—Applying Beading and Edging.

The beading can be set on as described in Chapter XX for a beaded seam (see Fig. 140, p. 262, and Fig. 151 on this page). When there is no material left on the beading, place the beading right side downward on the right side of the material, with the latter projecting about ⅛ inch above the corded edge. Then roll this little turning toward you over the corded edge and whip the two together the reverse way—that is, with the beading facing you and the material turning rolled over the corded edge.

To apply the embroidery edging to the beading, cut off the required amount of plain material, then proceed as just described. In Fig. 151 the edging

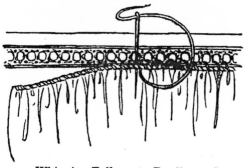

Fig. 152.—Whipping Fullness to Beading or Insertion.

is lace, so the work is even simpler, and the needle is inserted from the back instead of from the front.

When setting on beading to full material, the latter should be rolled and whipped as described on p. 58, then the two must be whipped together as in Fig. 152.

Applying Embroidery Insertion

There are at least three ways of applying embroidery insertion.

A. If the insertion is to have plain material at

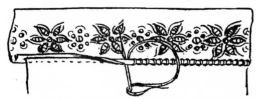

Fig. 153.—Applying Embroidery Insertion to Plain Edge.

each side, place the embroidery with right side to right side of the material, and run together finely. Then cut off the turning of the garment to $\frac{1}{16}$ inch, and that of the insertion to a thread or two more. Roll over the two edges towards you, and then use the needle as in Fig. 153. The other edge of the insertion may be applied to plain material in the same way, or may be whipped to beading or edging as before described for beading.

B. When the insertion has a corded edge, cut off the plain material .close up to it, then tack the insertion with its right side to that of the material; but leave a little turning of the latter above the insertion. Roll this turning toward you over the insertion and whip together in the usual way.

C. Enclose the insertion in a French seam. Place the wrong sides of insertion and material together and run or machine them just under $\frac{1}{4}$ inch from the insertion edge. Cut off turnings as far as is safe, turn to wrong side, and run or machine close up to the insertion edge.

PICOTING

First read the paragraph on this subject on p. 175. It is possible to have almost the whole of a garment made at the machine shop—seams and hems being hemstitched, and any frills and neck and sleeve edges finished with picoting. This is quite satisfactory when very thin fabric such as ninon is in use. The seams must first be tacked, but not as for hand-sewing. One edge should be laid flat over the other as shown in Fig. 141A, and a line of tacking made through the two fitting-lines. If the lower edge is to be picoted, the line for this must be tacked, leaving at least 2 inches below. But if there is to be a hemstitched edge, this cannot be done until the seams have been treated, and so a second visit to the machine shop will be necessary. Any edges, such as those of frills, must be tacked along the fitting-line; turnings of from $1\frac{1}{2}$ to 2 inches should be left, and where any edges are much curved they should be tacked onto tissue paper. But if a good length of frilling is needed and a large piece of material is available, a simpler way is to measure the frilling on this with a ruler, so as to get the exact depth, and to tack the dividing lines finely. The stitch will be worked on these lines, and all that will be needed is to cut through the stitching.

When the garment returns, cut off the seam turnings on both sides as close to the stitching as possible, but on any outside edges cut through the middle of the stitching. Hems may be tacked with either a single or a double turn. If the former, then tack up at an even height all round above the lower edge of the garment, leaving a turning of at least 1 inch above the tacked line; if the latter, make the two turns of the same depth when the fabric is transparent, then tack close to the turned-in edge; but when the fabric is not transparent, the raw edge should be turned in for at least $\frac{1}{4}$ inch. The hemstitching will then come half on the hem and half on the single material. One thing should always be remembered—that is, always to tack for hemstitching or picoting with matching thread, as it will be caught in with the machining and cannot be removed.

TUCKS

Full directions for making several varieties of tucks are given on pp. 153–6, and any one of these is suitable for lingerie, with the exception of corded tucks. Tucks are often alternated with lace or embroidery insertion with good effect.

PLEATS

These are not used much for lingerie, except for the fullness which is often placed in the side seams of petticoat-slips to give ease for walking and yet at the same time preserve a slim outline. Inverted pleats are most suitable here, and they are described on pp. 161–2.

GATHERS

Read the instructions for gathers on p. 166. Note that most of the materials now in vogue for lingerie are sufficiently supple to allow the stroking stitch to be dispensed with, though this is necessary with the old-fashioned stout fabrics such as long-cloth or cambric. This stroking, when it must be used, is worked in the following way.

Mark off the edge to be gathered in quarters to correspond with similar marks on the band or edge to which the gathers are to be joined. Then gather on the fitting-line (see Fig. 25, p. 56). A second row of gathers *above* the first makes them set better. Draw up the threads fairly tightly and twist them

K   (Dress)

round a pin which is set in point downward at the left end. Hold the gathers in the left hand, and with the eye of a coarse sewing-needle or the blunt end of a wool needle press each little fold into place against the thumb of the left hand, working from left to right. This stroking must be done very gently, and on no account should the sharp point of a needle be used, or the material will be scratched and its surface ruined. Stroke in the same way on the wrong side, then let out the gathers to the required width.

Setting Gathers Into a Band

When setting gathers of stout material into a waist-band or sleeve-cuff, etc., proceed as follows :

The waist- or sleeve-band will be cut out with the warp threads running round the figure for strength. If the band is to be in the form of a ring, join up the ends on the wrong side and press the turnings open; if the ends are to be open, fold the band down the middle on the wrong side and join up each end. Now in either case turn up $\frac{1}{4}$ inch or less on each edge of the band. Quarter the band and mark with pins, then match up with the quarterings on the gathered edge, and pin together there. Lay the turned-up edge of the band over the gathers on the right side so that the lower gathering thread is just covered. First pin into place, then tack finely through the folded edge. Now fell the folded edge between the gathers—one stitch to each gather—producing upright stitches. When finished, turn to the wrong side and tack in the same way, except that the fold should come the slightest bit higher than on the right side in order that the second set of felling stitches will not show through on the right side.

When Using the Sewing Machine

After letting out the gathers to the desired width, take the band and crease one edge only; then lay this right side downward on to the right side of the gathers and tack very finely through band and gathers on the creased line, which should come exactly over the lower gathering thread. Now turn the garment to the wrong side and turn up the band on the lower edge; then tack it over the gathers with the fold just a shade below the fold on the right side. Now stitch from the right side close to the fold of the band; and if the ends are open, then carry the stitching up the ends also.

For Very Thin Fabrics

For the thin fabrics, now generally used, the gathers are usually set into bands similarly to the method used for machining just described, but with a fine running stitch over the first row of tacking (before the band is turned up), and felling on the wrong side, as for the hand-sewn method. But when the fullness is set onto a single edge it must be done by rolling and whipping.

Waist Fullness at Side of Petticoat

In a princess petticoat or slip there is often a horizontal cut on the waist-line at each side of the under-arm seam, into which fullness on the lower edge is set. Stitch the side (under-arm) seams as you prefer—usually French seams—then take two bias strips of the same material ¾ inch wide. Place one strip on the upper side of the cut with right sides together and raw edges level; tack the two together. Turn to the wrong side and tack the other strip over the cut in the same way, then run or machine together as close to the raw edges as is

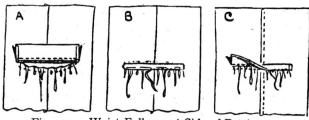

Fig. 154.—Waist Fullness at Side of Petticoat.

safe (see Fig. 154A). Gather the lower edge to fit the upper, then turn in the edge of the strip on the right side and tack it over the gathers. Fell this into place by hand, or machine close to the turned-up edge (see Fig. 154B). Tack down the strip on the wrong side in the same way and fell into place (see Fig. 154C).

SMOCKING

This may often be employed in lingerie, particularly when the gathering is fine and the fancy stitches firm and close, so that they do not get disarranged in washing. (Smocking, of course, is always in favour for children's frocks, and from time to time it is fashionable for blouses for adult wear.)

The amount of fullness required for smocking

varies with the thickness and texture of the material, and also with the stitches to be used. The average amount required is three times the width of the finished measurement, but thicker materials will not need so much fullness, and very fine ones can take more.

Preparation

The preparation of the material for the fancy stitching, by means of rows of gathers, is all-important. To ensure perfect regularity there are two methods.

1st *Method.* Buy a transfer of rows of evenly-spaced dots. On fine materials the dots should be from $\frac{1}{4}$ inch to $\frac{3}{8}$ inch apart, while on thicker ones $\frac{1}{2}$ inch is usual. See to it that the top edge of the material is cut by a thread. Place the transfer on the *wrong* side of the material with the rows of dots on the straight thread.

Calculate how many rows of gathers you will need for the fancy stitches and add one extra for the top row, which will usually be set into a band of some kind. Tack the paper into place on the *wrong* side of the material with the row of dots on the same thread, then apply a hot iron.

2nd *Method.* Take a ruler and pencil or chalk and rule horizontal lines the required distance apart, keeping on the straight thread. Now cross these lines with downward ones to form perfect squares.

The Gathering (Fig. 155)

This is done on the wrong side with fairly thick but soft cotton. Make a large knot on the cotton, which cannot be pulled through the fabric. Now begin at the right hand by taking a stitch under a

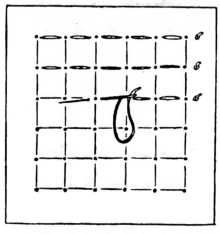

Fig. 155.—Foundation Gathering for Smocking.

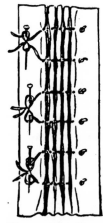

Fig. 156.—Drawing up the Gathers.

few threads exactly on the dot or at the crossing of the lines on the squares. Continue to the end of the row, and here cut the cotton, leaving about 1 inch. Repeat until all the rows have been gathered, then make an extra row about $\frac{1}{8}$ inch above the top row, taking up the threads immediately above the stitches of the row below. (This extra row gives firmness.) Now draw up two threads at once from the left hand and twist them together round a pin placed vertically at the end of the two rows. Repeat until all the rows are drawn up to an equal width (Fig. 156). This should be almost as much as the desired finished width.

Planning the Stitches

It is necessary to have a clear plan in your mind before beginning the fancy stitches. This can then be drawn out on squared paper and consulted as you work. Almost any fancy embroidery stitch can be used—most usually outline, crewel, feather, chain, etc.—and some of the elaborate patterns are simply arrangements of one or two stitches in diamonds or waved lines. They are not difficult to carry out, but they entail careful counting of stitches and folds on the material so that a whole pattern, or else the division between two patterns, comes in the exact middle of the finished work.

Holding the Work

The material may be held in the left hand while being worked, or it may be tacked carefully to a piece of stout but pliable paper, and then the gathers should be stretched out to the exact width desired. Some stitches are worked from right to left, some from left to right, and for some others—such as chain stitch—the work must be turned so that the little folds come horizontally and the stitch is worked downward.

Fig. 157

This is a simple pattern to start with, being merely an arrangement of crewel, outline, and chain stitches. Ten rows of gathers are required, with an extra row worked ⅛ inch above the top row for strength. These two will not be worked on. Work a row of crewel stitch on the second and fourth gathered rows, and a row of chain stitch on the third

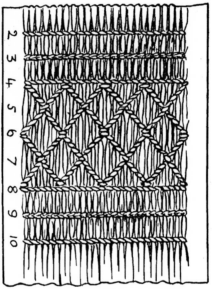

Fig. 157.—A Simple Pattern for a Start.

row of gathers. Repeat these on the eighth, ninth, and tenth rows of gathers. In the space left work a trellis band as follows :

Begin close up to the straight row of crewel stitch at the left hand. Bring out the needle to the left of a fold and * work outline stitches in a slanting row, making the fifth stitch **exactly** on the fifth gathered row, and bringing out **the** needle after the ninth stitch exactly on the sixth gathered row. Now work nine crewel stitches slanting upward to the straight crewel row. Repeat from *. Next start with a stitch on the sixth gathered row exactly underneath the first stitch of the previous slanting row of stitches. Now work a slanting row of crewel stitches to the fourth gathered row, immediately in the middle of the space. Then continue working downward and upward to cross the previous rows of stitches to form diamonds and triangles. Now repeat what has just been worked on the sixth, seventh, and eighth gathered rows.

Here is a reminder that when working outline stitch horizontally from left to right the needle is brought out *below* the previous stitch, while when working the same vertically the needle is brought out to the *right* of the previous stitch. But when working crewel stitch horizontally the needle is brought out *above* the previous stitch, while when working vertically it is brought out to the *left* of the previous stitch.

The border is finished with three rows to match the upper part of the border—a row of crewel stitch on the eighth and tenth gathered rows, and a row of chain stitch on the ninth gathered row.

Fig. 158

Eight gathered rows are needed for this pattern, adding an extra row for firmness immediately above the top row—neither of these being worked over, and not being shown in the diagram. Work over the second and fourth gathered rows in crewel

stitch, or outline, if preferred, and work over the
third gathered row in single feather stitch.* Join
the thread at the left hand close to the last row
of crewel stitch, and bring out the needle to the left
of a fold. Work five slanting outline stitches down
to the next (the fifth) gathered row; then work
upward to the fourth gathered row with five crewel

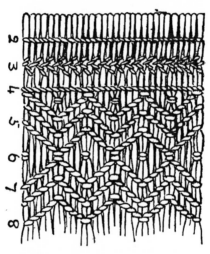

Fig. 158.—Waved Lines are Effective.

stitches. Repeat from * as required. (See that
the triangles thus formed are equally spaced.) Now
join on to the beginning of the fifth gathered row
and work as before between this and the sixth row,
and when this is done work another row midway
between the last two rows. After this join the
thread on the seventh gathered row immediately
under the first stitch on the fifth gathered row and
work three waved rows as before, but in reverse, so

as to form a row of diamonds between the two sets of three. Exactly in the middle of each diamond catch the two middle pleats together with two back stitches; finish off each pair of stitches separately so that the thread is not carried across at the back.

Honeycombing

This is the most elastic stitch of any used in smocking, and it may be used entirely by itself or combined with others. Fig. 159 shows exactly how it is worked. Bring out the needle to the left of a fold at the left hand of the work on the second gathered row. Take two back stitches over this fold and over the one to the right of it, and when making the second stitch insert the needle downward through the fold to the next gathered row, bringing it out there to the left of the second fold (which will be the first of the second pair). Now catch together this fold and the one to the right, as in the previous stitch, but in the

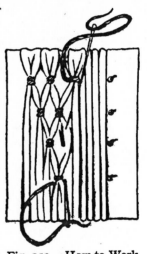

Fig. 159.—How to Work the Honeycombing.

last stitch pass the needle upward to the previous gathered row and bring it out to the left of the fold. (Both these movements are shown in Fig. 159.) Repeat these stitches on the two gathered rows alternately. To work subsequent rows repeat on the gathered rows below, either in the whole width of the material or in sets of diminishing stitches to form a vandyke pattern as in Fig. 160.

Fig. 160

Fourteen gathered rows are required for this, with an extra one just above the first—these two are not worked on, and are not shown in the diagram.

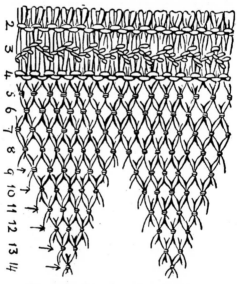

Fig. 160.—Honeycombing in Points.

Work cable stitch over the second and fourth rows. This is similar to crewel stitch, but the needle is brought out above and below the previous stitch alternately. Work double feather stitch over the third gathered row. Honeycombing is worked over the next four gathered rows right across, and then the points are formed over the remaining six gathered rows.

Embroidery Threads

For lingerie it is well to choose a rather tightly twisted silk or cotton, with its thickness in proportion to the texture of the material. Stranded cotton may frequently be used, with the number of strands appropriate to the pattern and fabric. A fine crewel needle is the best to work with.

Finishing Off

After all the fancy stitches have been worked, and before taking out the gathering threads, place the work on an ironing blanket with wrong side upward. Pin out the edges straight, then place a damp cloth over the back of the work and pass the iron lightly over it. On no account press the work, or the whole effect will be spoiled. Then remove the damp cloth and hold the iron over the material, but not touching, until the steam has evaporated. Leave for a few minutes, and then withdraw the gathering threads. This process sets the gathers and gives a professional look to the work.

CHAPTER XXIII

LINGERIE (*continued*)

FASTENINGS

BUTTONS and buttonholes or buttons and loops are the most usual fastenings for lingerie. Hooks and eyes are taboo, and although press studs are sometimes seen on crêpe-de-chine and satin slips and petticoats, these neat little fastenings are frowned upon by experts on account of their unsuitability for washing.

Buttons and Buttonholes

Buttons for lingerie are generally either small pearl ones or small unpierced linen ones—the latter for lawn and cotton fabrics. The pierced linen ones are never used on dainty garments, and in any case buttons should always be as small as efficiency permits, for large ones are both clumsy and out of place, and are calculated to mar the beauty of an otherwise attractive and well-made garment. The buttons should be sewn into position before the holes are cut, or their positions should be marked with pencil or cross stitches, and the spaces between should be measured carefully with a ruler. (When many buttonholes are to be made, it is a good thing to space the positions out on cardboard and thus make a gauge to cut them by.) Buttons and buttonholes should, with very rare exceptions, always be on double material, and when there are several in line, as for instance on front, back, or side fastenings, the edges should either be hemmed back or faced with a strip of self-material. When the buttons and buttonholes are isolated, so that neither hem nor facing is practicable, a small square of material cut on the same grain as the button or buttonhole site should be placed beneath it and felled all round.

Use strong double silk or cotton, according to the material, for sewing on buttons. First make two small back stitches on the button site on the right side of the material, then place the button exactly over them and bring up the needle and thread through one of the holes in the button. Place a pin across the button and take the stitches over it. When there are four holes, make a cross of two stitches each way; if there are two holes, make four stitches across, then pass the needle to the back of the button, between it and the material; withdraw the pin and twist the thread three or four times round the sewing-on stitches to form a " neck ". Pass the needle to the back, make one or two back stitches and cut the thread (see Fig. 71, p. 123).

For Shank or Covered Buttons

Moulds are sometimes covered with a circle of the garment material—this being gathered round the edge and drawn up into the centre of the under side. For these, and for buttons with a shank, the method of sewing is to start as before with small back stitches, then to pass the needle through the shank (or through the gathered covering of a mould), and then through the material and back again, repeating this as required for strength. In the case of a covered button a " neck " should be made as described for the button with holes.

For Linen Buttons

When linen (unpierced) buttons are used, begin work on the button site with two back stitches, then place a pin across the button and bring the needle out on the top. Carry the single thread four times over the pin and across a little space not more than one-third the width of the button and exactly in the middle of it; then bring the thread to the right side, remove the pin, and work loop stitch over the strands (as shown in Fig. 76, p. 129); make a " neck " as before, and secure the end of the thread.

Buttonholes

These are like those used in dressmaking, but not in tailoring. When the buttons have been sewn on, place the buttonhole side of the opening over them and mark the place of each button with a pin. Now either chalk or pencil the line for each buttonhole, using a ruler. The buttonholes should be on the straight thread, if possible, though this cannot always be managed, and if not, care must be taken that the slits are not stretched, and to prevent this it is wise to overcast the slit very lightly. The length of the slit should be $\frac{1}{16}$ inch more than the width of the button, if this is a flat one; if it is a dome-shaped one, then $\frac{1}{8}$ inch more. (But it is a good plan to cut experimental slits in a spare piece of material to make sure.) The distance of the buttonholes from the edge of the material should be enough to allow ⅛ inch, at least, beyond the buttons when they are fastened, so that this all depends on their size. Cut each slit as required, to avoid stretching.

Method of Working

Coarser thread than is used for the sewing of the garment should be employed for the buttonholes, and silk on all materials except cotton ones. (See Fig. 73, p. 127, for method.) Stitches should be as short as is compatible with strength, and they should be placed closely together with not more than a hair's breadth between them. The thread should be drawn up tightly to make a good knot after each stitch, and so that this knot comes exactly on the edge of the slit; but it should not be drawn up *over-tightly*, or it will tear the fabric.

To begin, secure the thread at the left end (that farthest from the edge of the material). Bring out the thread there just below the cut and begin to work the stitches from left to right as shown. After inserting the needle, take the thread coming from its eye and draw it round under the point from the left side, then draw up the needle to form the knot. When you reach the other end fan out the stitches (five or seven), and continue along the other side until you reach the starting point. Here pass the needle into the slit and out again at the beginning of the first stitch you made. From there take two or three stitches across the end of the buttonhole and bring out the needle at the left hand again. Then work buttonhole stitch over these strands, keeping them free of the material. Pass the needle to the back and finish off there. When making button-holes downward (as for the front fastening of a shirt blouse) both ends must be barred.

Buttons and Loops

When the material is not firm enough to serve as a foundation for buttonholes, loops should be used instead. The buttons should be sewn on as before, and the position of the loops marked accordingly on the other side of the opening. Sometimes (*a*) the loops are made just under the edges so that the buttons are covered, and at others (*b*) they are made on the extreme edge. You must make your own choice. In any case the right side should be hemmed or faced to make it double.

Method A

Attach the thread for the loop to the left end of the right side of the garment (holding the edge to-wards you). Bring out the thread for the loop just under the edge and carry a strand across the space for the loop, which should be the width of the button. Leave this strand very slightly loose from the material. Make a tiny stitch through the fabric, then ,carry the thread back again to the starting point and take a tiny stitch there. Now test the loop over the button and adjust if necessary. Carry two more strands across in this way, and then work over them in loop stitch (see Fig. 76, p. 129). When you finish at the right-hand end you may fasten off there with a few tiny back stitches, or, if you have enough thread, you may pass the needle through the material and bring it out at the next position and repeat.

Method B

Work as before, but on the extreme edge. Note that when round or dome-shaped buttons are used a looser loop will be needed, but this can only be decided by experiment.

Cord Loops

These are made in the same way as for dressmaking (described on p. 128 and illustrated in Fig. 75), but with one slight difference—in lingerie the edge for the cord must be hemmed before the cord is sewn on.

CASINGS FOR ELASTIC

These are needed at the waist and knees of directoire knickers. When the edge is on the straight, tack a hem one-and-a-half times the depth of the elastic, and stitch by machine on both top and bottom of the hem—hand sewing is not firm enough. Make an opening for elastic, preferably by unpicking the little bit of seam in the hem at the centre-back of a waist edge, or at the inside seam of knee edge. Buttonhole the edges of the opening. When there is not sufficient material for a hem, or the edge is curved, cut a bias strip twice the width of the elastic. Turn down and press the edge of the garment, then do the same to the raw edge of the bias strip and tack it just below the turned-down edge of the garment. Arrange the opening to come at the ends of the strip at the place suggested for a hem. Turn back both ends of the strip and button-hole them as before. Turn up the other edge of the strip and tack it into place, then stitch on both edges as near the turn as possible.

Inserting Elastic

Pin a small safety-pin to one end of the elastic and run it through the casing. Join the ends of elastic by overlapping them for $\frac{1}{2}$ inch and sewing firmly all round. If there is a small placket in the garment the elastic must not be joined, but the left end should be turned back twice and have a button sewn on it. This will keep the elastic from running back. On the other end of the elastic a hem should be made, and a buttonhole loop made on its extreme edge to pass over the button. Each end of elastic must be secured to the garment with a few stitches, but it can be removed easily if it is not desirable to wash it. If strings are to be used instead of elastic, the casings are made in the same way.

Other Casings

Sometimes a small casing is needed on the waist-line at the back of a petticoat or other garment. In this case a strip of material cut on the selvedge threads is necessary, and it should be twice the width of the elastic, tape or ribbon. Top and bottom edges should be turned down narrowly, and rather more at each end. Then the upper and lower edges should be tacked into place and machined close to the fold, but the ends should be left open. If only one string is used, pass it through the casing and sew it through the middle of the strip with an upright row of back stitch or else a large cross stitch. If two strings to cross are used, sew one to each end of the casing before it is applied, then lay the strings flatly over one another, and tack and stitch the casing into place with one string emerging at each end. Be sure to keep clear of the strings when you are machining.

BUTTONHOLED SLOTS FOR RIBBON

These slots are often used round the waist and neck of nightgowns and petticoats. They must of necessity be in single material, and so this must be firm, even though at the same time it may be fine. The slots are always upright, never horizontal. Draw them on the material with pencil and ruler. They should be $\frac{1}{16}$ inch longer than the width of the ribbon. They are usually in pairs about 1 inch apart, leaving about 2 inches between the pairs. The slots must be worked very lightly in buttonhole stitch, but without pulling tightly on the corded edge, and both ends must be the same— either barred or round. On very fine material— say lawn, crêpe-de-chine or silk—the slots may be whipped as in *broderie anglaise* in the following way : Pencil the slot, but do not cut it. Take needle and fine embroidery cotton for lawn, or twisted embroidery silk for silk, and run finely round the mark on both sides. Then cut the slit and work close over-and-over stitches from right to left all round over the running stitches, turning down the extreme edge with the needle as you go along.

SEWING ON STRINGS

If ribbon strings are to be set into the ends of hems, they should be sewn on before the hems are sewn. Arrange the hem, then tack the end of ribbon for ¾ inch to the inside of the hem and stitch the hem. If hand-stitched, then the ribbon must be felled to the hem at each end, but if machined the line of stitching may be carried up the ends of the hems. When the ribbon is not to be in a hem, but sewn inside the ends of an opening, place the end of the ribbon—right side downward—about ¾ inch from the end of the garment. Run the ribbon to the material, then turn the ribbon over and fold it backward to meet the edge of material. Seam the two together, and then flatten out the seam, after which fell the side edges of the ribbon.

SHOULDER STRAPS

Ribbon or double strips of the garment material are generally employed for the shoulder straps of cami-knickers, petticoats, etc., when these have straight-edged tops. Their position depends on the figure, and should be marked with pins after trying on the garment. Sew them on as described for ribbon strings. The stitches should not show on the right side, so, if the material is thin, it is best to make a small bow of ribbon, or a rosette, to cover any stitches.

Mark the position of the straps, then make a buttonhole slot (vertical) in the garment at each position. If the material is single, it must be backed with small pieces for strength, felling these finely all round. Hem each end of the ribbon and sew a flat button on the under side of each, covered on the right side with a bow or rosette. The button goes through to the inside of the garment.

To Prevent Straps Slipping

On the turnings of each shoulder seam of a frock attach a little strap of double material near the neck. Fasten the other end by means of press studs either to the turnings near the armhole seam, or to the end of the sleeve extender. Pass the petticoat straps under this little strap and you will be spared the discomfort of shoulder straps halfway down the arm.

CHAPTER XXIV

RENOVATION AND RE-MODELLING

MOST home-dressmakers find renovation a fascinating occupation—indeed, there are many who consider it more interesting than working in new materials. It can be a great money-saver if planned with foresight; but, on the other hand, it can be a sheer waste of time and money. For success it is necessary that the fabrics should be in good condition, with a reasonable amount of wear left in them; there should also be ample material to carry out your designs, and it should not be necessary to buy new materials or trimming—or, at any rate, the expenditure for these should be very small. I have known enthusiastic renovators to spend much time and money in making over materials which were shabby and almost worn out after a few weeks' wear in their new guise.

If renovation is a hobby of yours, then you should have it in mind when you make your original purchases of new materials; choosing them of good quality and of fast colour, and also, if possible, doubly reversible—that is, not only does the surface look the same from whichever end it is viewed (so that for economy's sake the different parts of the pattern can be placed either up or down), but also that both right and wrong sides are equally attractive, so that the wrong one may be used for the outside in the re-making.

You will be wise to buy an extra yard beyond what you need for the original garment. You should select a simple style for the first time of making, and one with few seams, so that the material is not cut up unduly; this will facilitate the re-cutting for the second style, and fewer joins will be required to provide for new shapes of the different parts. In the original make-up do not use any ornamental or outside stitching, and avoid much trimming, either applied or in the way of pleats, gathers, etc., as these entail stitch marks and pressed folds which are often difficult to remove, and remain as a constant reminder of re-making. Also use a larger machine stitch than you would otherwise employ, as being easier to unpick. Make up as lightly as is consistent with firmness, and let the inner neatenings be light also. Another invaluable warning is, do not wait until the frock or other garment is really shabby before essaying renovation, or you cannot be sure of either a good appearance or of getting the desired amount of " wear ".

CHOOSING A STYLE

In selecting the second style you may choose a rather more elaborate one than before, if you wish; but in any case do avoid one in which there is great strain on any part. Also try to arrange the cutting so that those parts which originally have had much strain, as the front of a skirt, may be put in a less conspicuous position. From time to time Fashion favours a combination of contrasting colours or different fabrics, and this is fortunate for the renovator, for quite possibly she may have two garments which will combine successfully—in fact, the far-seeing shopper will have anticipated this when buying both materials.

UNPICKING

The best method of unpicking machine-stitched seams is to withdraw the under thread with a strong darning needle. This will not prove difficult if the stitch, as has been suggested, is fairly large. This method prevents loose ends of thread being left in the garment, and also the accidental cutting of it with scissors. When the fabric is a substantial one it will be found better to rip the seams with a safety razor. In this case you should either pin one end of the seam to a table, or get a friend to hold it, wrong side upward, and then begin to cut towards yourself from the farther end. Of course, great care must be taken that you cut the stitches only and not the fabric, but this is not difficult. The only drawback is that small pieces of thread are left in the material, but these can be drawn out with tweezers. When, however, the pieces of material are large, and there is no fear of shortage, you may save much time and patience by cutting the seams right out as close to the stitches as possible.

On no account re-make soiled material, so, should there be any stains, plan out your pattern roughly to see if these can be avoided—if not either send the whole of the material to the cleaner's or do the work of removal yourself. (See Chapter

XXVI for methods.) Those places needing repair should be run round with white cotton so that they may be avoided in re-planning, or at any rate placed in an inconspicuous part. (See Chapter XXVI for repairs.) After this each piece must be pressed on the side which will in future be the wrong one. This should be done before cutting out, to ensure perfect accuracy. Any stitch marks, folds or crinkles must be pressed out with the aid of a damp cloth (as described in the beginning of Chapter XV), as, if they are first pressed dry, it will be most difficult to press them out afterwards, even with the aid of moisture.

The planning and cutting out should be done on the same principles which apply to new material, and due regard must be paid to placing the parts of the pattern on the correct grain, as in some fabrics this is not very easy when the selvedges have been removed.

INGENIOUS RE-MODELLING

It is surprising how nimble one's wits may become under the spur of necessity! Scarlet O'Hara illustrated this to perfection in " Gone With the Wind ", when she tore down a pair of handsome velvet curtains and hastily made them into a ravishing cloak! In a recent autobiography a lady of title described how in her childhood's days she and her sister lacked suitable frocks for a party to which they were invited, and finally these were provided by a resourceful nurse, who cut up a pair of frilled white muslin curtains and transformed them into two dainty, frilly, fairy-like frocks. Of course, the making of children's clothes from those of adults of either sex is an easy matter, and it is scarcely necessary to remind readers that a boy's suit may be cut from a man's overcoat or trousers; a boy's or girl's coat from that of an adult; a girl's frock from a woman's frock or skirt; a woman's blouse or child's frock from a man's shirt, etc. All these present no difficulty.

A Woman's Suit from a Man's

This is a piece of work which calls for ingenuity in planning and for tailoring skill; but it is one well worth while for the worker who has these qualities, and from personal experience I can vouch that the finished product need not proclaim its origin. (It is an advantage when the original wearer is well-built and the prospective one not above the average.) If the coat lining is suitable for re-use, it should be cleaned or washed after removal—but in any case this may be done, for, as linings for masculine garments are always of good quality, they will " come in " eventually for some purpose. Then the seams of the suit must be unpicked carefully, and also the buttonholes in the coat. If the cloth can be turned, so much the better, as the fronts will then be reversed, and the buttonholes can be either re-worked or bound. If turning is not possible, the slits must be fine-drawn (see p. 352, Fig. 173) and if pressed well they will be unnoticeable when the coat is unbuttoned.

The sleeves need care in planning, and if the

pattern of the sleeve is cut with a full head, arranged in darts or pleats, small wedge-shaped pieces may have to be added at each side of the upper sleeve. Needless to say that these must match in grain and weave to a thread, and, if pressed well, the joins will be invisible. In planning the skirt, the trousers should be turned upside down. If more fullness is needed at the hem, pleats made from spare pieces may be inserted at the seams.

The above remarks refer to a lounge or jacket suit, but when the cloth is fine and thin, it is possible to make a frock from it, particularly if contrasting cloth is used for trimming. From a dress suit a very smart suit for a woman can be made, as the tails give extra material.

BLANKETS ARE CONVERTIBLE

More uncommon, but equally successful, are frocks, coats, and dressing-gowns made from blankets, or from large-sized table-cloths, etc. Let me enlarge upon this, for the idea is worth consideration.

One cold winter, when a new warm frock became a necessity, and my purse was thin, I hunted through the house for suitable material for a make-over. In exploring the blanket chest, I was struck by the very attractive texture of a blanket which must have been at least sixty years old. It was delightfully fine in weave, and age had denuded it of its fluffy nap, leaving a fabric with a hand-woven appearance. It was light in weight, too, so I despatched it to the dyer with a pattern of the desired colour—a shade of dead-leaf brown—with, it must be confessed, many hopes but more fears. But the result was better than I had dared to hope, and I made it up into a most attractive bolero and skirt—the former trimmed with a little wool embroidery to conceal an unavoidable small darn. The sole outlay for this was merely the cost of dyeing.

A Dressing-Gown

Another blanket I converted into a cosy dressing-gown. It was almost new, and had not been washed. Then why cut it up? Well, the reason was that a careless person—I won't say who !— had burnt several small holes in it with a taper, and as the consequent darns did not please me, and I urgently needed a dressing-gown, I cut one from the blanket and made it up in the regulation style with stitched edges to the revers and cuffs. I need not tell you what a treasure it is.

CRETONNE CURTAINS

I always like to apply the principle of devolution in both clothes and household furnishings. For instance, when new overalls or aprons are needed at the same time as new cretonne curtains, I cut up the old curtains into overalls, etc., and buy only material for new curtains. There is often a good deal of hard wear left in cretonne or linen loose covers even when they are too faded for their original purpose; but their faded condition is of no consequence when aprons for kitchen wear are required—and anyhow, a cheap patterned material used for them would quickly fade.

SMALL COTTON TABLECLOTHS

There are usually a few of these in use in most households. When mine begin to show signs of wear I turn them into aprons, instead of mending them. A thirty-two inch size is the most useful for

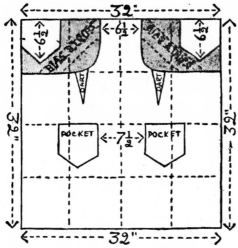

Fig. 161.—An Apron from a Tablecloth.

a medium figure, but for a larger figure the square should be in proportion. (Of course, a square of any other washing material—cretonne, crash, etc. —will serve.) Look at the diagram in Fig. 161, and fold your square as shown, *i.e.*, fold in half, then fold over again; then open out the square and fold twice the opposite way, and when the square is opened out you will find sixteen small folded squares. Now with coloured chalk draw according to the thick lines on the diagram. Cut the pockets from the spare pieces by the bib. Note the dart at each side of the bib. All figures will not need them, but if you use them they should be from 1 to 1½ inches wide at the top and about 2½ inches long.

Stitch the darts, press to one side. Hem the top of the pockets, turn in the raw edges, and stitch at a convenient height on the apron. Make narrow hems on the sides of apron and bib, and wider ones on lower edge and top of bib. Face the waist edges with bias strips cut from spare parts, and sew on tape strings (or strips of material) to tie at the back.

COTTON FROCKS, ETC.

Old cotton fabrics can often be transformed quite quickly into either petticoat-slips or overalls. If cut on slender lines, the sleeves may be removed and the armholes widened, also the neck cut down in front and back and the hem turned up a little— this will give a useful petticoat; while for an overall the sleeves, if wide and full, may either be set into wristbands with button and buttonhole fastenings, or may be cut to any length desired; unless it is preferred to remove them entirely and widen the armholes. Then the back should be cut down the middle from top to bottom and hemmed on both sides. The neck should be cut down all round, all raw edges should be bound with bias strips, and button and buttonhole fastenings should be made at waist and neck. One or two pockets should be cut from spare pieces and stitched on the front at convenient height. If the frock has a front fastening it is often possible to turn it back to front, especially if the front is at all shabby. The old bodice front may be cut off at the waist-band and at under-arm seams and shoulders. Then from the old back a bib may be cut, and this may be either pinned up or may have a strap of material sewn to each corner to be passed over the head. The old front of the skirt part should be cut from waist to hem and be hemmed on the raw edges. The skirt may be shortened if necessary. The apron may tie or button at the back.

TO MAKE BOLEROS AND COATEES

There is nothing to equal a bolero or coatee for cheering up a passée evening or afternoon frock. If it is short-sleeved it takes very little material, and when only small pieces are available it is often feasible to join these to the desired shape, if the joins are planned first, so that they become part of the design and there is no need to disguise them. Here are some of the sources from which I have seen good results : the best parts of an old skirt, frock or coat, if of suitable fabric; any old garment of velvet, satin, or brocade—even an old Victorian " dolman " ! Besides these, old furniture brocades and hand-printed linens have possibilities, especially if the design is touched up a little in various parts with silks or gold thread. Of course, any striking material should be worn with a quiet-looking frock,

L   (Dress)

and it is a good rule for one to be plain and the other patterned. If the bolero or coatee is required for winter wear and its material is thin, an interlining of domette, flannel, flannelette, or knitted fabric should be inserted, and the lining should be of silk, satin, or crêpe-de-chine—possibly the remnants of an old frock. Bits of fur may be used as trimming, and a chilly person will find a little upstanding collar of fur—merely a straight strip—a great protection from draughts.

I have seen a most attractive bolero cut from an old taffeta coat. The sleeves were cut off at the elbow, and the fronts were rounded so that the lower edge all round just escaped the waist-line. The whole of the fronts and back was worked over in large flowers in wool and silk, touched up here and there with gold thread. These poppy-like blooms were evenly spaced and carried out in bold stitches, leaving a good deal of the background showing inside the outlines. The sleeves were left plain except for a few lines of stem stitching in four or five colours round the lower edge. The maker had not intended this embroidery, but when she had cut down the coat she discovered several cuts in the taffeta, and therefore added the stitchery to conceal them—with very happy results.

TO MAKE BLOUSETTES AND WAISTCOATS

These attractive but deceitful little articles are quickly made for almost nothing. I say deceitful, for when worn under the coat of a suit or an odd bolero one imagines a complete garment, while in reality it is but a front or fronts attached to a back of net or other thin material. The home dressmaker's piece box will provide scraps of lace, satin, and other dainty materials for a blousette, and very often the back of a crêpe-de-chine or other blouse will be intact when all the other parts are outworn, and this will need but little adaptation for the same purpose. Rather more substantial fabrics are used for waistcoats, but, as there will be two fronts, even smaller pieces can be used, such as odd pieces of cloth, velvet, or brocade, etc. Plain materials may be embroidered or left plain, and if the latter, handsome buttons may be used with good effect.

Knitted Fronts

Only a very small amount of wool is needed to make what is apparently, when worn under a coat or jacket, a pullover. If sufficient wool of one colour is not available, two, three, or more colours may be used in horizontal stripes. Cast on a sufficient number of stitches to make a width of about 9 inches. Work a depth of $2\frac{1}{2}$ inches in knit one and purl one (or knit two and purl two) rib, then change to stocking stitch, or a fancy pattern, and work until, when you place the ribbing round the front waist and hold the knitting upward, the strip reaches the neck. Now shape the top like the front neck of a pullover, and work on until the side parts reach the shoulders, then cast off. Take up the neck stitches and cast on more at each end of the needle to make the first row of a collar which shall meet in the middle of the back neck, and be fastened there with press studs. Knit a roll collar to match the waist ribbing, or if you prefer a straight stand-up collar, this is equally suitable. Now take up the stitches on the left-hand side of the ribbing and knit a strip of garter stitch long enough to reach round the waist to the middle of the back, then work off in a point. Knit in the same way at the other end of the ribbing, but finish off the end with a buttonhole before the point. Sew a button on the left end.

TO WIDEN SKIRTS

To widen a narrow skirt often entails a good deal of ingenuity, and no hard-and-fast rules can be given. Here are methods which have proved successful, and may suggest others to the reader.

1. A skirt of four or more gores, too tight in its whole length, may be treated in this way. Unpick each seam, then press the fold of each turning (double) on the wrong side. Take a strip of material (either the same as the skirt or contrasting in some way—either in colour or texture) about $1\frac{1}{2}$ inches wide and backed with lining, if thin. Tack the folds of the matching gores to this strip, leaving an even space all the way down. The width must be proportionate to the amount of enlargement needed, as the spaces must be equal throughout. A striped skirt should have the stripes cut with the stripes running across, or else be of plain fabric. Plain material could have similar strips, or of checked material cut on the bias, but a checked skirt will look best with plain strips. Bias velveteen, sold ready-cut by the yard, will also serve very well.

Tack the folded edges down finely, then press the strip on the wrong side and stitch on the right side, either close to each fold or $\frac{1}{8}$ inch from it (Fig. 162),

2. An alternative method is better when the enlargement required is not the same for the whole length of the skirt. Unpick all the seams and re-fit the skirt with the turnings on the *right* side. Tack the seams according to alterations needed, then pin a strip

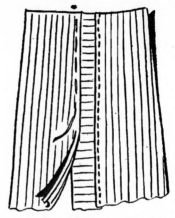

Fig. 162.—Widening a Skirt.

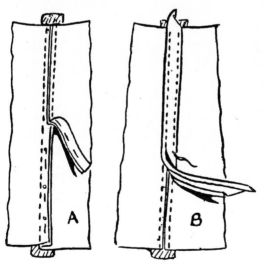

Fig. 163A and B.—Making Strapped Seams to Enlarge.

of lining about 1¼ inches wide under each seam, tack from the right side about ¼ inch each side of the tacked seam, then cut off the turnings, including the tacking (Fig. 163A). Now a take a bias strip of cloth (edges turned back and pressed if material is a fraying one, or cut with a knife on a board if very firm and close) and tack on the right side with the meeting edges of the gores exactly in the middle (Fig. 163B). Stitch the strip on the right side as close to the edges as possible. Braid might serve equally well, and it should be felled very neatly with silk on the extreme edges. If bias strips are used they must be stretched well under the iron in preparation.

3. If a skirt is too long as well as too tight, it is an easy matter to remove it from the band and raise it on the figure until it fits correctly round the hips; then the excess above the waist-line should be cut off, any necessary alterations made in the seams at the hips, or in the darts, and finally the skirt should be remounted on the waist-band and any needed re-adjustment made in the hem.

4. Here is an attractive method when the shape of the skirt allows it—for instance, a two-piece skirt with a seam at each side. Unpick the seams and insert a strip of material not less than 3 inches wide (without turnings) all the way down; after tacking, stitch down the turned-in edges of the skirt about ¼ inch from the turn. This would give a total extra width of 6 inches, and where this would be too much, the sides of the skirt pieces should be trimmed off and turned in afresh, so as to give the correct width

measurements after the insertion of the pieces.   If still more width is required at the hem, it may be given by making each strip wide enough (for about 10 or 12 inches from the bottom edge, plus turnings, according to fashion) to make an inverted pleat at each side.   This entails adding 4 inches or more at each side of the strip.   The join must come under the turned-back edge of the skirt piece.

5. For a skirt with seams at back and front a similar plan may be followed by inserting strips there. Certainly there should be pleats at the lower edge, their height being according to current fashion. There may be two pleats instead of one at each side of the opening, if the material is not bulky, and these would come on the top of one another.

Note.   These inserted pieces may be of contrasting colour, or a skirt of plain colour could have them striped or checked.   The stripes should be used horizontally.   It is a good plan to make experiments in pleating in paper before cutting material, to avoid mistakes.   When making these alterations the skirt hem should be unpicked for a few inches at each side of the seam, and a hem of the same depth arranged for on the inserted pieces, then, after pressing the seams, the hem may be re-adjusted and the pleats pressed again.

Widening on the Lower Part Only

When a skirt needs widening below the knees only, this may be effected by means of inverted pleats, either single or double, at each seam (Fig. 164A, B, and c) ; and in the case of wide gores vertical slits may be made also for pleats. The same, or contrasting fabric may be used. In a thin material godets

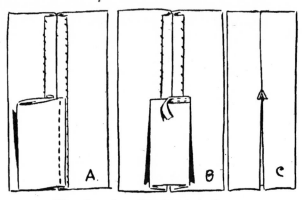

Fig. 164.—Inserting Pleats in Seams.

may be used instead of pleats (see Fig. 105A and B, p. 165, and instructions for making on pp. 164–5), and a tight-fitting evening skirt of silk or satin can

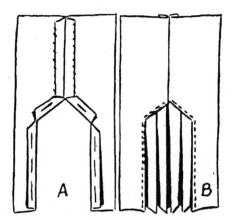

Fig. 165.—Another Method of Widening a Skirt.

be renovated effectively by the insertion of ninon or georgette godets in several vertical slits.

Another method of inserting pleats is shown in Fig. 165. Here the two gores are cut away on each side of the seam as in A, and the turnings tacked back and pressed. A piece of material, cut on the straight, is laid in four pleats—two at each side with folds toward the middle. After being pressed they are tacked behind the turned-in edges of the opening and stitched as in Fig. 165B.

TO WIDEN A BLOUSE OR BODICE

In thin fabric it may be possible to give the required extra width by inserting two or three strips of lace or ribbon down the front (or fronts) and back, stitching these in by machine or joining them in with a faggoting stitch. Another plan is to cut away a strip from the middle of the front and to insert a sham waistcoat of different material, or a vest of tucked georgette or net.

TO LENGTHEN A SKIRT

A full gathered skirt of thin fabric may be lengthened in the following way :

If the material is a patterned one, add a straight band of plain material to tone, about 12 inches deep, to the lower part of the skirt; or cut off an even depth from the lower part and insert a straight band of another colour. This band should be rather narrower than the band of the original material below it. In the first method the lower part should be turned down on its upper edge and stitched over

L 2   (Dress)

the skirt at the desired height (the original material behind being cut away); while in the second method both edges of the added band should be turned down and stitched over the raw edges of the skirt. When the skirt is on a curve, great care should be taken

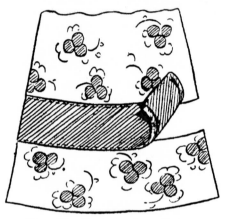

Fig. 166.—Lengthening a Skirt.

to get the band on the same curve as the lower edge of the skirt (see Fig. 166). In the case of very thin material, the edges of both skirt and added band may be pressed back, stitched once close to the turn, then joined by means of faggoting.

Add a Shaped Flounce

This method is only suitable for a fairly soft, though not necessarily very thin material, and it requires a good deal of extra fabric—exactly how much depends upon the particular style chosen. Cut off the lower part of the skirt so that the remaining upper part finishes at least 10 inches above the desired hem-line, then add a shaped flounce of the necessary depth. This method also serves well for combining two old frocks. The flounce would be cut from the second frock and the same material introduced as a trimming on the upper part of the first frock, perhaps as a yoke and sleeves.

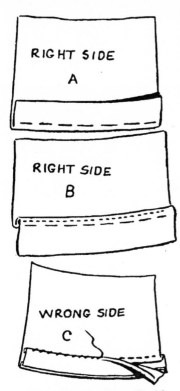

Fig. 167.—Re-making a Shabby Hem to Lengthen.

For Fairly Firm Fabric

This is a suitable plan for thin woollens, substantial silks, cottons, etc. When the additional length required is not more than 1 inch and there is a hand-sewn hem in good condition inside (this is important) and not less than $2\frac{1}{2}$ inches deep, proceed as follows :

Unpick the hem and press out all creases. Fold back the hem to the RIGHT side on the old turning and tack $\frac{1}{2}$ inch from the fold (Fig. 167A); then go to the right side, turn down the material below the tacking and tack through the three layers close up to the tacking (Fig. 167B). Press on the wrong side as flat as possible and stitch by machine on the right side just below the fold. Press again on the wrong side, then turn up the lower edge to the correct depth and face with a piece of lining or spare material cut to the shape of the lower edge, and sufficiently deep to be felled on its upper edge behind the first stitching (Fig. 167c).

CHAPTER XXV

RENOVATION OF KNITTED WEAR

NOT all knitters realise that there are many short cuts in their craft which will reduce labour and economise materials. I have often seen knitters laboriously pulling back a jumper of which they have grown tired or which has proved ill-fitting, when it could so easily have been altered in style without re-knitting, or enlarged or made smaller in order to improve the fit. Of course there are cases where re-knitting is the only cure. When this is the case, unpick the seams of the garment most carefully, to avoid breaking the wool. If they are sewn up by the edge loops with matching wool, you should begin unpicking where the seam was finished off. Use a blunt wool needle or a bodkin to find the last stitch. When this has been found, unpick a few stitches, then pull the wool gently, and when you have drawn out a few inches, cut it and straighten out the seam. The cut end will now be visible, and you can repeat this process probably for a good length of seam. Should there be a stoppage, the stitches should be unpicked one by one until the wool can be drawn out as before. When all seams have been undone, find the casting-off of the front or back and proceed to unravel the knitting. Do not pull the wool more than you can help, and do not make into balls, but wind round the back of a chair or a wide piece of card to produce skeins. Tie up each skein loosely at each end. Wash them quickly in a warm lather, holding them up by the tying threads. Dry quickly —in the open air, if possible, or otherwise before a good fire. When the wool is dry wind it into loose balls and avoid stretching.

You will now find that the yarn is thinner than it was originally, and also it will have shrunk in length, so that unless you decide to make a smaller garment, you will need extra wool. Do not try to match the old, but choose a different colour of similar thickness, and use this for trimmings, such as yoke, collar and cuffs, etc. Suppose that you have unravelled two garments of different colour but of the same ply, and you find that after washing the wool is thinner, you may, if the colours are harmonious, knit up the two together, and thus obtain a charming mixture effect. Silk and wool may often be combined attractively in the same way.

TO SHORTEN A JUMPER

There are two usual methods. (1) If the jumper has been knitted from the top downward unravel it from the bottom upward to the desired height above the ribbing, then re-knit this. (2) This serves whether the knitting has been done downward or upward. Cut off the garment at the required height above the ribbing and unravel the lower part. Take up the stitches and re-knit the ribbing. A better way is as follows.

Insert pins at the side seams to show where the top of the ribbing should come on the shortened jumper. Then at one of the seams cut (with great care) an edge loop at the level marked. Pull the cut end very gently, and you will find you can trace the strand straight across to the other edge. Cut the loop there, and the lower part will drop off. Treat the other half of the jumper in the same way. If you wish to use the original ribbing, you may either unravel the unwanted part above it or else cut it off as just described; then take up both sets of stitches on no. 12 needles and graft them together. Should you wish the ribbing to fit more tightly than before, turn back a sufficient piece at each end and take up the discarded stitches on safety-pins. After taking up the remaining stitches on a no. 12 needle, knit a row on the stitches of the upper part, but take two together at intervals to reduce the number to correspond to the number on the ribbing. Now graft the two sets together. Sew up the sides of the ribbing, turn back the unwanted pieces and secure the loops left on the safety-pins to the back of the ribbing.

Note that this method of cutting knitting may be used for any other part of the garment.

TO LENGTHEN A JUMPER

If a jumper is too short between the armhole level and the ribbing, it is possible to add the desired length by means of stripes of a different colour. Cut off the back and front at the bust-line by the method described above, then take up the stitches of the upper part on needles the correct size, and with the new wool knit an inch either in garter

stitch or a fancy stitch—that is, if the jumper is
worked in stocking stitch, but if a fancy stitch this
may be continued throughout the stripes. Pull
back the wool of the lower part, wind it in skeins and
place it on a rack above a bowl of hot water so that
the crinkles will be steamed out. Now knit an inch
or more, as desired, with the original wool to match
the original part, and repeat these two stripes as

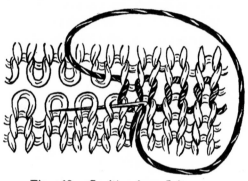

Fig. 168.—Grafting for a Join.

often as required to get the correct length, but
contrive to finish with one of the jumper wool, even
though it may be deeper than the others. Graft
the last row of stitches to those of the ribbing, or
else knit new ribbing. (It will be found a good plan
to work out the number and depth of the stripes
on paper by finding the number of rows to the inch,
before beginning them.) It is desirable to add
stripes to correspond on the sleeves at the same level,
also collar and cuffs, of the new colour.

Grafting is shown in Fig. 168, above. If the
knitting has been washed the stitches will be firm,

and may be joined as shown, pinned and tacked to a piece of paper; but if newly-knitted the stitches should be left on the needles.

TO WIDEN A JUMPER OR CARDIGAN

If the garment is tight round the bust only, and not round the lower part, unpick the under-arm seams from the armhole downward as far as seems desirable. Try on the garment and note the extra

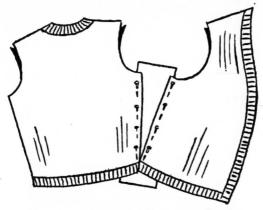

Fig. 169.—Widening a Jumper or Cardigan.

width needed at the bust-line. Cut a long strip of paper 1 inch wider than this extra width, and pin the edges of the under-arm seam to this strip, leaving the exact width needed at the top and then gradually narrowing the strip of paper off to nothing. Mark the shape between the knitted edges on the paper with pencil and take out the pins. Of course, should extra width be needed all the way down, the seam must be unpicked entirely, and the sides separated on the paper as much as is necessary.

Now knit two pieces to the required shape, using the same wool and stitch as the garment. Press well, then sew the pieces into the seams in the usual way, and press the seams (see Fig. 169). When the sleeves are tight in the upper part, wedge-shaped pieces may be inserted on the same plan, otherwise the armhole seam should be unpicked for 2 or 3 inches at each side of the inserted piece between the back and front, and the sleeve stretched to fit the armhole.

FOR A STOUT FIGURE

The ordinary type of jumper or cardigan proves unbecoming to the figure which is large in front in

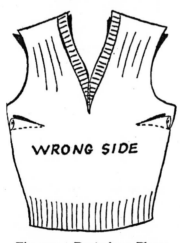

proportion to the back, which is often the case with a stout figure, and the garment is consequently tight across the bust and short from the neck to the lower edge. Here is the remedy.

Unpick the underarm seams, then take up a dart on each side edge of the front about 2 inches below the armhole. These darts should run straight

Fig. 170.—Darts for a Plump Figure.

across, and the amount taken up will depend on the figure (Fig. 170). Stitch them by machine

as you would stitch them in material, and be sure
to taper them nicely, so that a poke is avoided.
(However, if one does result, it can be got rid of
in the following way. Make a circle of fine running
round the poke, place it right side downward on an
ironing blanket, lay a damp cloth over the circle
and press with a hot iron, and allow the wool to
dry before removing the running thread.) Press the
darts up or down, but on no account cut them open.
The side edges of the front will now be shorter than
those of the back, and you must join up the under-
arm seams from the waist, leaving the excess on
the back. When sewing in the sleeve, this excess
will form a graduated turning which may be pressed
back and caught lightly to the back threads of the
knitting. If this method does not seem feasible,
the back must be shortened as required, as described
in the directions previously given for shortening a
jumper. Note that darts may be placed in any
other part where needed, and if well made they will
be quite inconspicuous.

A PETTICOAT FROM A SKIRT

A very satisfactory petticoat can be made from
a skirt, especially if it is a slim-fitting one with three
or four seams. Suppose that you have one consisting
of four gores of similar size. It may be possible to
use this just as it is, after removing the waist-band
and substituting one of elastic; but if the skirt is
too wide for its new purpose, the seams may be
taken in a little. If too long, a really shapely
full-length petticoat (see Fig. 171) can be made in
the following way :

Put on the skirt and draw it up on the figure until you get the lower edge at the desired level, then pin the top all round to the under garment. Get someone to fit the lower part, taking in the seams

if required. Measure the length in front from the front neck to the top of the skirt, and the width across the chest from armhole to armhole about half-way between neck and bust. Remove the garment from the figure and stitch any alterations. Now knit back and front yokes from any wool which will " go " with the skirt, even if of a different colour. For the front yoke cast on sufficient stitches to produce the chest measurement you took. Knit in stocking stitch—garter stitch drops too much— and decrease at both ends of the third row and of

Fig. 171.—A Petticoat from a Skirt.

every alternate row afterwards until the yoke is about 3 inches narrower than the chest measurement you took. Continue without decreasing until the yoke, when attached to the lower part, reaches 2 inches below its desired position. Then work the remaining 2 inches in knit one and purl one rib, using finer needles than before.   Make the back yoke in the same way, but continue the stocking stitch for 1½ inches more than at the front, and work the last 2 inches as before.   Note that instead of casting-on you may take up stitches from the top of the skirt for the yokes.   If possible, use the original front gore of the skirt for the back of the petticoat to equalise the wear.

To complete the petticoat, knit shoulder straps 1½ inches wide in garter stitch, and stretch them well before sewing to the front and back yokes.   If short of wool, the straps may be made of ribbon or double strips of silk or sateen.   A hand-knitted skirt has been in mind in describing this renovation, but a machine-knitted one may be treated in the same way.   If preferred, instead of adding knitted yokes, a short petticoat bodice may be cut in sateen with a back opening, and sewn to the wool skirt.

DISCARDED JUMPERS AND CARDIGANS

When these are of light colour they may often be adapted for night wear over thin lingerie.   A touch of simple embroidery in wool may be added.   A plain, short jumper with V neck may have sleeves removed, and may then be worn as a spencer under thin blouses.   A hip-length, sleeveless jumper, with rather low neck will often serve as a vest, and if too short it may be possible to remove the ribbing on the lower edge and knit on the desired additional length.

A NEW WAY OF TREATING OLD "KNITTEDS"

Accidents often suggest novel ways of overcoming difficulties.   I entrusted the washing of an outsize jumper in plain style to an inexperienced laundress, and it came back so shrunken that it was firm and close like cloth, with no " stretch " left in it. Enquiries disclosed that she had washed it in hot, soapy water, and dried it slowly. It was too small to be worn in that state, and it could not be unravelled, as it was much too felted, and I was at a loss how to deal with it until I hit upon the idea of treating it like cloth. So I cut from it a bolero with short sleeves, laying a paper pattern on it as though cloth were being used, and leaving the usual turnings. I made it up on the same method, but without neatening the outside edges. I cut a lining in some old silk and tacked it round the edges, but felled the under-arm turnings over each other, also the shoulder turnings. Then I cut off the turnings off the outer edges on the fitting-lines and bound the raw edges with silk braid.

The result was so successful that I have since shrunk knitting purposely to use in similar ways; for instance, a pair of knickers for a toddler can be made from a full-sized jumper. No lining is needed, but after the seams have been stitched the turnings should be pressed open, then tape or bias binding should be tacked over each raw edge and the edge on the turning should be stitched by machine, while the other edge should be felled by hand to the back threads of the knitting. The upper edge of the knickers should be faced similarly with a piece of sateen.

The above examples are only given as suggestions, and other methods will speedily be thought out by the ingenious needlewoman.

USES FOR OUTWORN GARMENTS

Knitted fabric, whether hand- or machine-made, should never be thrown away, however old, for in its final stages it can be used for a variety of purposes.

1. It may be tacked to thin silk or cotton and used as an interlining for coats.

2. After being washed and shrunk, pieces of various colours may be laid on an old sheet and their edges cut to fit until the whole surface is covered. The edges should then be tacked into place. Both sides should be covered with thin cotton material, preferably patterned, and the whole lightly quilted in large diamonds, after which the edges should be bound with a bias strip of the same, or contrasting, material. This makes a cosy quilt for a bed, and may be made in any size desired.

3. Kneeling pads may be made by sewing several layers together and binding the edges with broad braid.

4. Seat cushions for chairs may be made with several layers of knitting covered with cretonne, etc. They may be buttoned down at intervals like mattresses, if liked that way.

5. When the arms or seat of an armchair become somewhat flat they may be padded up with pieces of knitting of graduated size, and then, when the desired result has been obtained, the knitting should be covered with a piece of thin material (a piece of an old garment will do), which should be catch stitched lightly to the upholstery. Of course, this presupposes that the chair has a loose cover. Por-

tions of knitting may be unravelled, and then used for padding up small depressions to the desired shape.

REPAIRING THIN PLACES OR HOLES

If possible, the repair should be done before a hole has developed, so, while a garment is in use, the vulnerable parts, particularly cuffs and elbows

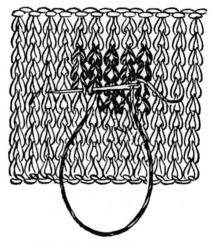

Fig. 172.—Swiss Darning.

of sleeves, should be watched. Thin places may be darned on the wrong side, using matching wool— dividing it if it is too thick for its purpose; or it may be possible to match the colour in darning wool. Place the thin part over an " egg ", but do not stretch it. Then darn upward and downward through the back loops of the knitting, with a wavy edge at top and bottom, and leaving the wool there rather loose to allow for shrinking in the wash. Do not darn across unless the place is very thin; but in that case it is best to turn the knitting to the right side and try to imitate the knitting stitches as much as possible. A better effect may be obtained by tacking the worn part, wrong side downward, to a piece of card, then working over the stitches as in Swiss darning (see Fig. 172).

When there is only slight thinness, darning may not be necessary, but a piece of thin net should be tacked on the wrong side to cover the worn part, allowing a good margin of net all round. The corners of the net should be rounded off, and then the edges should be herringboned with silk to the back threads of the knitting. If the elbows show signs of strain and the sleeves have a head with a symmetrical curve, you may take out the sleeves and transpose them, thus bringing the strain to a new place. (When the elbows have become baggy they should be shrunk as described for the top of a dart.)

A More Decorative Way of Repairing

If the defective spot, be it hole, thin place, or stain, is in a suitable position for ornamentation, the best thing is to work an embroidered motif or spray of flowers in coloured wools over it. I once put away a cardigan for a few weeks, and on taking it out found it moth-eaten on the left front near the shoulder and also on the lower part of each sleeve. I tacked a piece of net under the holes on the front and worked a spray of multi-coloured flowers over them and through the net; but on the sleeves the holes were too numerous to be treated similarly, so I cut the knitting across just above the elbow, turned up an inch, and herringboned the raw edge to the back threads of the knitting. A good pressing followed, and the result was most effective.

CHAPTER XXVI

CARE AND REPAIR OF CLOTHES

WHEN the home dressmaker has satisfactorily replenished her wardrobe, her work is by no means over—that is, if she is to get full value out of her clothes in regard both to appearance and durability. Their care is a continuous process, and cannot be confined to stated periods. Each time they are taken off they should be looked over and any necessary repairs or cleaning noted, and then carried out as quickly as possible, for delay always makes stains, etc., more difficult to remove. This daily lookover soon becomes a habit, and if nothing else is needed, a brushing of suits and cloth frocks, and a shaking of thin frocks, are generally called for. A stiff brush is required for cloth and firm materials, a softer one for thin fabrics and velvet, and velvet pads for silk and satin, etc. After each time of wearing it is also a good plan to air the discarded garments over a towel airer, either in the open air or near a moderate fire.

Any stains or grease spots should be removed at the earliest opportunity; and even should your garments be free from them, yet those of cloth and substantial fabric are improved by a general sponging-over with a cleanser from time to time. There are many excellent cleansers on the market, in the way of liquids, soaps, and cloth balls, and they should be applied according to the instructions which

347

accompany them. But there is a good home-made cleanser which will serve the double purpose of stain-remover and general reviver.

HOME-MADE CLOTH CLEANSER

Shred 2 oz. of Castile soap into a pan containing one pint of water. Boil until the soap is dissolved, then add 2 oz. of lump ammonia, 1 oz. of glycerine, 1 oz. of ether, and 2 quarts of water. Mix well, put into bottles and cork tightly. Dilute with water before using, as required. (It is the best plan to use a piece of the same material as the garment when applying this mixture, and if this is not forthcoming, then to use the nearest you can get.)

If the stains do not yield to the action of the cleanser, try one of the remedies which follow. But although all have been tried and found efficacious, yet it cannot be guaranteed that they will be successful in every case. Differences in the texture of the material, or in the nature of the dye used, may prove a deterrent. It should be borne in mind that all strong acids, such as oxalic acid, must be used with caution, and they should first be tested on the turnings of the garment, for there is always the chance that the colour might fade. As a general rule, after using oxalic acid the material should be sponged with ammonia, followed by the application of warm water.

A Stronger Cleanser

When simpler methods have proved unsatisfactory try the following :

Dissolve 2 oz. of oxalic crystals in one pint of water, then bottle and cork tightly. When required for use dilute with twice its own quantity of water. Moisten the stain by means of pieces of cotton wool dipped in the solution. Repeat until the stain disappears, then sponge with ammonia, followed by warm water. Peroxide of hydrogen is often successful on silks and thin woollens.

REMEDIES FOR STAINS

Ink

There are many reliable ink removers on sale, but all may fail at times, as has been explained in reference to home remedies. Here is the simplest remedy for ink-stains, and I have seen it bring out a small bottleful of ink and leave no trace behind. On the other hand, sometimes it has failed for an unknown reason. It should be remembered that if the stain is allowed to dry it is extremely difficult, and sometimes impossible, to remove it. It is best therefore to put the stained part in lukewarm water until milk or other remedy can be obtained.

1. Whether the material is linen, silk, or wool, white or coloured, put the stained portion into milk and leave for several hours. If not successful, then try again or use one of the other treatments suggested. In either case, wash out in warm water first.

2. Use tomato juice in the way described for milk.

3. Moisten the ink-stains with turpentine and leave for half an hour, adding more turpentine if the fabric shows signs of drying up. Then rub the stained part between the hands as if washing.

Now sponge with cold water, whether successful or not, and then, if the stain has gone, rub dry with a piece of the same material.

4. Wet thoroughly with peroxide of hydrogen. Rub with a piece of self material, and when the stain has gone sponge over with weak ammonia and rub dry with a piece of the same material, but dry.

Fruit

Fruit-stains often prove most difficult to remove, though some yield almost at once to warm water or milk, especially when they are tackled immediately. A method which is often successful is to soak the spot in chloroform, and then in ammonia. Repeat several times, if necessary, then sponge gently with warm water.

Mud

Do not attempt to remove mud while it is wet. When dry lift off what you can with a penknife, then brush well, and afterward rub with a slice of raw potato, followed by a sponging with ammonia. Instead of potato, pure alcohol may be used. (This latter should always be used in the case of silk.)

Paint

If the paint is wet, remove at once with a piece of self material and then rub with a fresh piece until the mark has gone. If it is obstinate, rub with chloroform, or with a mixture of turpentine and ammonia. Finish off by sponging with warm soapy water, and rubbing until dry with a piece of self material. If the paint is hard, saturate the spot with turpentine and ammonia and renew as required until the spot is soft.

Machine Oil or Grease

Use ether, benzine, or turpentine. (Either of the first two should be used for silk or delicate fabrics.) Take a piece of the same material or similar, dip it in one of the liquids and apply in a circle wide of the stain; then gradually work up to it and rub as required. (This is to avoid a ring mark.) When the grease has disappeared rub until dry with a piece of the same or similar material—the wrong side of another part of the garment will serve. When the grease is only slight, place the stained part between two pieces of blotting-paper and pass a warm iron over the paper next to the stained side of the material. This method often drives the grease completely into the lower paper, but should a mark remain, remove it with benzine or ether.

Tar

Cover the spot with oil of eucalyptus. When softened, remove with benzine or methylated spirit, and finally sponge with warm water.

REPAIRS

These should be done before you press the garment or before it is sent to the cleaners.

Buttonholes

When these are broken, turn the part right side downward on an ironing blanket, draw the edges of the buttonhole together and press on the wrong side under a damp cloth. Then carry two strands of buttonhole twist (if this has been used for the buttonhole) round the edge of the slit, and with fine matching silk (finer than the original silk used) work all round with buttonhole stitch over the two strands, but making the stitches shorter, and taking them between the original stitches. If the bar is broken, cut it off, and work a new one. Press on the wrong side.

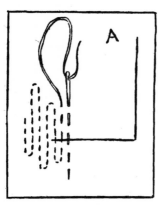 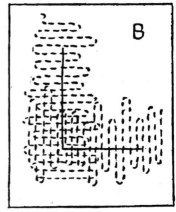

Fig. 173.—A Three-Cornered Tear.

A Three-cornered Tear

If the garment has a lining, unpick this behind the damaged part, then tack the tear, right side downward, to a piece of thin card, drawing the edges of the tear together to meet exactly. Thread a long fine needle with fine matching silk (or a strand of the material if this is fine and loosely woven) and darn across the torn edges just on the uppermost threads, as no stitches must show on the right side, working from left to right and starting from a little beyond the closed end of the tear. Let the stitches ' end in wavy lines (see Fig. 173 A). Make two or three lines of darning beyond the corner, then cut the silk. Start again at the other closed end and work as before (see Fig. 173 B). If you think the angle of the tear needs greater strength, darn across the two sets of darning stitches diagonally, though this is not done in the illustration. On the right side scratch up the cloth a little with a needle over the darn, then press on the wrong side.

Note that there is a mending tissue, and also a mending solution, on the market, by which small patches may be applied over a tear, either without darning or after darning as just described. These are sold under trade names, and are usually most satisfactory.

Torn Pocket-ends In Coats

Make a buttonhole bar in strong silk across each end (see Fig. 76, p. 129), or work a small arrowhead in these positions, with the broad end at the pocket opening (see Fig. 174).

Weak Places

When a place begins to show signs of weakness without the threads being broken—for example, the elbow of a coat—any bagginess which may have formed there should first be shrunk out (see Chapter on Shrinking). A small circle should next be run in silk to enclose the baggy part, and then this fullness shrunk away with a wet cloth and hot

M   (Dress)

iron. After this the weak part may be darned
across the back threads on the wrong side with fine
silk. (It is best to tack the part face downward
on a thin card as for the three-cornered tear.) The
silk must not be drawn tightly, and the lines of

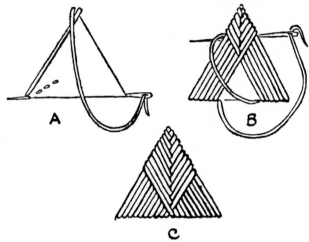

Fig. 174.—Sprat's Head or Arrowhead.

stitches should end irregularly to avoid a ridge on
the right side. Instead of this, a piece of fine net
might be tacked on the wrong side, the corners
rounded off, and then the raw edges of the net
lightly herringboned to the cloth with silk.

PATCHING

Always avoid a patch in a conspicuous place, if
possible, as it is difficult to make one perfectly
invisible. The simplest method is to use one of the
tissues which are sold for this purpose, by which

patches are applied with a hot iron without sewing. But however they are applied, patches should always match the damaged part in grain, also in pattern when there is one. If possible, the patch should not be of new material, but should have had the same exposure to the air as the garment, and it may be necessary to cut a patch from an inconspicuous part (perhaps the turn-up of a skirt or the front facing of a coat) and to replace the part taken away by a new piece, either matching or as near so as possible.

A Fine-drawn Patch (Fig. 175)

First draw on the right side of the garment with tailor's chalk a square or oblong to enclose the hole or tear, ruling by a thread. Then draw the patch to the same size, matching the enclosure on the garment in grain. Place the garment over a board or piece of glass and cut along the lines with a sharp penknife and a ruler. Cut the patch in the same way. Remember that the patch must not be even a shade smaller than the hole. Place the material right side downward on a piece of thin card and, without stretching it, tack finely all round. Then drop the patch in, secure with a large cross in the middle, draw its edges to meet those of the hole, and tack finely all round, seeing that the corners are perfectly exact. Now work through the meeting edges as described for the three-cornered tear. Finish off in the same way. Note that this method is only suitable when the cloth is firm and non-fraying. When it is more loosely woven, par-

M 2 (Dress)

ticularly when it is of the hopsack order, the following method is good.

A Darned-in Patch

Cut a piece of material 4 inches larger each way than the hole. It should be square or oblong, and

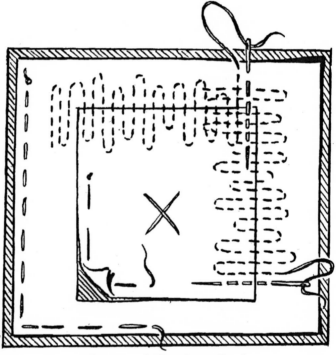

Fig. 175.—A Fine-drawn Patch.

should match it in grain—that is, the warp threads of both should run the same way, and if there is a nap (which is not likely), it should run the same way in both patch and garment. Fringe the edges of the patch all round for $1\frac{1}{2}$ inches, and about $\frac{1}{4}$ inch from each corner on all sides draw out a few more threads, so that the corners are no longer sharp. Now tack the hole onto thin card, right side upward, and tack the patch exactly over the hole, matching the grain. Thread up in turn each strand outside the patch into a needle and darn into the surrounding material, following its weave. The best way of doing this is first to darn in the needle only, leaving the eye close up to the patch, then to thread the strand through the eye, and pull out the needle by the point. Leave the edges of the stitches irregular, then draw the strands to the back of the material and cut off each. When finished lay the patch right side downward and press from the wrong side.

Darning Tweeds

Some tweeds are very easy to copy with the needle. In that case a worn part may be reproduced easily, either by using warp threads pulled out of a spare piece or from the turnings. If this cannot be managed, it may be possible to buy darning wool to match. Take a piece of thin net behind the garment, then darn through both tweed and net to reproduce the pattern. If the tweed is not thick it is best to tack it to a piece of thin card. Of course a good final pressing is needed.

Holes in Thin, Patterned Fabrics

These may be repaired invisibly in two ways.

1. Cut a patch about 2 inches larger each way than the hole, matching the design perfectly, and

round off the corners. Now apply this patch to the under side of the garment with the special liquid sold for the purpose.

2. To be quite successful the pattern of the material should be large and bold. Cut out a largish piece of the fabric matching the part where the hole is, then cut round the edges of the different parts of the design as far as possible, leaving a turning of about ⅛ inch. Place over the damaged part and tack finely and plentifully so that the patch does not move. Now begin to fell on the patch all round, turning in the raw edges bit by bit as you do so, and changing the colour of the sewing silk as the colour of the pattern changes.

Another way, instead of felling the edges, is to cut them off close to the design and then to work fine satin stitch over the raw edges with matching silk.

CARE OF COAT LINING

If a coat lining is soiled it is a good plan to remove it and wash it; and when it is at the same time outworn it should be replaced by a new one— probably an old frock of rayon, crêpe-de-chine, or thin silk would provide the material. If you find that you have not sufficient of one material a second one may be used for the sleeves, or perhaps for the lower parts of them, where it will not show. The new lining should be cut from the old one and inserted as described in Chapter XIX. But while the coat is without lining it is a good opportunity to brush it well, inside and out, and to sponge it all over with cleanser. Necessary repairs should also be made, and the coat then pressed according to rules given in Chapter XV. If the padding round the armholes and on the shoulders has worn thin it may be renewed or added to with extra layers cut to the original shape, tacking these lightly into place and then fraying out the edges with the opened points of the scissors. When it is desired to build up the shoulders, pads should be bought or made and inserted, after which the lining should be sewn in as described in Chapter XIX.

TO REMOVE BAGGINESS

A cloth skirt is liable in course of wear to develop a bulge at either back or front, or both. Run a circle very finely with silk, large enough to enclose all the bagginess. Place this face downward on an ironing blanket and cover with a large piece of the same material as the skirt, or similar, which has been wrung out of water. Apply a hot iron all over the baggy part with a dabbing movement, not allowing it to stay long at each dab, but being sure that the whole area of the bagginess is touched by the iron. Allow the steam to escape, then repeat the process several times. Then remove the wet cloth and hold the iron over the exposed part very closely, but without touching it. When dry, if not sufficiently shrunken, repeat the treatment. Finally press with the iron, but take care not to stretch the material which has just been shrunk. Then turn to the right side and rub the part downward (particularly if there is a nap) with a piece of the same material—another part of the skirt will do.

If the side seams appear to be out of shape owing to stretching in wear, it is a good plan to unpick them and to straighten the fitting-lines with chalk and a long ruler, after which the seams should be re-stitched on the chalked lines and pressed. To help to keep either the front or back gore in shape cut a piece of strong lining the shape of the upper part of the gore, and reaching below the area of the former bulge. Hem the lower edge lightly or notch the raw edge, then fell in the turned-in edges at the waist and down the seam turnings.

TO REPAIR TORN INVERTED PLEATS

Sometimes inverted pleats in a skirt seam tear away at the top. Here is a remedy. Tack the pleats as they should be and press them. Take a

Fig. 176.—Repairing Torn Inverted Pleat.

piece of the same material, if you have any, otherwise velvet or silk of the same colour will serve. Cut a triangle in canvas, each side measuring not more than $1\frac{1}{2}$ inches. Place this on a piece of the chosen material, turn back the edges, tack, and press them. Then machine as shown in Fig. 176. Press again, then tack over the top of the seam opening and slip stitch neatly

into place.   If untidy at the back, face the damaged
part with a triangle of lining.

GARMENTS OF THIN MATERIALS

These, when tumbled and crushed, look a sorry
sight; but discretion is needed in pressing, and only
a light iron and moderate heat should be employed.
It is really better to try steaming before pressing.
Place the garment on a coat hanger in a steamy
bathroom and leave for several hours.   After this
you will probably find that all creases and crinkles
have smoothed out—if not, you can then go over
the frock lightly with a moderate iron.   But remember that after either steaming or pressing a
garment should be allowed to dry very thoroughly
or it will crease at once, more deeply than before.

STORING CLOTHES

As a rule clothes are better hung than folded, and
they should be placed on padded hangers, while if
not in general wear, or delicate in colour, they should
be covered.   Old nightdresses make good covers
as the lower edges may be buttoned together or
fastened with press studs.   When special sizes are
needed they may be made from old sheets or table-
cloths.   Full sleeves should be stuffed with tissue
paper.   A frock with frilled skirt should be hung
upside down so that the frills fall over, as then they
will look fresher when worn.   Hang a lavender bag
in each garment for moth prevention.   There are
many good moth preventives, but generally their
smell is both unpleasant and clinging.

Furs

These are best stored in special moth-proof bags; failing these, newspapers may be stitched up into bags with moth balls inside them, and then the edges of the paper should be pasted together to enclose the furs and exclude the air. Furs not so stored are best hung in a wardrobe and taken out daily for inspection, and also beaten with a cane in the open air very frequently. Valuable furs should be put into cold storage for the summer months.

Folding clothes

If you must store clothes in drawers because of lack of space, use the longest ones you have so as to avoid many folds in the garments. Any necessary folds should be arranged in such a position that if creases are formed they will be inconspicuous when the garment is worn. Keep the frock, etc., right side out, and make large rolls of tissue paper to extend large sleeves or draperies. Very soft frocks, such as those of lace, crinkly fabrics, and uncrushable velvet, may be stretched out to their full width, then rolled downward and laid like that in a drawer, inserting rolls of paper in any folds.

WARNING

It is most important, and it cannot be impressed too strongly, that on no account should any garments which are soiled, spotted, or damp be put away for even a few days, as it is such things which attract moths, and which they attack first. Washing frocks and blouses should be washed and rough-dried. The wardrobe, cupboard, or drawers should be free from dust and perfectly dry, and a moth preventive should be sprinkled in all corners. A cover (one made from an old sheet will serve) should be laid over the contents of any drawer.

INDEX

APPARATUS, dressmaking, 9–12
Apron, from small tablecloth, 319–320
Arrowhead Tack or Sprat's head, 162, 192, 353

Balance marks, 76, 242
Band (skirt or waist), 84, 90–91, 190–92, 339
Beading, applying, 261–62, 285–86
Bias : bind, 171–72 ; binding, 267 ; cutting on, 32, 44–45, 67–69 ; fold, 171 ; seam, 209 ; sleeve cut on, 112
Blankets, convertible, 317–18
Blouse(s) : cutting out, 70 ; fancy, 202–3 ; jacket-, 203–204 ; jumper-, 203 ; making shirt, 196–202 ; tacking-up, 80
Blousettes and waistcoats, 322–23
Bodice(s) : boned, 210–11 ; correcting pattern of, 34–37 ; fitting, 84–88 ; foundation, 13–16 ; tacking-up tight-fitting, 79–80 ; taking measures, 28–30 ; turnings for tight-fitting, 69
Bodkin, 255, 274
Bolero(s), 204, 321–22
Braiding, 174–75
" Break," 148, 151, 232, 241
Bridle, 151 ; see also " Stay tape "
Brocade, 47–48, 50, 321
broderie anglaise, 259, 309
Buttonholed loops, 129 ; scallops, 268 ; slots, 309

Buttonhole(s) : bound, 126–28, 246 ; dressmaker's, 126 ; lingerie, 304–307 ; on coat cuff, 250 ; position of, 123 ; repairs to, 351–52 ; scissors, 10, 212 ; silk (or twist), 123–24, 129, 212, 255 ; tailor's, 123–25
Button(s) : and cord loops, 128, 138, 306–307 ; for lingerie, 302–304 ; linen, 304 ; sewing on, 123, 255, 304 ; position of, 122 ; shank, 255, 303 ; thread, 255
Buttons and buttonholes : for coat, 217 ; for lingerie, 302–306 ; for shirt cuff, 140 ; for tight-fitting coat, 245–46

Calico (unbleached), 12–18, 34
Canvas, tailor's, 51, 134, 142, 192, 212, 230 ; shrinking, 185
Canvasing coat fronts, 214–15, 223–24, 243
Cardboard, sheets of, 12, 72
Casings, for elastic, etc., 307–309
Chalk, tailor's, 11, 71, 212
Chalking fitting-lines, 10–14, 71–74, 242
Clothes : cleansers for, 347–49 ; folding, 362 ; re-modelling, 312–17 ; repairing, 351–61 ; stain removers for, 349–51 ; storing, 361
Coat(s) : coffee, 50 ; short, tight-fitting, 227–57 ; simple tailored, 212–26
Coatee(s), 204, 321–22

365

INDEX